STRIKING BACK

OVERT AND COVERT OPTIONS TO COMBAT RUSSIAN DISINFORMATION

By Thomas Kent

The JAMESTOWN FOUNDATION

Washington, DC
September 2020

THE JAMESTOWN FOUNDATION

Published in the United States by
The Jamestown Foundation
1310 L Street NW
Suite 810
Washington, DC 20005
http://www.jamestown.org

For more information on this book of The Jamestown Foundation, email pubs@jamestown.org.

ISBN: 978-0-9986660-9-9

Cover art provided by Peggy Archambault of Peggy Archambault Design.

Jamestown's Mission

The Jamestown Foundation's mission is to inform and educate policy makers and the broader community about events and trends in those societies which are strategically or tactically important to the United States and which frequently restrict access to such information. Utilizing indigenous and primary sources, Jamestown's material is delivered without political bias, filter or agenda. It is often the only source of information which should be, but is not always, available through official or intelligence channels, especially in regard to Eurasia and terrorism.

Origins

Founded in 1984 by William Geimer, The Jamestown Foundation made a direct contribution to the downfall of Communism through its dissemination of information about the closed totalitarian societies of Eastern Europe and the Soviet Union.

William Geimer worked with Arkady Shevchenko, the highest-ranking Soviet official ever to defect when he left his position as undersecretary general of the United Nations. Shevchenko's memoir *Breaking With Moscow* revealed the details of Soviet superpower diplomacy, arms control strategy and tactics in the Third World, at the height of the Cold War. Through its work with Shevchenko, Jamestown rapidly became the leading source of information about the inner workings of the captive nations of the former Communist Bloc. In addition to Shevchenko, Jamestown assisted the former top Romanian intelligence officer Ion Pacepa in writing his memoirs. Jamestown ensured that both men published their insights and experience in what became bestselling books. Even today, several decades later, some credit Pacepa's revelations about Ceausescu's regime in his bestselling book *Red Horizons* with the fall of that government and the freeing of Romania.

The Jamestown Foundation has emerged as a leading provider of information about Eurasia. Our research and analysis on conflict and instability in Eurasia enabled Jamestown to become one of the most reliable sources of information on the post-Soviet space, the Caucasus and Central Asia as well as China. Furthermore, since 9/11, Jamestown has utilized its network of indigenous experts in more than 50 different countries to conduct research and analysis on terrorism and the growth of al-Qaeda and al-Qaeda offshoots throughout the globe.

By drawing on our ever-growing global network of experts, Jamestown has become a vital source of unfiltered, open-source information about major conflict zones around the world—from the Black Sea to Siberia, from the Persian Gulf to Latin America and the Pacific. Our core of intellectual talent includes former high-ranking government officials and military officers, political scientists, journalists, scholars and economists. Their insight contributes significantly to policymakers engaged in addressing today's newly emerging global threats in the post 9/11 world.

For Sophie Arielle Kent

my muse and counselor

Table of Contents

Introduction: The Upside-Down War

Russia's Offensive

The Russian assault on democratic states has turned the usual nature of war on its head. Bereft of an inspiring ideology, constrained by a weak economy and unable to project decisive force beyond its own neighborhood, Russia has been forced to seek unconventional tools to remain relevant as a world power. It has found them.

Democracies that had hoped to settle into a post–Cold War world of nonviolence and political consensus have been shocked by Russia's embrace of murder, invasion and organized crime as tools of policy. More insidious—and the central subject of this study—are aggressive Russian information operations (IO) aimed at undermining national cohesion and public order within democratic societies.

It would be unfair to credit Russia alone for the impact of its tactics on democratic nations. Starting at the end of World War II, successive leaders of democratic states began to bank on the idea that civilization had reached a turning point—that education, trade and technology would erase such eternal traits of society as nationalism, tribalism and competition for geopolitical advantage.

These leaders were wrong about their own societies, discovering that policies based on globalism and white-collar outlooks ignited sharp and sustained turmoil at home. They were certainly wrong in expecting Russia, with its historically well-justified fears of foreign aggression, to gamble its security on Western promises of economic progress and general kumbaya.

As a result, states that had bet on a new stage in human development came face-to-face with an unreconstructed Russia. Political freedoms peaked under Mikhail Gorbachev and Boris Yeltsin but faded again under Vladimir Putin. As the West clung to the idea that the Cold War was dead, Moscow sliced with tanks into neighboring countries, rebuilt influence over formerly Soviet states, and strived to reassert itself in Latin America and Africa.

The West's responses to all of this were minimal. Even when Russia invaded Georgia and Ukraine, neither the United States administration of Barack Obama nor its allies in the North Atlantic Treaty Organization (NATO) deployed a single soldier. Major Western countries imposed biting economic sanctions on Moscow, but they never really expected Russia would surrender its territorial gains. Western nations also kept pursuing new business deals with Russia. Hope sprang eternal that enough trade and investment would ultimately bring an end to Kremlin aggression. After all, in the West's view, whatever Russia had done, the geopolitical balance was still grossly tilted against the Kremlin. Eventually it would have to join the Western system.

Russia not only did not change its course but intensified its efforts. Along with its military adventures, it intruded increasingly over the past decade into the domestic affairs of new and old democratic states. In major Western countries, it sought to exacerbate the fractures that globalism and the 2007 recession had already created. It worked to destabilize formerly Soviet countries that had joined the European Union and NATO. It encouraged anti-US actors in Latin America. In Africa, it tried to revive Cold War relationships based on anti-colonialist solidarity and arms-dealing.

At first, Western governments largely ignored all these actions. They felt that the Russian impact on major Western societies was minimal and post-Soviet countries could be secured through sufficient EU aid. In line with long-standing habits, the West focused little on Latin America and Africa. Some analysts saw Russian actions there as mainly a small-scale response—even an understandable one—to NATO and EU encroachment into the formerly Soviet Europe's East.

However, under pressure by legislators, media and civil society, some countries felt increasingly obligated to address the Kremlin's penetration of their populations and politics. Especially after revelations of Russian IOs during the 2016 US elections, politicians and intelligence officials in Europe became aware of the complex web of information assets that Russia had already deployed within their societies. In fits and starts, Western governments and civil society began increasingly to enter the information war.

A War Like No Other

The characteristics of the information conflict with Russia are far different from the wars that major Western democracies have known. In almost every respect, this war is upside-down:

• The challenging power, Russia, is led not by a madman or a shadowy Politburo, but by one of the longest-serving leaders in the world. Vladimir Putin is well-spoken, personally engaging and deeply experienced in both international diplomacy and covert tradecraft. In his frequent interviews, he easily comes across as at least the intellectual equal of the leaders of major Western states, many of them newcomers to their jobs with backgrounds mainly in domestic politics.[1]

---

[1] See, for instance, "Interview with The Financial Times," President of Russia website, June 27, 2019, http://en.kremlin.ru/events/president/news/60836.

• The traditional wartime advantages of highly industrialized states are of little use. Russia's capture of Crimea had much more to do with special forces and psychological tactics than with military iron. The West's vast military assets were irrelevant to the situation. Even in the case of Russia's more traditional tank-led assaults on Georgia and eastern Ukraine, the absence of even token Western mobilization sent a powerful strategic message: though the West possesses overwhelming military power, it lacks the unity and will to even threaten to use it.

• Russia's information offensive is not entirely led or controlled by the Russian state. A thick array of private contractors, hackers and social media artisans, some loyal to Moscow and others just looking for money, all play a role in sowing chaos in the West. Often their messages seem inconsistent and even contradictory. The upside for Russia is that multiple actors with varying goals and styles bring creativity and entrepreneurship to the overall effort. For Russian purposes, confusion can be useful, too.

• The West's response to Russian IOs has no clear leader. Democracies habitually look to Washington. Much of Congress and the government are uncompromising toward Russian disinformation and propaganda. Yet, President Donald Trump has undermined the United States' leadership role by his ambivalence toward Russian disinformation in the United States, his insulting behavior toward US allies and general cultivation of authoritarian leaders. All this has come despite his continuing military buildup and support for sanctions against Russia. The Washington-based Center for Strategic & International Studies (CSIS) says "international allies and partners are more distrustful of U.S. narrative campaigns and less likely to partner with U.S. projects because of credibility concerns."[2] Pro-

---

[2] Kathleen H. Hicks, Melissa Dalton, et. al., *By Other Means, Part II: U.S. Priorities in the Gray Zone* (Washington: Center for Strategic & International Studies, August

democracy organizations abroad routinely express fears they will be abandoned by the Trump administration.

• While armies always try to fight on the enemy's territory, the information conflict is being fought almost entirely on the territory of the West. Democratic states have shown little interest in an information offensive against Russia's own population. Instead, their efforts have been devoted almost entirely to trying to shield themselves from Russian IOs by such defensive measures as media literacy programs for their populations and attempts to crack down on the West's own social platforms.[3] "In terms of Russian operations, people have gone from ignorance to denial, then to recognition, then to defense. But not yet to deterrence," says Petras Auštrevičius, a Lithuanian member of the European Parliament.[4]

• In past contests of public persuasion, democracies calculated they had "a better story to tell" and would therefore triumph. In the Cold War, the West's main information problem was simply finding a way to pierce its winning message through to Soviet-controlled populations. Today, the "story" the West has to tell is not as persuasive. The West's killer arguments against the Soviet Union— that it locked its citizens in, allowed no opposition and could barely feed its people—have dissolved. Russians travel freely, a token political opposition exists and shopping malls glitter like those anywhere else. Russia now projects its own confident "story" of strength, national pride and conservative social values. It helps mediate international conflicts and sends aid to countries in distress

---

2019), 35, https://csis-prod.s3.amazonaws.com/s3fs-public/publication/Hicks_GrayZone_II_full_WEB_0.pdf.
[3] Typical is the EU's 2018 "Action Plan Against Disinformation," which focuses on better identification of disinformation, possible regulation of social networks, and boosting media literacy and independent journalism. European Commission, "Action Plan Against Disinformation, December 5, 2018, https://eeas.europa.eu/sites/eeas/files/action_plan_against_disinformation.pdf.
[4] Petras Auštrevičius, interview with author, June 25, 2019.

(Russian aid to some countries during the coronavirus pandemic is an example).

• In past wars, almost all disruptive IOs came from abroad, usually by radio, leaflets or through identifiable enemy agents. In this conflict Russian interests are often advanced by citizens inside democratic countries. This raises by many degrees the complexity of a response, since democratic governments stand for freedom of speech and are not built to propagandize their own people.

• While the start of a war used to be obvious to everyone, opinions vary widely in the democratic world as to whether a significant conflict is even underway. Certainly, no spirit of wartime mobilization exists, on the information or any other front. No Western leader speaks in the style of Ronald Reagan, who summarized in five words his strategy toward the Soviet Union: "We win and they lose." As for Russia, its military theoreticians publish ample clues to suggest they are already waging war, alternating between IOs and armed action depending on tactical needs.[5] Yet, given the way Moscow interweaves doctrine and propaganda, it is hard to tell if it is truly conducting long-term, coherent warfare or is just engaging in opportunistic adventures that often happen to go quite well.

• Even if we accept that a conflict is under way, it may never have an end. Sean McFate of the National Defense University says that in the new age of warfare, "There's not going to be a decisive USS *Missouri* moment like at the end of World War II […] It's going to be more like business. Coke doesn't defeat Pepsi and obliterate them forever. You

---

[5] Valery Gerasimov, "Ценность науки в предвидении" [The value of science in prediction], *Voenno-Promyshlenny Kurier*, No. 8 (476), February 27–March 5, 2013, https://vpk-news.ru/sites/default/files/pdf/VPK_08_476.pdf.

have better quarters, you have worse quarters. That's what war is turning into."[6]

The Western Response

Russia has faced a daunting task in trying to manipulate the world's information space. The West has enjoyed crushing information dominance worldwide for a century. Its movies, music, mores, news, politics, jeans, fast food, social networks and pop stars have become ubiquitous. They have made deep inroads into the world's consciousness and lifestyles and attracted countless immigrants. It seems the whole world has a brother in Brooklyn. Amid this torrent of Western influence, Russia's international visibility has been miniscule.

However, while Western companies never relent in defending their brands and market share, Western democracies took for granted after the Cold War that political liberty had become the world's natural condition. Efforts to campaign for democracy abroad, and to teach civic consciousness at home, declined in what policymakers increasingly saw as a post-conflict world. "We're now reaping the costs of having stopped explaining the benefits of democracy to our own people and to the world," says Thomas O. Melia, Washington director of PEN America, who held senior posts at the State Department and USAID during the Obama administration. "We thought that it was preposterous that anyone would argue against democracy. We thought it was simply a matter of time until even

---

[6] *"The New Rules of War: Victory in the Age of Durable Disorder, with Sean McFate,"* video, Carnegie Council, March 13, 2019, https://www.carnegiecouncil.org/studio/multimedia/20190313-new-rules-war-victory-age-durable-disorder-sean-mcfate.

Russia would inevitably institutionalize democratic governance, as they seemed to be doing in the 1990s."[7]

The West remained comfortable with its historic attachment to the concept of a "marketplace of ideas," where righteous ideologies naturally triumph of their own virtue. It largely stuck with the view of Thomas Jefferson: "Truth will do well enough if left to shift for herself. [...] She has no need of force to procure entrance into the minds of men." Or as *CNN* founder Ted Turner put it ebulliently in 1980, "See, we're gonna take the news and put it on the satellite and beam it down to Russia. And we're gonna bring world peace and we're all gonna get rich in the process!"[8]

Russia saw the situation differently. Soviet leaders since 1917 recognized that the survival of their state depended on their ability to publicly communicate the attractiveness of Communism and covertly undermine capitalist societies. Russia has always understood that the information marketplace is as unsentimental as any other: products move depending not only on their inherent value, but on how good they look, their emotional appeal and the recommendations of friends. Products also sell because they fill a need. Russia recognized that the speed of social and economic change in the West had left millions feeling frightened by globalization, unmoored in society and abandoned by their nations' elites. People were looking for a way to make sense of it all. The situation was ideal for Russian information operators promoting conspiracy theories and grievance.

Russia discovered that the information technology created by democratic societies provided an ideal platform for this work. No longer did it have to depend on unreliable leftist parties in the West, or hope people were listening to Radio Moscow through a scratchy

---

[7] Thomas Melia, personal communication with author, March 25, 2020.
[8] Cited in Hank Wittemore, *CNN: The Inside Story* (Boston: Little, Brown, 1990), 124.

ionosphere. Facebook allowed Russian operators to microtarget any segment of Western populations they wanted. Especially in the absence of pushback from respected national leaders and institutions, Russian use of social networks in democratic states could inflame existing tensions and make wobbly governments wobblier. Best of all was the minimal cost. Russia's Internet Research Agency is estimated to have spent only $1.25 million a month during its campaign to influence the 2016 US elections.[9] Some pro-Russian sites even make money, collecting fees for displaying ads from Google and other advertising networks.

It remains debatable whether Russian efforts have changed the outcomes of any Western elections or have divided societies more than disinformation from purely local actors would have. Sometimes Russian operators simply hang on to the coattails of domestic disrupters. Yet, constant Western exposures of what Russia does manage to accomplish have been valuable propaganda in themselves. As the Hungarian think tank Political Capital put it in 2019:

> Vladimir Putin's Russia has been rather unsuccessful since the annexation of Crimea in employing traditional soft power tools; i.e., in making Russia more attractive. However, it has been highly successful in a certain sense of sharp power; i.e., in creating the illusion of near omnipotence in influencing Western policy processes, changing electoral outcomes and replacing leaders. This mystification of Russia in the whole Western world is the

---

[9] This estimate includes not only the cost of Russian advertising on social platforms, but the personnel and technical costs of human operatives and bots that used individual free accounts. *Report of the Select Committee on Intelligence on Russian Active Measures, Campaigns and Interference in the 2016 US Election, Volume 2: Russia's Use of Social Media with Additional Views,* 7 (Washington: United States Senate), July 25, 2019, 7, https://www.intelligence.senate.gov/sites/default/files/documents/Report_Volume2.pdf.

greatest result that the Kremlin's spin doctors might have achieved so far.[10]

In many of the countries that are most vulnerable to Russian information operations, government responses have been weak and confused. Part of the reason is simply shock: Western elites never anticipated something as audacious as an information assault by Russia, whose credibility in the information space they had rated at zero. It was a failure of imagination on the level of underestimating al-Qaeda's ability to attack inside the United States, or the power of a pandemic. Westerners never conceived that Russia could analyze their political landscapes in painstaking detail, master the communication skills to precisely target the most vulnerable citizens, and then use that penetration to batter their societies from within. Russia also proved highly adept at wrapping its IOs into the domestic politics of target countries, making its campaigns almost indistinguishable from those of militant local groups and conspiracy theorists. With no commitment to an ideology, Russia could join forces with whichever local actors promised to bring the most disruption. Often Russian operators simply retweeted the angriest messages posted by local extremists. This tactic had an additional advantage: when governments and civil society called out Russia for its actions, they could be made to look as if their real motive was to attack domestic political opponents.

Democratic nations were also plainly frightened by Russia. They had let their militaries atrophy, discouraged patriotic sentiments (especially in the EU) and allowed political, economic and cultural gulfs to open between elites and the rest of their populations. In

---

[10] Péter Krekó, Csaba Molnár, and András Rácz, "*Mystification and Demystification of Putin's Russia*" (Budapest: Political Capital, March 2019), 3, https://politicalcapital.hu/pc-admin/source/documents/pc_mystification_and_demystification_of_russia_eng_web_20190312.pdf.

Western Europe's philosophy, the great lesson of World War II was not that armed aggression from anywhere must be stopped, but that the biggest threat to peace was nationalism and bigotry in Western Europe itself. As for Russia, European leaders were convinced that trade and respect could mollify any of its worries, and that because NATO members themselves had no intention of invading Russia, Moscow would attach no importance to the post-Cold War expansion of the alliance.

But suddenly facing Western nations was a Russia that was not supposed to exist in the new international order: flag-waving, rapidly rearming, apoplectic over NATO's expansion, nonchalant about invading its neighbors, and overtly contemptuous of Western democracy and social liberalism. The aphrodisiac of business failed to seduce as Russia stolidly endured sanctions rather than retreat from its adventures. For good measure, Russia also boasted about new "unstoppable" nuclear weapons, while experts worried aloud that Russia's cyber armies could destroy Western energy grids and communications at will.

Against this background, NATO and EU countries failed to implement their best tactic against Russian IOs and other adventurism short of military action. They never took a strong, united political stand. Such a stand could have been backed up by clearly enunciated threats of even more trade sanctions, the expulsion of Russian students and businesspeople, seizures of Russian assets and the cancelation of industrial and energy projects. The United States could have been the driver of such a position. Yet, successive US administrations showed little interest, and no other Western country put itself forward to lead a coalition.

Another obstacle to effective responses to Russia, especially in the information space, was Western nations' commitment to their own democratic ideals. Most countries decided their values were inconsistent with blocking Russia's freedom of speech, and even granted Moscow channels on their local television systems. A few, including the Baltic States, Ukraine and Moldova, banned Russian television or social networks as a danger to their societies. French and British regulators publicly condemned *RT* television in 2018 and 2019 for manipulating coverage of Syria and other stories, but they never took it off the air. However, these were exceptions. With *RT* responding to every challenge by portraying itself as a martyr for press freedom, democratic countries feared doing anything that could make themselves look censorious.

Most democratic states—the Nordic and Baltic countries were notable exceptions—also shied away from sustained internal campaigns against Russian disinformation. To be effective, such campaigns required calling out Russia by name. Few governments had the stomach for persistent, on-the-record denunciations of Moscow, especially since many of Moscow's talking points were the same as those of domestic political opponents. Governments also feared they would be accused of becoming "propagandists" themselves—even if they were simply reasserting the values of free societies. France and Germany, during their 2017 elections, worked publicly to raise awareness of Russian IOs and warned Moscow against interference. After the elections, however, they returned to broader agendas of trying to improve ties with the Kremlin.

Yet another impediment to an effective response to Russian IOs was instability in many of the formerly Soviet-controlled states of Europe's East. In principle, Russia's former East European satellites should be the most sensitive to renewed machinations from their eastern neighbor. Yet Russia has been active in each of them with such tactics as backing pro-Russian politicians, making common cause with extreme right and left forces, collaborating with corrupt powerbrokers and whipping up opposition to NATO and the EU. Responses by these states to Russian influence has varied greatly depending on the party in power and the local allies it needs to cultivate—reputable or otherwise—to survive the next election.

Given these obstacles, in few countries is there a long-term, coordinated effort by governments to respond to disinformation narratives by Russia and its allies. Efforts often include generic media literacy campaigns that can be portrayed as broad efforts to fight misinformation in general, not aimed at any country specifically. It is difficult, however, to make people resilient against dangers that are never identified out loud.

The Role of Non-Government Actors

Fortunately, there is an entire plane of resistance to IOs by Russia and its local allies that has little to do with governments. This is the work of such private-sector actors as civil society NGOs and independent journalists. A central contention of this study is that the importance of these organizations is far greater than generally recognized. They are likely democratic societies' most effective tools in the information war. "Little by little, over time, we have seen people become more aware of disinformation, more suspicious," says Tomáš Kriššák, who has been active for years in anti-disinformation efforts in Slovakia.[11] Even if Western governments become emboldened against Russia— perhaps due to new leadership in Washington in 2021—these organizations will remain key to a speedy, flexible response.

The very terms "civil society," "NGOs" and "independent journalism" are inadequate to convey the dynamism of some of those opposing Russian IOs and domestic radical actors. Civil society and NGOs commonly evoke thoughts of panel discussions and little-read reports. Independent journalism brings to mind a few crusading editors. In fact, non-government actors (I shall refer to them in the aggregate as

---

[11] Tomáš Kriššák, interview with author, April 29, 2020.

NGAs) have built themselves into a dense system of constantly changing and interlocking parts that represent a growing and increasingly coordinated challenge to Russian IOs.

Many are traditional civil society organizations campaigning for democracy, clean government and respect for facts. Others are much more aggressive. Some NGAs battle online against Russian trolls. Still others develop software to unmask troll and bot networks and compel social platforms to shut them down. NGAs campaign for advertisers to boycott disinformation sites. They slip into chat rooms and comment boards to push down hostile comments under dozens of moderate posts. They lure frequent posters of conspiracy narratives into private chats where they try to deprogram them. A few NGAs operate inside Russia's own information space, challenging Kremlin policies and even tangling online with Russian soldiers. NGA members from different countries come together regularly to sharpen their techniques against not only Russian IOs, but against corrupt actors and extremists in their own countries. Many activists have no fear of engaging in aggressive persuasion—some might call it propaganda—though many insist they do not spread disinformation. They are extremely courageous. Their members often work at significant personal risk in countries where political violence is common.

Their funding consists of grants from Western governments and private foundations, supplemented at times by public fundraising. Their work appeals to donors because NGAs are quicker than government bureaucracies and freer to do whatever they want. "Governments are limited by laws, but NGOs can do anything," says an East European specialist in psychological warfare who advises NGAs. The NGAs' funders benefit from deniability, since they work from a distance and can know as much or as little as they wish about the groups' more aggressive activities. NGAs are particularly active in Europe, though some are growing elsewhere.

Along with civil society groups, independent journalists and factcheckers in Europe, Africa and Latin America have become an increasing force against disinformation, corruption and conspiracy theories. Some of them would strongly reject the label of pro-democracy activists. They consider themselves objective journalists, ready to expose malfeasance by East or West, though the bulk of their work tends to favor democratic causes. Other journalists specifically target Russia and its allies. Spread across multiple nations, they use the latest tools of artificial intelligence and geolocation to expose closely guarded money transfers, military movements and intelligence operations. For them, the line between journalism and militancy is thin; some people work simultaneously for news outlets and more combative NGA groups. For journalists of all stripes, exposing Russian disinformation, local bigots or corrupt businessmen takes substantial personal courage. Journalists realize they can be killed for their work. Some have been.

NGAs innovate quickly, discarding approaches that do not work and moving on to something new. NGA groups morph constantly into new coalitions, changing their names and methods. A Russian investigator trying to monitor their activities might perceive the tradecraft of covert organizations working to avoid detection. In fact, many of the changes have less to do with deceiving Moscow than with off-the-cuff reorganizations to meet the vagaries of different funders. However, such maneuvers do provide a fringe benefit of making NGAs harder to track.

NGAs' work can eventually flow into far greater "people power" movements that, around the globe, have toppled leaders, exposed corruption and forced economic reforms. Nancy Lindborg, president of the United States Institute of Peace (USIP), says this resurgence "probably won't be driven by partner nations, heads of state or US leadership. Instead, it will come from people themselves, who have imbibed the powerful ideas and values of democracy and are demanding that vision for themselves."[12] That is equally true in the information realm, where civil society has targeted disinformation as one of the greatest dangers to democracy. In the view of Jonathan Pinckney of USIP, the coronavirus may add new strength to "people power" efforts: "As people in countries around the world are responding negatively to perceived failures of government response, we're going see that being used by movements as a mobilizing tool."[13]

It is essential, however, not to overstate the power of NGAs. In many countries, their numbers are small. Members are largely volunteers, devoting what time they can while holding down full-time jobs. Not all agree on tactics. There may be competition and jealousy among and within groups. Members who lose courage or interest must constantly be replaced. Foreign grants are often small and unpredictable. Many journalistic groups work on a shoestring because of minimal revenue from subscriptions and ads.

Activists may overstate their accomplishments; in candid moments, many say their efforts are a drop in the bucket compared to the deluge of disinformation and propaganda they seek to confront. Yet, NGAs possess characteristics of adaptability and self-direction that make them ideal actors in the current struggle, where Russian IOs are also highly agile and opportunistic. They can take on local groups that spread deceitful messaging with none of the concerns their governments feel about challenging domestic opponents. They do not need to fight the whole Russian state, but only limited sets of actors and narratives in their own countries.

---

[12] Nancy Lindborg, "Revolutions of our time: Freedom without US leadership," *The Hill*, Nov. 2019, https://thehill.com/opinion/civil-rights/471481-revolutions-of-our-time-freedom-without-us-leadership.

[13] "On Peace," podcast, United States Institute of Peace, April 29, 2020, https://play.google.com/music/listen?u=0#/ps/Iijmiabq66jjzbtkv6v3rzn3ycq.

They are particularly useful instruments for the situation in which the West finds itself: one where ample money exists to counter disinformation actors, but many governments are reluctant to enter the fight because of domestic politics, fear of retaliation or qualms about engaging in "propaganda." Since this war does not require military iron, there is no reason NGAs—properly reinforced—cannot conduct a good deal of the campaign. Governments and foundations can provide support overtly or covertly, depending how much visibility they feel comfortable with. In an upside-down war, the most successful tactics may be upside-down, too.

Civil society groups "are going to be the heroes of counter-disinformation techniques," Daniel Fried, a former US ambassador to Poland and now an Atlantic Council fellow, told the House Foreign Affairs Committee in July 2019. "They, not government bureaucracy, are going to be able to expose, in real time, Russian and other disinformation operations. We ought to put our trust in them. We ought to put some of our resources behind them."[14]

About This Book

This book is based on more than 160 interviews with diplomats, military and intelligence officials, civil society activists and academic specialists in the United States, Europe, Africa and Latin America. It also draws from my own experience as an anti-disinformation practitioner at *Radio Free Europe/Radio Liberty*, where I was president and CEO, and as a journalist and journalism ethicist.

---

[14] *Russian Disinformation Attacks on Elections: Lessons from Europe,* hearing of the Subcommittee on Europe, Eurasia, Energy and the Environment, House Foreign Affairs Committee, July 16, 2019, https://www.youtube.com/watch?v=U3heju1HIQE&feature=youtu.be&t=2545.

I argue for a significantly stepped-up campaign that stresses democratic values while opposing disinformation by Russia and its allies. This includes more messaging to Russia's own citizens.

The book attaches central significance to strengthening non-governmental actors in at-risk countries (those highly vulnerable to Russian IOs), in concert with democratic governments and non-government funders.

I begin with a close look at the forces—governments, NGAs and others—available to contest IOs by Russia and its allies. I assess the strengths and weaknesses of each. I then ask what can be done to multiply these actors' scale and skills. Next, I turn to questions of truth and propaganda—whether a more aggressive information effort by pro-democracy forces means "becoming propagandists ourselves." (Russians might die laughing that we think this is even an issue, but it is a common concern among Western policymakers.)

The study then moves to concrete information actions democracy activists might undertake in at-risk countries, including through social networks. The next topic is the goals and techniques of messaging directly to Russia's population. This is followed by an assessment of the pluses and minuses of covert action by Western countries and local NGAs against Russian IOs, up to and including the democracy movement deploying disinformation of its own. Lest anyone be shocked by such notions, democratic countries long ago lost their virginity in this area. They have used covert IOs before, during and since the Cold War, and no law prevents them from being used again. The question is whether they should be. The study concludes with a limited set of recommendations that would be the most effective in responding to Russian information violence.

The scope of these recommendations is limited to what democratic countries can undertake in the information space. Many other kinds of action are available, and have been used, to retaliate against Russia for its military and political adventurism: trade restrictions, sanctions against individual Russians, military buildups and cancelation of intergovernmental programs. This study concentrates on options in the information sphere, which has received less attention from policymakers.

My focus is resisting Russian operations in Europe, but I refer also to Latin America and Africa, whose democratic governments I include in the general category of the "West." Many of these nations are also at risk from a competition between democratic values, which most of their populations appreciate in principle, and anti-democratic forces that prey on persistent poverty and corruption and a sense that globalization has failed to deliver on its promise. Some Latin American and African states have seen limited, if any, Russian IOs. However, adopting some of the measures described here can advance democracy in general and guard against Russian and other foreign operations in the future.

This study does not deal with political jousting, within a country or from outside, that is based on facts. I recognize that, like any other country, Russia has the right to advance its political arguments in a public and transparent way. The focus here is on communication that directly or indirectly advances Russian interests through deceitful content aimed at destroying democracies' national unity and social fabric.

I use the terms "democratic" and "pro-democracy" in a limited way. Democratic states, in my definition, are those where citizens can expect fair elections, rule of law and basic civil and economic freedoms. The term does not necessarily imply specific social policies, or the lifestyle of major Western democracies. My test is simply whether national policy is set by democratic processes and most members of the population feel they have an opportunity to express their will.

This analysis differs from studies that offer dozens of proposals, broken down into tasks for governments, social media platforms, civil society and others. Instead, it identifies a small number of approaches, many of which can be carried out by either government or NGA actors, depending on capabilities and comfort levels from country to country. Unlike many other proposals, the approaches advocated here do not depend on some sudden sea change in Western governments' understanding of the Russian IO threat, or congressional action that would force US social networks to be more responsible and transparent. All of this would be welcome. However, my recommendations are designed to be executed within the reality of the current political environment, where united, assertive action—or even united statements—by the governments of democratic countries are far from assured.

Some initial caveats:

• Information wars are hard, both to wage and to measure who is winning. There is no silver bullet for disinformation. "Give me the person who has the magic formula and I'll give him a million dollars," says Tatyana Margolin, regional director for the Open Society Eurasia Program.[15] Sometimes Americans tend to believe that any problem can be solved with enough resources. As Washington has found in its overseas engagements, this is often not the case. Months of expensive and painstaking information efforts can be upended in an instant by a sudden world event or even a sensational news photo showing Abu Ghraib prisoners or rioting in American cities. It is not even clear when an information war has been won; an actor must precisely define the attitudes and actions it hoped to encourage in a target

---

[15] Tatyana Margolin, interview with author, February 26, 2020.

population, and then have the capacity to measure if the desired effect occurred.

• Russia is unlikely to ever fully renounce the IOs that have been a core part of its survival strategy since the Bolshevik Revolution. These operations today are aided by a host of surrogates, many of which have built their own political or money-making agendas on top of Russian narratives. For its part, the West, with its crushing economic and cultural power, has a bottomless well of marketing skill and a growing number of NGA allies. Game theory teaches that as the number of players increases, the harder it is to control events. Even if Russia or Western governments suddenly agreed to stop all information efforts undermining each other, they would have no chance of doing so.

• The cosmos has not ordained that Russia and democratic states must eternally be enemies. Some analysts believe Putin, conscious of his legacy and economic reality, will moderate his course. Russia may also be concerned in the long run more about China than Western countries. A stronger response to Russian influence could help to restore the West's nerves and stabilize its overall dynamics with Moscow, just as equivalent nuclear capabilities have. This would allow both sides to concentrate on the strategic issues and economic goals that are the most significant to their peoples.

Chapter I: Who Can Respond to Russian IOs?

One reason for the effectiveness of Russian IOs is that they are flexible, decentralized and benefit from the skills of many actors. Putin's Presidential Administration is widely believed to approve general concepts of the countries to be targeted and the outcomes the Kremlin would like to see. It also is likely to establish some rules of engagement for those serving the Russian state—if not moral principles, at least guidance about the level of risk to be taken. Beyond that, the Kremlin grants substantial freedom to a dizzying variety of government agencies, oligarchs, social media influencers, populist haranguers and for-profit entrepreneurs to create information products that serve Kremlin interests, while often advancing their own goals as well.

Pro-democracy forces have their own broad range of actors. These are associated even more loosely than pro-Russian forces; while the Kremlin provides a common reference point for its allies, there is no one headquarters for democracy. Viewed together, these forces have substantial power. This chapter is devoted to identifying the main forces on the democratic side of the information conflict and the strengths and weaknesses of each. The next chapter will consider how these forces might work better together, and force multipliers that could add dramatically to their combined strength.

Governments

The broad variety of information actors that currently serve Russian interests are not the kind of challenge that Western governments are used to dealing with. In the Cold War, Soviet IOs could be easily identified as such: *Radio Moscow* broadcasts, pro-Communist newspapers and unions, and front organizations that parroted Soviet viewpoints. When Moscow changed its propaganda line, all these actors turned on a dime to reflect the new position. The overall goal was to paint an alluring portrait of Soviet life, energize anti-military sentiment in NATO countries and spread rumors in developing nations about malevolent Western intentions. Soviet efforts were predictable, and all originated at the same place.

Facing Soviet IOs of this kind, directly financed and tightly controlled from Moscow, Western countries responded with their own government-run strategies that were appropriate for the time. Government spokespeople and publications relentlessly highlighted Soviet internal repression and Moscow's arms buildups. They portrayed NATO as essential to block Soviet tanks from pouring through the Fulda Gap. With the Soviet economy obviously floundering, the capitalist market system was the only reasonable option for Africa and Latin America. Western information efforts were conducted in a top-down process similar to what the Soviets used: centralized decision-making that was then carried out by a variety of officially financed or controlled agencies. In the United States, the billion-dollar US Information Agency (USIA) was charged with telling a positive story about America. The Active Measures Working Group (AMWG), created by the Reagan administration in 1981, had the separate job of countering Soviet IOs. The AMWG grouped the Defense Department, Central Intelligence Agency (CIA), State Department, Federal Bureau of Investigation (FBI) and USIA, and issued a stream of public reports exposing Soviet falsehoods and forgeries.[1] The AMWG operated until 1992, a year after the Soviet collapse. USIA was shut down in 1999, many of its functions merged into the State Department.

Officials today often wistfully recall the era of the USIA and AMWG as a golden age of response to Russian disinformation. "Perhaps a similar interagency effort and strategic communications strategy is required today if we are to successfully combat the Kremlin's influence and disinformation campaigns both here in the US and abroad," Rep. Hal Rogers, a senior Republican on the House of Representatives Appropriations Committee, mused at a hearing in 2019.[2] Congressional Republicans have called for USIA to be re-created.[3] Yet, the playing field has changed radically since the days of the Cold War.

Actions so Far

If Western governments today had the courage and unity of purpose of Cold War times, they might be able to lead an effective struggle against disinformation now. Governments can expose disinformation

---

[1] For details of the AMWG's work, see Fletcher Schoen and Christopher J. Lamb, "Deception, Disinformation, and Strategic Communications: How One Interagency Group Made a Major Difference," *Strategic Perspectives* 11, Institute for National Strategic Studies, June 2012, https://ndupress.ndu.edu/Portals/68/Documents/stratperspective/inss/Strategic-Perspectives-11.pdf.

[2] *United States Efforts to Counter Russian Disinformation and Malign Influence*, hearing of the Subcommittee on State, Foreign Operations, and Related Programs, House Foreign Affairs Committee, video, July 10, 2019, https://appropriations.house.gov/events/hearings/united-states-efforts-to-counter-russian-disinformation-and-malign-influence.

[3] "Strengthening America & Countering Global Threats," Republican Study Committee, US House of Representatives, 80, June 10, 2020, https://rsc-johnson.house.gov/sites/republicanstudycommittee.house.gov/files/%5BFINAL%5D%20NSTF%20Report.pdf.

tactics, focus populations on the danger, threaten adversaries with retaliation and pour resources into civil society efforts. Various Western governments have done each of these things to some degree, especially since Russia's intervention in the 2016 US elections—but with little consistency.

On the plus side, the US government's 2018 National Cyber Strategy vowed to use "all appropriate tools of national power to expose and counter the flood of online malign influence and information campaigns and non-state propaganda and disinformation."[4] Although Trump is openly dismissive of Russian IOs directed against the United States, his administration's 2021 budget request provides $21 million specifically to counter Russian disinformation in Europe, Eurasia and Central Asia. The request more than doubles the budget of the Global Engagement Center, the closest thing the US has to an information warfare coordinating center, to $138 million.[5] Congress may increase counter-disinformation funds even more.

USAID and the Defense Department have built up their own programs to fight Russian information and cyber operations. The Treasury Department has sanctioned Russian individuals involved in that effort. To secure the 2018 US midterm elections, the Pentagon used authorities granted by Trump to launch a cyberattack on the Internet Research Agency on Election Day, and reportedly peppered individual Russian cyber operators with messages saying their identities were known.[6] More broadly, the State Department spends

---

[4] The White House, *National Cyber Strategy of the United States of America,* September 2018, https://www.whitehouse.gov/wp-content/uploads/2018/09/National-Cyber-Strategy.pdf.

[5] US Department of State, "State Department and U.S. Agency for International Development (USAID) FY 2021 Budget Request: Fact Sheet," February 10, 2020, https://www.state.gov/state-department-and-u-s-agency-for-international-development-usaid-fy-2021-budget-request/.

[6] Julian E. Barnes, "U.S. Begins First Cyberoperation Against Russia Aimed at Protecting Elections," *The New York Times,* October 28, 2018,

more than $2 billion annually on "public diplomacy"—the ensemble of its international information, media, cultural and educational exchange programs, all of which have value in the information struggle.

Meanwhile, the United Kingdom said in 2019 that it will spend £18 million ($22 million, in June 2020) over three years to counter disinformation and fake news across Eastern Europe and strengthen independent media in the Western Balkans.[7] The EU's Stratcom East unit, which exposes Russian IOs on its frequently sarcastic *EUvsDisinfo* website, saw its 2019 budget boosted to €5 million ($5.6 million, in June 2020) from €1.9 million ($2.1 million) in 2018.[8] The EU also announced it would put more staff in non-EU member states to run anti-disinformation campaigns. EU foreign affairs chief Josep Borrell of Spain, appointed in 2019, has received good reviews internally for his awareness of Russian IOs. He has noted that "today soft power is becoming a kind of hard power also, and we [the EU] have to learn to use all of our capabilities […] in order to defend our interests with the same assertiveness that others do."[9]

---

https://www.nytimes.com/2018/10/23/us/politics/russian-hacking-usa-cyber-command.html, and Ellen Nakashima, "U.S. Cyber Command operation disrupted Internet access of Russian troll factory on day of 2018 midterms," *The Washington Post,* Feb. 27, 2019, https://www.washingtonpost.com/world/national-security/us-cyber-command-operation-disrupted-internet-access-of-russian-troll-factory-on-day-of-2018-midterms/2019/02/26/1827fc9e-36d6-11e9-af5b-b51b7ff322e9_story.html.

[7] Foreign & Commonwealth Office, "UK steps up fight against fake news," news release, July 7, 2019, https://www.gov.uk/government/news/uk-steps-up-fight-against-fake-news.

[8] European Union, "Questions and Answers—The EU steps up action against disinformation," news release, December 4, 2018, https://ec.europa.eu/commission/presscorner/detail/en/MEMO_18_6648.

[9] "Brussels Forum 2020: A Conversation with Josep Borrell," video, German Marshall Fund, June 22, 2020, https://www.youtube.com/watch?v=LrEdjsmB3j8&list=PLRlpW88SeBSPD79WFzP9jpawQGDyapjYM&index=16&t=905s.

EU Vice President Věra Jourová, who grew up amid Soviet-era propaganda in Czechoslovakia, has been assigned to develop in a new 2020 European Democracy Action Plan against disinformation. The EU allocated €2.5 million ($2.8 million, in June 2020) in 2019 for a European Digital Media Observatory to fight disinformation. A host of EU national governments are running their own projects to contest disinformation in general or Russian IOs in particular. The Swedish government has mailed leaflets to households about the disinformation threat. Angelina Jolie agreed to produce television programs to teach young Britons about disinformation. Other countries with such programs include Finland, the Baltics, Spain, France, the Czech Republic and Poland. Interestingly, efforts targeted specifically at disinformation seem the most extensive in smaller countries; in the larger democracies of Western Europe, the information conflict has largely become a subtheme of existing political conflicts.

A Lack of Unity

"The West is far more powerful than Russia. If we're in any way united, they don't have a leg to stand on," John Sipher, the former head of the CIA's Russia operations, told a 2020 conference on disinformation in Brussels. Yet, despite everything Western governments have done, Russia would be correct to view their actions as patchy and uncoordinated. Many do not even have a central "rumor control" site or social network feed where the government spotlights dangerous and false information—from Russia or elsewhere—and gives its response.[10]

---

[10] When the coronavirus broke out, officials in the four Visegrad countries tried to counter false information by pressing into service a variety of websites and Facebook pages that citizens were not used to routinely referring to. See "COVID-19 in CEE," *GLOBSEC*, April 17, 2020, https://mailchi.mp/GLOBSEC/covid-19-in-cee-weekly-roundup_corona-disinfo-and-impact-on-democracy-

As for Russian IOs in particular, EU and NATO countries hardly have a unified view of them. Some believe Russian IOs are far from a top priority. To the Italian government, migration and North Africa are bigger foreign concerns, while Russia looks more like a trading opportunity. Some countries are befuddled by the Kremlin's intertwining of its messages with those of domestic political opponents, or the beliefs of religious or ethnic communities. If top Spanish or Italian officials were to declare war on Russian narratives, they could be seen as attacking right-wing parties in their own governing coalitions, which promote the same ideas as Moscow. A 2018 assessment by the hardline European Values Center for Security Policy listed only five of the 28 EU members—the now-departed UK, Sweden and the three Baltic republics—as "full-scale defenders" against Russian subversion. The center counted nine more as "the awakened" and the rest as "hesitant," "in denial" or outright "Kremlin collaborators."[11]

The effect of EU disunity has been to keep actions by the central EU bureaucracy to minimal levels. The European Commission official who announced the €5 million counter-disinformation budget, Vice President Andrus Ansip, complained afterward it was meager. Ansip, an Estonian, said pro-Kremlin information channels have budgets of €1.1 billion ($1.2 billion, in June 2020) a year.[12] The EU's small

---

k4kbhjppfm?e=9421bc0cee. An example of an always-on government fact-checking service is Panama's Pacto Ético Digital. It was initially aimed at pre-election disinformation but now functions as a general fact-checking site that has also been active amid disinformation on the coronavirus. See https://twitter.com/pactoeticodg?lang=en.

[11] *2018 Ranking of countermeasures by the EU28 to the Kremlin's subversion operations*, Kremlin Watch Report (Prague: European Values Center for Security Policy, 2018), 7–8, https://www.kremlinwatch.eu/userfiles/2018-ranking-of-countermeasures-by-the-eu28-to-the-kremlin-s-subversion-operations.pdf.

[12] "Ansip uncovered: Commission Vice-President on disinformation, Huawei, copyright," *EurActiv*, January 23, 2019, https://www.euractiv.com/section/cybersecurity/interview/ansip-uncovered-commission-vice-president-on-disinformation-huawei-copyright/.

Stratcom task force even lacks funds to publish its exposés of Russian disinformation in East European languages. The US and, by some reckoning, even the UK outspend the EU's central apparatus on anti-IO activities. After Russia invaded Ukraine, the EU decreed significant sanctions in response to its military actions. The EU's initiatives against Russia's information offensive have amounted mainly to bureaucratic restructurings and declarations that propose, but do not require, responses by member states.[13] Occasionally the EU's calls to resist disinformation have sounded like they are aimed less at Russia than at people in EU member states who have populist sympathies or distrust EU institutions.[14] Messages of that flavor are more likely to further antagonize Euroskeptic EU citizens than to strike a blow against the Kremlin.

French President Emmanuel Macron proposed in 2019 a new European Agency for the Protection of Democracies to advise EU nations on resisting IOs and cyberattacks.[15] If such an agency is ever created, its success will depend on how many nations are interested in its advice. The experience of the EU's Rapid Alert System is not encouraging. Its official mission was to help coordinate responses to hostile narratives, but a less-publicized goal was simply to push details of Russian activity into the consciousness of governments reluctant to recognize the problem. An EU official said the system, established in 2019, had minimal effect because countries unconcerned about Russia

---

[13] For examples, see European Union, "Questions and Answers," and European Council, "Countering hybrid threats: Council calls for enhanced common action," news release, December 10, 2019, https://www.consilium.europa.eu/en/press/press-releases/2019/12/10/countering-hybrid-threats-council-calls-for-enhanced-common-action/.

[14] Martin Williams, "EU vs Fake News: The truth about Brussels' fight against disinformation," *4News*, December 18, 2018, https://www.channel4.com/news/eu-vs-fake-news-the-truth-about-brussels-fight-against-disinformation.

[15] Emmanuel Macron, "Pour une Renaissance européenne [For a European renaissance]," Elysée, March 4, 2019, https://www.elysee.fr/emmanuel-macron/2019/03/04/pour-une-renaissance-europeenne.

paid it little attention, and countries with valuable intelligence were reluctant to share it for fear it would not stay secure. Strong joint actions by EU countries against disinformation seem unlikely given their lack of unity even against murder. In 2018, nine member states abandoned EU solidarity and refused to order expulsions of Russian diplomats over the poisoning of Sergei Skripal and his daughter in the UK. [16] With the UK's absence, pressure within the EU to stand up to Russian IOs is likely to diminish further.

Bureaucratic Confusion

Even in countries with strong commitments to opposing Russian influence, government bureaucracies are frequently divided on the best kind of response. Focus on exposing false narratives at home, or go on the offense and take the information war to Russian citizens? Work to bring down Putin, or try obtain the best possible deal from him for fear a successor could be even worse? (A British intelligence officer who contributed to this study said he struggles with whether there truly are worse characters in the Kremlin wings, or if that idea, too, is a creation of Russian disinformation.)

Along with unclear goals, governments must deal with siloed information within their own bureaucracies. Foreign and defense ministry officials interviewed for this study—even in small countries—said they only had a hazy idea of what their own intelligence services were doing about Russian IOs. Disputes continue within the US national security establishment as to what tools and goals should even be on the table.

Strategy disputes and compartmented information can bring policy paralysis unless some powerful authority has the clout to break deadlocks. Congress has assigned the State Department's Global

---

[16] *2018 Ranking of countermeasures*, 13.

Engagement Center (GEC) to "direct, lead, synchronize, integrate, and coordinate efforts of the Federal Government to recognize, understand, expose, and counter foreign state and non-state propaganda and disinformation efforts" against the United States and its allies.[17] But even with that sweeping mandate, questions continue in Washington about the precise role of the GEC. It is unclear how the center, consisting of little more than 100 people and based inside the State Department, can impose its vision and priorities on the Defense Department, the Department of Homeland Security and other formidable Cabinet-level agencies—especially without backing from a powerful White House or National Security Council (NSC) official committed to fighting disinformation.

At the start of its work, it took the State Department a year to cajole the Pentagon to send $40 million from its budget for the GEC's needs, despite a direct order from Congress that it do so. Discussions abound on whether the GEC should be moved out of State, to some higher level befitting its mission to oversee all the government's counter-IO efforts. The task of countering Russian IOs becomes additionally complicated when it comes to the US population, since regulations restrict the State Department's ability to monitor activity inside the United States and do messaging to the US public.

Yet another question is how public the GEC's work should be. Its head said, in March 2020, that "sometimes publicly revealing what we're seeing is actually counterproductive to higher-level efforts being made to build cooperation [with states that spread disinformation], and sometimes it's a matter of making sure that our policy makers and our leaders are fully informed of what we're seeing."[18] Five months later,

---

[17] H.R. 5515 National Defense Authorization Act for Fiscal Year 2019, Sec. 1284, Modifications to Global Engagement Center, https://www.congress.gov/115/bills/hr5515/BILLS-115hr5515enr.pdf.
[18] "Briefing on Disinformation and Propaganda Related to COVID-19 (remarks by Lea Gabrielle), US State Department, March 27, 2020,

however, it publicly released a 77-page report that detailed and condemned "Russia's disinformation and propaganda ecosystem."[19]

The NSC has created a Policy Coordination Committee on Information Statecraft. But like another separate interagency mechanism, the Russia Influence Group, its role appears to be largely a place to exchange ideas. In the view of many lower-level US officials, the White House and its political appointees in the NSC do not consider opposing Russian IOs an important mission—either because such action could anger Trump personally, or because it hurts efforts to secure Russian cooperation on specific issues like the Middle East. Clarity about Washington's policy toward Russia has deteriorated sharply since a 1983 US National Security Decision Directive declared:

> U.S. policy must have an ideological thrust which clearly affirms the superiority of the U.S. and Western values of individual dignity and freedom, a free press, free trade unions, free enterprise, and political democracy over the repressive features of Soviet Communism.[20]

The effect of the current uncertainty is to put a damper on the enthusiasm of rank-and-file officials to present proposals to battle Russian IOs.

---

https://www.state.gov/briefing-with-special-envoy-lea-gabrielle-global-engagement-center-on-disinformation-and-propaganda-related-to-covid-19/.

[19] "GEC Special Report: Pillars of Russia's Disinformation and Propaganda Ecosystem," Global Engagement Center, August 2020, https://www.state.gov/wp-content/uploads/2020/08/Pillars-of-Russia%E2%80%99s-Disinformation-and-Propaganda-Ecosystem_08-04-20.pdf.

[20] "US Relations With the USSR," National Security Decision Directive No. 75, January 17, 1983, https://www.reaganlibrary.gov/sites/default/files/archives/reference/scanned-nsdds/nsdd75.pdf.

At a 2019 hearing, Rep. Nita Lowey, head of the House Committee on Appropriations, worried, "I see little evidence that we are successful in using all our tools of public diplomacy to get our message out, win the hearts and minds. [...] We have in the United States the best technology and marketing minds in the world. Are we harnessing our talent in this area?"[21]

Perhaps the best thing that can be said for the lack of high-level US coordination is that it could leave individual agencies freer to experiment with different techniques against Russian IOs on their own. However, bureaucracies are risk-averse when there is no strong leader to approve proposals and take the heat if something goes wrong.

The United Kingdom created in 2018 a National Security Communications Team based in the Cabinet Office, which directly supports the prime minister as well as several intelligence agencies.[22] When Sergei Skripal and his daughter were poisoned, the Foreign Office reacted with a strong public diplomacy campaign, posting videos on social media directly accusing Russia of spreading disinformation and hiding its chemical weapons program. One video warned, "Think critically about information shared by Russian state accounts and state media."[23] However, a report by Parliament in July 2020 severely criticized the government for an inadequate response to Russian influence in Britain overall.

---

[21] *United States Efforts to Counter Russian Disinformation and Malign Influence.*
[22] HM Government, "Government Communication Plan 2019/20," 2019, https://gcs.civilservice.gov.uk/communication-plan-2019/strengthening-our-democracy/.
[23] Foreign Office (@foreignoffice), "This is how the Russian state is spreading disinformation following the Salisbury attack. We know the tactics they use, but they don't change the facts," *video*, Twitter, March 29, 2018, 8:24 a.m., https://twitter.com/foreignoffice/status/979333458131607553?lang=en.

Governments fighting disinformation must also contend with conflicting priorities. A state may be corrupt and close to Russia, making its government a likely target for messaging against false Russian narratives. At the same time, it may, for example, be a strong opponent of the Islamic State (IS) or helpful to the West in some other way. In the State Department system, an embassy that has cultivated such a government in order to accomplish some specific goal can refuse "post clearance" for a democracy program that could put the government in danger. Shifting priorities can also hijack messaging units like the GEC, with focus suddenly pulled off a target like Russia to focus in a crisis on Venezuela, Iran or elsewhere.

Speed and Credibility

Governments also are not adept at the quick, nimble social media and web campaigns needed to fight disinformation today. Political messaging is no longer a matter mainly for press conferences and newspapers, as in USIA and AMWG days. Today's information wars leap in seconds from news apps to podcasts to social networks to video games. Veronika Špalková of the European Values Center in Prague estimates that a response to disinformation must come within two hours to have a chance of countering a false narrative.[24] Russian operators are known for their freedom to throw multiple, even contradictory, lines of argument at a problem to see what sticks. Government bureaucracies, by contrast, are built to maintain maximum discipline over public communication. Messaging with a government imprimatur often requires extensive internal discussion and clearance from a host of sub-bureaucracies. Richard Stengel, who tried to remake the State Department's international messaging, recounts a case where posting a news-related banner on a State website took ten days to shepherd through the department's clearance process, and would have taken longer if he had not gone directly to

---

[24] Viktoria Spalkova, personal communication with author, March 18, 2020.

the secretary of state's office.[25] Former FBI agent Clint Watts, a student of Russian and Islamic extremist IOs, argues:

> [S]uccessful social media influence messengers must be human to be social, nimble to be effective, timely to be relevant, and adaptable to be successful. This is the appeal of President Donald Trump, whose personal Twitter posts, whether one likes them or hates them, effectively engage, enrage and mobilize audiences. Sadly, no other American government leader or representative is given the autonomy to engage without scrutiny and joust without doubt the way the president does from his private platform. America's official social media messengers are neutered from the outset."[26]

One reason Kremlin messaging is agile is that it uses outside contractors. The Internet Research Agency is not a government organization but an enterprise of Yevgeny Prigozhin, "Putin's chef" and a major government contractor. Western governments have their own traditions of entrusting projects to "implementers" and subcontractors. A later chapter will discuss these implementers in more detail.

Even if government messaging is efficient, the government sending the message must have credibility. No major government today, East or West, has the credibility of the major powers of old.[27] The US

---

[25] Richard Stengel, *Information Wars: How We Lost the Global Battle Against Disinformation and What We Can Do About It* (New York: Atlantic Monthly Press, 2019), 64.

[26] Clint Watts, *Messing with the Enemy* (New York: HarperCollins, 2018), 194.

[27] A 2020 survey asking people in ten countries whom they trusted most for information on the coronavirus found only 51 percent trusted their national leaders. "Trust and the coronavirus," Edelman, March 6, 2020, 9, https://www.edelman.com/sites/g/files/aatuss191/files/2020-03/2020%20Edelman%20Trust%20Barometer%20coronavirus%20Special%20Repor t_0.pdf.

government's image has been clouded by decades of hapless military adventures, Trump's constant false statements, America's racial violence and poor performance in the coronavirus epidemic. Though many abroad still respect the United States' democracy and prosperity and wish the same for themselves, they hardly take at face value everything that America says. US claims that Iran shot down a Ukrainian aircraft in 2020 might not have carried the day over Iranian denials had Iran not eventually admitted what it did. In many other democratic countries, leaders are new in office, struggling for authority amid polarized societies and widespread cynicism. Putin may be listened to with somewhat more attention, but mainly out of fear that he is more likely to deliver on a threat. In the days of the AMWG, US representatives met regularly with newspaper editors worldwide to brief them on the latest Kremlin disinformation. Such a project would be much harder today. Not only has US credibility declined, but major media outlets have more trouble preserving their own credibility in the storm of social media chaos.

Resorting to Legislation

Legislation is exclusively a prerogative of states, so governments turn to it instinctively to solve problems. Thus, has it been in the disinformation realm. Dozens of countries have adopted or are debating legislation aimed at banning hate speech, disinformation and inauthentic social media activity. In authoritarian countries, such laws are often just a cover for additional censorship. That is usually not the intent in democratic societies, but any law on information is risky where free speech is valued.

In 2018 both France and Germany passed laws aimed at disinformation. In France, the Law Regarding the Struggle Against the Manipulation of Information includes a ban on "false information" within three months ahead of an election. Courts must rule within 48 hours on whether a statement brought before them is false or not, and they have wide discretion in terms of how to stop its spread. Germany's Network Enforcement Act, or NetzDG, requires online platforms to remove "obviously illegal" posts within 24 hours of their being reported. Systematic failure to delete them can lead to fines of up to €50 million ($56 million, in June 2020).[28]

Both laws have drawbacks. France's measure, which has never been used, contains vague descriptions of false information that leaves it open to challenge in European courts. (A French law similar to NetzDG was overruled by France's own Constitutional Court in June 2020.[29]) The draconian fines and 24-hour time limit prescribed by Germany's NetzDG legislation create a better-safe-than-sorry incentive for social platforms to haul down anything that could conceivably violate the law, even if it might turn out on closer inspection to have been legal.

These laws aside, the tide in the EU has been toward extreme caution over anything that might be classified as government censorship. An EU-appointed High-Level Expert Group on Fake News and Online Disinformation declared in 2018:

> Legal approaches amounting to well-intentioned censorship are neither justified nor efficient for disinformation. Right of defence and speed are incompatible. Public reaction to censorship will backfire, as "the establishment" or "parties in power" could be (mis-)perceived as manipulating the news to their advantage.[30]

---

[28] At issue is content that is already defined as illegal under existing German law. Examples include libel, incitement to hatred, posting of violent images and invasion of privacy.

[29] "Décision n° 2020-801 DC du 18 juin 2020," French Constitutional Court, June 18, 2020, https://www.conseil-constitutionnel.fr/decision/2020/2020801DC.htm.

[30] *A multi-dimensional approach to disinformation: Report of the independent High Level Group on fake news and online disinformation* (Brussels: European Union, 2018), 30, http://ec.europa.eu/newsroom/dae/document.cfm?doc_id=50271.

Ukraine, the recipient of massive Western aid, including for free media, is considering a drastic anti-disinformation law that includes government regulation of media and imprisonment for journalists convicted of spreading disinformation.[31] It has brought well-merited international condemnation. For many, its fate will be viewed as a litmus test of Ukraine's commitment to democratic principles.

International Broadcasting

Often unappreciated as powerhouses of Western influence are government-financed broadcasters. These include the *BBC*, the *Voice of America*, *Radio Free Europe/Radio Liberty*, *Deutsche Welle* the networks of France-Médias-Monde and others loosely organized in an alliance known as the DG7.[32] These companies have largely abandoned static-prone shortwave transmission to become active across the web, online social networks, FM radio and television. They operate in more than 60 languages. They display a nimbleness their governments lack as they report breaking news and constantly experiment with multimedia innovation.

For audiences in some authoritarian countries, these voices are the main alternative to official media. They not only report events and call out disinformation but serve as a model of journalism that speaks truth to power. They are a powerful tool of soft power because the

---

[31] "Media Freedom Groups Express Unease Over Ukrainian Disinformation Bill," *Radio Free Europe/Radio Liberty*, January 23, 2020, https://www.rferl.org/a/media-freedom-groups-express-unease-over-ukrainian-disinformation-bill/30393814.html.

[32] Other members include the Australian Broadcasting Corporation, the Canadian Broadcasting Corporation and Japan's NHK. The coalition undertakes joint projects and adopts positions on press freedom and disinformation issues. See, for example, https://www.usagm.gov/2019/12/05/dg7-international-public-service-media-organizations-launch-project-against-disinformation/.

reliability of their reporting builds respect for the values of the countries where they are based.

Interestingly, although authoritarian regimes often see their content as aimed at undermining them, the broadcasters do not consider themselves government communication tools. They endorse their governments' broad goals of advancing democracy and free speech, but see themselves as engaged in independent journalism—not in public diplomacy or sending specific messages. As early as the initial postwar years, the UK Foreign Office found the *BBC* unwilling to follow its direction in broadcasts to Russia: "[W]here the Foreign Office pressed for hard-hitting broadcasts in Russian programmes, attacking and denouncing the actions of the Soviet Union and its propaganda activities, the *BBC* resisted, warning against 'thinking too exclusively in terms of counter-propaganda.' "[33]

The debate continues today. Journalists at *Radio France Internationale* protested vehemently in 2019, when Premier Edouard Philippe suggested that France-Médias-Monde might serve as a "diplomatic influence operator." They declared, "No, Mr. Prime Minister, public media is not state media, and *RFI*'s job is not to be 'the voice of France.' "[34] Amanda Bennett, director of the *Voice of America*, told a 2019 conference, "The word 'message' is a very, very

---

[33] Alban Webb, "Iron Curtain: How did the BBC's response to the descending Iron Curtain shape its Cold War broadcasting style?" *History of the BBC*, undated web presentation, https://www.bbc.com/historyofthebbc/100-voices/coldwar/iron-curtain.

[34] Société des journalistes de RFI (@sdjrfi), "Mr le Premier Ministre, un média public n'est pas un média d'Etat, RFI n'a pas vocation à être 'la voix de la France.' Nous appelons le gouvernement à investir dans des médias internationaux de qualité et non à tenter de les transformer en opérateurs de communication," Twitter, February 21, 2019, 8:37 a.m., https://twitter.com/sdjrfi/status/1098577560370323458?ref_src=twsrc%5Etfw%7Ct wcamp%5Etweetembed%7Ctwterm%5E1098577560370323458&ref_url=https%3A %2F%2Ffr.africacheck.org%2F2019%2F03%2F14%2Fblog-media%2F.

dirty word at the *Voice of America* because that implies that you are deliberately moving your content in order to achieve a particular end." *VOA*'s job, she said, is exporting "the First Amendment, neutral news, truthful news, not messaging, independent of a government."[35]

It is not unreasonable to ask, however, if truthful news is always neutral news. Should these broadcasters provide a fully balanced diet of news, including detailed coverage of whatever good things dictatorial regimes do? Or should they be "alternative" news outlets, devoting their limited airtime and internet resources to what authoritarian governments do not reveal? The concept of complete balance is at odds with the fact that many audience members come to foreign outlets specifically because they want to hear the other side of what their leaders are telling them. They already know all the benefits of the new bridge the dictator announced this morning; what they want to learn is which of his brothers got the contract. Many also continue to believe, as I do, that highlighting what is legitimately positive about Western broadcasters' home countries is not inappropriate. If Western countries do not promote their own accomplishments, no one else will do it for them.

For its part, Russia refuses publicly to accept that these broadcasters are independent, calling them outlets of government propaganda that only claim to be free media. However, it tacitly acknowledges their independent status by aiming retaliation for their broadcasts against the outlets themselves, rather than at their home governments. After accusing Western broadcasters of interfering in its 2017 and 2019

---

[35] "Stemming the Tide of Global Disinformation," conference transcript, Council on Foreign Relations, October 11, 2019, https://www.cfr.org/event/stemming-tide-global-disinformation. Legislation on what US international broadcasters are supposed to be doing is contradictory. See Thomas Kent, "Congress needs to clarify mission and oversight of Voice of America," *The Hill*, April 28, 2020, https://thehill.com/opinion/technology/494957-congress-needs-to-clarify-mission-and-oversight-of-voice-of-america.

elections, virtually all Russian threats were directed against the broadcasters' bureaus and correspondents in Russia.

Beyond political issues, the government broadcasters suffer from a content problem. Except for the *BBC,* most lag far behind commercial networks, including Russian ones, in the attractiveness of their programming. They lean toward standard-style newscasts and round tables of experts, rather than the dynamic, opinionated news and news-comedy shows that are so popular with audiences. Amid current budget-cutting and reluctance to confront Russia directly, the broadcasters may never obtain the funding they truly need, or venture too far into politically edgy content. The broadcasters also suffer from increasing competition, such as *Al Jazeera* and Turkey's *TRT,* that portray themselves as objective networks outside the DG7 umbrella.

This survey of government responses to Russian IOs shows some strong responses but a critical lack of unity and coordination. Messaging created directly by government bureaucracies suffers from glacial decision-making in an area where fast reaction is critical. Legislation against disinformation has been spotty and controversial. Attempts to ban Russian media risk making democratic countries look as censorious as the Kremlin. Finally, government-funded international broadcasting can be highly effective in terms of general soft power but cannot be counted on as a tool of government messaging.

In all, most democratic governments lack both a sense of urgency about Russian IOs and the tools to contest them. "The lack of an organized Western response shows politicians and agencies don't feel real pressure on this issue, and so they go on to other things," says the head of a government security service in East Europe.

To the extent that the information conflict with Russia is a war at all, democratic governments are fighting it poorly. The "whole of government" response to Russian IOs that some argue for is worth little if government lacks focus and capabilities. We must look to other actors to do what government cannot.

Non-Government Actors

This study contends that the most energetic force against Russian IOs may be non-government actors. Many are already working to counter IOs by Russia and its allies. They include civil society activists, journalists and media literacy trainers in individual countries, strengthened by transnational coalitions and centers of training and expertise. They are backed by substantial sources of funding.

Local NGAs

Local non-government actors provide authentic, close-to-the-ground activism that has the best chance of resonating with populations in their own countries. Despite the value of foreign resources like the *BBC* and the *Voice of America*, local actors have the greatest credibility. "Psychologically, people are inclined not to want 'the truth' from abroad," says Sergey Parkhomenko, a Russian journalist and senior advisor at the Kennan Institute in Washington.[36] When programs have minimal political coloring, like generic media literacy efforts, direct foreign participation is usually not a problem. When efforts are directed specifically against Russian IOs and their allies, however, local NGAs have far more credibility because they are local people defending their own countries. Even if they receive funding from abroad, they bring their own names, on-the-ground expertise and native enthusiasm to the task. They may also derive strength from pro-democracy local politicians and parliamentary members as well

---

[36] Sergey Parkhomenko, interview with author, May 12, 2019.

as city and regional governments, even if their national governments on the whole are unhelpful to their efforts.

Some of the most active NGA groups model their work on the Lithuanian "elves," who began operating on the internet after Russia's invasion of Ukraine. They are loosely organized, claim to number in the thousands and are known for leading energetic social network campaigns. When Adidas in 2018 marketed a Soviet-retro sportswear line bearing the letters "USSR" and the hammer and sickle, the Lithuanian Foreign Ministry accused the company of abetting Soviet "imperial nostalgia." The elves then took up the campaign. By the next morning, they had created a #StopAdidas hashtag and began posting to the Adidas Facebook page memes showing an Adidas logo on a Soviet labor camp and images of the clothing with the Soviet imagery replaced by a swastika. After more than 6,000 #StopAdidas posts had appeared, Adidas stopped selling the products.

During the COVID-19 pandemic, elves infiltrated conspiracy-oriented chat rooms to battle claims that US soldiers brought coronavirus to Lithuania and that vaccines will contain nanochips to let people be controlled by 5G cellphone signals. Administrators of the chat rooms blocked them but the elves kept coming, using new names and accounts.

Perhaps ten countries now have groups that work actively to undermine IOs by Russia and its allies. Some call themselves elves; others do not. Their work is highly varied. A few examples:

• The InformNapalm investigative group, uniting 30 analysts in 10 countries, publicly identifies individual Russian service members who have fought in Ukraine, Georgia and Syria. It posts lists of soldiers and officers who secretly received decorations for fighting in Ukraine, and the effort has publicized the identities of 116 members of a Russian air force group that bombed Syria.[37] Such "doxing" opens soldiers to online harassment and could make them fear they will be barred from traveling to Western countries. InformNapalm postings also suggest that their identities may come before the war crimes tribunal in The Hague.

• In another country, activists who consider themselves a "secret organization" identified a set of Facebook groups that were being fed, by just a few people, with a steady stream of pro-Russian, conspiracy and hate content. After the activists compelled Facebook to close the groups down, they recreated them under the same names and attracted back about 20 percent of the original members. They then began posting more moderate content, and found this led people who had been gleefully exchanging conspiracy theories in the old groups to become more rational in their comments.

• Before the February 2019 Moldovan elections, the Trolless group, operating with US and German support, tipped off Facebook to some 700 accounts and pages trafficking in disinformation and false identities. Facebook did its own investigation and removed nearly 200.[38]

• Campaigners in the Czech Republic, Slovakia, France and elsewhere are pressing companies to withdraw advertising from sites that spread false news and conspiracy theories. Since many of these sites exist mainly to make money, cutting their revenue may be the best weapon against them.

• Also in Slovakia, members of a civic initiative divided themselves into teams that work their way into closed social media groups. There

---

[37] "About Us," *InformNapalm*, accessed July 10, 2020, http://informnapalm.rocks/.
[38] "Civil Society Tracks Trolls and Fakes, Prompts Facebook Action in Moldova," *Internews*, February 21, 2019, https://internews.org/story/civil-society-tracks-trolls-and-fakes-prompts-facebook-action-moldova.

they take on trolls and try to convert individual people to more democratic perspectives. They also try to influence conspiracy-oriented email chains favored by the elderly.

These activists do not only work in national silos. In recent years, training sessions, largely funded by Western governments and foundations, have brought together NGAs from various countries. Topics at such sessions include how trolls work, how best to communicate with elderly people, and how to do "open-source" investigations based on publicly available information.

Such an investigation might involve a photograph making waves on social networks. Working in teams under an instructor, activists at one conference learned how to use websites like Google Earth and Tineye to determine where the photo was actually taken, and if it might have appeared in a different form years earlier on the internet. They learned to use more advanced software that can even determine the time of day a photo was taken based on the size and direction of shadows.

Perhaps most importantly, training sessions present opportunities for NGAs from different countries to exchange experiences. Conversations at meals crackle with war stories about which tactics worked and which did not in battling Russian IOs and corrupt local figures. Such exchanges lead to further communication and joint projects.

The training sessions have not escaped Russian notice. In 2019, *Sputnik* denounced a conference in Moldova of civil society activists, journalists and artists organized by the Prague Civil Society Center. *Sputnik* called the gathering a "coup factory" and said that "in an atmosphere of strict secrecy and with American money, volunteers were told about strategies for fighting the authorities and about the organization of and media support for mass protests." Participants denied that Russian influence was a focus of the meeting.[39]

Journalists

Independent journalism can be a potent force against Russian IOs, but journalists conceive of their roles in very different ways. Some are of the "objective" school, claiming to simply cover the news without advocating for any cause. Their principles prevent them from taking political positions, teaming up with activists or, often, taking government money. First Draft News, an organization of journalists and academics that has studied Russian disinformation efforts, refuses to hold closed meetings with government officials or prepare reports for them unless the work can be made public.[40] In contrast to the objective camp, independent journalists can be "point-of-view" reporters, openly standing for a cause. From their perspective, this does not keep them from working ethically and grounding their work on facts; they just believe the facts are on their side. Point-of-view journalists may be the majority in at-risk countries, where Western traditions of journalistic impartiality can seem secondary to an immediate need to counter corruption and conspiracies. To point-of-view journalists there is nothing unethical in openly labeling Russia as a major threat to free societies and targeting it specifically in investigative reporting. Such journalists also have no problem partnering with, and taking training and funding from, foundations and governments that share their views.

Journalistic groups that focus on exposing disinformation may be denounced by Russia as propaganda tools or even intelligence

---

[39] "*Sputnik* Moldova Painted Media Forum as a Coup Factory," *Polygraph.info*, November 1, 2019, https://www.polygraph.info/a/fact-check-sputnik-moldova/30248595.html.

[40] "About," *FirstDraft*, accessed July 10, 2020, https://firstdraftnews.org/about/.

operators for Western governments. While some do receive grants from governments or government-financed foundations, they tend to have other sources of support as well, including private donors, subscriptions and crowdfunding. Among such groups is Bellingcat, a collective of researchers in more than 20 countries that has published deep reporting on Russian actions and disinformation in Ukraine and Syria.[41] It won a European Press Prize in 2019 for identifying the agents who committed the Skripal poisoning. Another group is the Conflict Intelligence Team, whose coverage areas include Russian mercenaries abroad. (The team insists its members should not be called journalists, because they use "techniques deemed unethical by journalists [...] hidden filming, field surveillance, working under legends with soldiers, militia fighters and their relatives. In especially important cases we pay our informers."[42] Exiled Russian industrialist Mikhail Khodorkovsky runs media projects including MBK Media, a Russian-language website dedicated to exposing Kremlin corruption and disinformation,[43] as well as Dossier Center, which shares with journalists its investigations into "the criminal activity of various people associated with the Kremlin."[44] *Coda Story*, with sites in English and Russian, focuses on disinformation, migration, authoritarian uses of technology and LGBT rights, all of them hot-button issues in the information conflict.[45]

This study will consider all independent journalists to be NGAs, although the objective contingent would bridle at the suggestion they are soldiers for one side in an information war. Democratic societies

---

[41] "About," *Bellingcat*, accessed July 10, 2020, https://www.bellingcat.com/about/.

[42] "About our Conflict Intelligence Team (CIT) and our investigations," *Conflict Intelligence Team*, accessed July 10, 2020, https://citeam.org/about-our-team/?lang=en.

[43] "MBK Media," *Khodorkovsky*, accessed July 10, 2020, https://khodorkovsky.com/mbk-media/.

[44] "The Dossier Center," *Khodorkovsky*, accessed July 10, 2020, https://khodorkovsky.com/dossier-center/.

[45] "What is Coda?" *Coda Story*, accessed July 10, 2020, https://codastory.com/about/.

always benefit in the long run from independent journalism, whether it is objective or responsibly point-of-view. Almost all journalists, even those working for outlets that espouse objectivity, intrinsically favor a free press because their work depends on media freedom.

In the past decade, a new phenomenon has massively multiplied the power of investigative journalism: large-scale international reporting projects targeting corruption and disinformation, some of it Russia-related. Leaders in the movement are the Organized Crime and Corruption Reporting Project (OCCRP)[46] and the International Consortium of Investigative Journalists (ICIJ),[47] which use sophisticated artificial intelligence tools to analyze mountains of data. Both were involved in the 2016 Panama Papers investigation, a team effort by journalists in 80 countries. Based on 11.5 million leaked documents, the reporting implicated close associates of Putin in corrupt financial activities. (The independent Russian newspaper *Novaya Gazeta* was a participant.) In Africa, the Code for Africa project unites investigative reporters and data journalists in 19 states.

Fact-Checkers

Fact-checking is an offshoot of journalism but open to civil society NGAs as well. Fact-checking organizations have been growing at enormous speed worldwide; in April 2020, there were nearly 240 active organizations in some 80 countries, an increase of 26 percent in 10 months.[48] Fact-checkers not only make public judgments about whether statements by newsmakers are true or false but are moving toward trying to make sure those who lie face consequences. In June

---

[46] https://www.occrp.org/en.

[47] https://www.icij.org/.

[48] Mark Stencel and Joel Luther, "Update: 237 fact-checkers in nearly 80 countries … and counting," *Duke Reporters' Lab,* April 3, 2020, https://reporterslab.org/category/fact-checking/#article-2656.

2019, three leading fact-checking groups based in South Africa, Argentina and the UK declared, "Fact checkers have concentrated on education for a long time. In the future it will be our job to agitate our engaged regular readers and to organise to challenge those powerful people and organisations that provide and promote misinformation without accountability."[49] Research collected by the three organizations suggests that pressure by fact-checking groups can make public figures and media outlets more accurate in their statements.[50]

Fact-checking, like investigative reporting, has become highly collaborative nationally and internationally. News organizations that normally compete for scoops often put their rivalries aside for fact-checking projects. "If you want to win battles, you need to go in unified," says Grégoire Lemarchand of Agence France-Presse, one of the biggest coordinators of international fact-checking work. In 2020, the International Fact-Checking Network (IFCN) organized more than 100 members in 45 countries to fight false information about the coronavirus. The previous year, 100 Argentine groups formed the Reverso project to judge statements by candidates in their national election. FactcheckEU, created by 19 European news outlets to monitor the campaign for the 2019 European elections, resumed activity again that year to identify false stories when fire struck Notre Dame Cathedral. Other joint fact-checking efforts have taken place in Mexico, Spain, Brazil and Bolivia.[51]

---

[49] Africa Check, Chequeado, and Full Fact, "Fact checking doesn't work (the way you think it does)," *Full Fact,* June 20, 2019, https://fullfact.org/blog/2019/jun/how-fact-checking-works/.

[50] Amy Sippitt, *What is the impact of fact checkers' work on public figures, institutions and the media?* (Africa Check, Chequeado, and Full Fact, February 2020), https://fullfact.org/media/uploads/impact-fact-checkers-public-figures-media.pdf.

[51] Cristina Tardáguila, "The rest of the world's fact-checkers collaborate on big elections—why won't they in the U.S.?" *Poynter,* June 26, 2019, https://www.poynter.org/fact-checking/2019/the-rest-of-the-worlds-fact-checkers-collaborate-on-big-elections-why-wont-they-in-the-u-s/; Philippe Papineau,

When false information about the virus started circulating in Slovakia, activists of a new group called the Digital Infospace Security Initiative[52] swiftly created a website, a campaign on Facebook and another on Instagram to debunk the most dangerous tales. In the course of a month, the shares and "likes" attracted by their warnings propelled their posts into the Facebook feeds of more than 130,000 people.

The speed of fact-checkers' interaction can be impressive. For example, a fact-checking group in France asked fellow members of the International Fact Checking network in May 2020 about a supposed Italian breakthrough that could lead to curing the coronavirus at home. Within 45 minutes, it received detailed responses from fact-checkers in the UK, Italy and Spain describing how the same rumor had spread in their countries and sharing detailed evidence that it was not true.[53]

Fact-checking has become one of the most dynamic movements in journalism and civil society. The IFCN attracted 241 participants from more than 50 countries to its 2019 Global Fact conference in Cape Town.[54] Fact-checkers share skills and software. They have created a common data format, Claim Review, that allows different organizations to aggregate their findings in common databases.[55] The

"Collaborer contre la désinformation aux élections" [Collaborating against election disinformation], *Le Devoir*, March 1, 2019, https://www.ledevoir.com/culture/medias/548950/collaboration-contre-la-desinformation-aux-elections.

[52] "Digital Infospace Security Initiative," *StratPol*, accessed July 10, 2020, https://stratpol.sk/digital-infospace-security-initiative/.

[53] International Fact Checking Network listserv, May 12, 2020.

[54] Baybars Örsek, "Fact-checking and the IFCN made big strides in 2019. Here's what's coming in 2020," *Poynter,* December 18, 2019, https://www.poynter.org/fact-checking/2019/the-state-of-fact-checking-and-the-ifcn-in-2019-and-whats-around-the-corner-for-2020/.

[55] As examples, Debunk.eu, a vibrant Lithuanian fact-checking site that has used Google funding to develop software, has shared technology with Alliance for

COVID-19 coronavirus is raising the visibility of fact-checkers to new levels.

Despite its growth, fact-checking faces challenges. Since 2016, Facebook has been a major financer of the movement (in 2020, it gave an extra $1 million for fact-checking on COVID-19), but fact-checkers often complain the platform is not transparent about how it uses their findings. Fact-checkers who come from objective journalistic organizations worry about being seen as advocates for one political side, especially when one party to a controversy tells more lies and therefore is cited more often for false claims. Even when fact-checkers efficiently correct one false claim, dozens more can be launched on the internet.

No IFCN-accredited team of fact-checkers operates in Russia. Thus, when the network's members from multiple countries collaborated to monitor each of their national leaders' speeches at the 2019 UN General Assembly, Putin's remarks were not subjected to fact-checking by anyone. Interviewed for this study, an executive of a foreign news organization with an office in Moscow said the bureau does not do fact checks on Putin's speeches for fear of repercussions against its staff. The IFCN includes an "offshore," Canadian-based fact-checking organization for statements by Iranian leaders, but none for statements from Russia. Fact-checking organizations also tend to lean toward political and other heavy topics; few have the resources to check celebrity and sports news, which might attract bigger audiences.

Further, there is always the danger that when fact-checkers highlight a false claim that a reader has not seen, the reader will remember the claim more than the knockdown. When fact-checkers go after outlets like *RT* and *Sputnik*, there may also be an implicit message that they

---

Securing Democracy's Hamilton 68 project. UK-based FullFact has provided software to Argentina's Chequeado. Trainers from Ukraine's StopFake project have shared their techniques with fact-checkers in Kazakhstan, Georgia and elsewhere.

are *worth* fact-checking; that is, they have enough journalistic standing to be checked, and whatever in their content is not exposed as false could be true.

Most critically, fact-checkers' products may never reach the online worlds where disinformation lives. Fact checks can exhibit the same technical characteristics online as disinformation—thriving in limited silos of like-minded people instead of reaching the population as a whole.[56] Meanwhile, just as the creators of disinformation are not wedded to the truth, they are not wedded to any one piece of disinformation, either. In the words of Rostislav Valvoda of the Prague Civil Society Center, "If one story line is discredited, the Kremlin will just find some new story line."[57]

Despite these downsides, fact-checkers will play an increasing role in the general information conflict, although—like other NGAs—they would benefit from more resources to publicize their findings. The Global Engagement Center, alert to the importance of fact-checkers, has begun supporting their work. The Atlantic Council partnered with a Mexican fact-checking team during that country's 2018 presidential elections. At the same time, fact-checking is a game anyone can play. *RT* and Russia's *Federal News Agency* run what they portray as their own fact-checking operations.

Investigative journalism and fact-checking are close to political activism. They are a serious threat to disinformation and to corrupt business interests. As the power of these non-government actors grows, especially through cross-border investigations, the risks they face increase.

---

[56] "How Effective Are Fact-Checkers?" *Alto Analytics*, July 12, 2019, https://www.alto-analytics.com/en_US/fact-checkers/.
[57] Rostislav Valvoda, interview with author, June 27, 2019.

According to the Committee to Protect Journalists, more than 500 journalists worldwide have been murdered since 2000 as a result of investigations into business, corruption, crime or politics.[58] Other forms of intimidation include attempts to obstruct journalists' work by trumped-up tax, extremism and libel charges or by denying them government advertising, an essential source of support for media in some countries. In 2020, many countries used the coronavirus outbreak to impose further press restrictions, including demands that media carry only official statements, sometimes of dubious veracity.

Disinformation operators also work to slip false information into legitimate news outlets. The time journalists have to verify facts is limited, and even professional reporters can miss obvious clues that a story is false.[59] Brian Fonseca describes the danger as it appears in Latin America:

> Latin American outlets have limited capacity to fact check everything, and in the race to ensure fresh content, find themselves re-publishing Russian media narratives. This gives the impression that Russia's message is consistent with Latin America's message. In fact, Moscow much prefers the message to come from Latin American media outlets because it carries more credibility.[60]

---

[58] Derived from the database at https://cpj.org/data/killed.

[59] See, for instance, an Estonian experiment showing gaps in the fact-checking skills of professional journalists. Marju Himma-Kadakas, " 'Sparing time from fact-checking': Journalists' skills and competences in recognizing and publishing false information," video, International Fact-Checking Network, June 17, 2020, https://www.youtube.com/watch?v=XrS7IHYNYj4&list=PLEcKYh_fjP9hsDdFjnRk xFdDKARmivAPg&index=2.

[60] Brian Fonseca, "Russian Deceptive Propaganda Growing Fast in Latin America," *Diálogo*, July 24, 2018, https://dialogo-americas.com/articles/russian-deceptive-propaganda-growing-fast-in-latin-america/.

"It is impossible to stop all extremist and propaganda sites," says Jakub Janda, head of the European Values Center. "But we must guard the borders against disinformation around major existing media."[61]

Independent media also face the same "leveling" problem as other media: all content looks about the same on social media and the web, whether it comes from a century-old news organization or a startup that opened last week. The most exciting headline, whatever its source, grabs the reader, and whoever grabs the most readers grabs the ads. Media with substantial readership in at-risk countries have attempted to monetize the depth and credibility of their coverage by putting their content behind paywalls. The Slovak independent daily *Dennik N* says its paywall revenue protects the publication from pressure from political and business interests.[62] However, disinformation is free, and readers who do not care enough about reliable news to pay for it will miss reliable reporting ensconced behind paywalls. Another source of support for independent media is crowdfunding. The independent Hungarian investigative site *Atlatszo* has 3,000 private donors, plus support from the Open Society Foundations.[63] Agora SA, the owner of Warsaw's independent *Gazeta Wyborcza*, has revenue from cinema and outdoor advertising.

In countries without strong civil society organizations and political centers, including many African and Latin American states, independent journalists and fact-checking organizations may be the non-government actors most able to expose disinformation. As of May 2020, there were 42 active fact-checking organizations in Latin America and 17 in Africa (in the Democratic Republic of Congo,

---

[61] Jakub Janda, interview with author, July 1, 2019.

[62] "95% subscriber growth in less than 3 years: How a news startup is driving reader revenue with its own CRM," *What's New In Publishing,* September 25, 2019, https://whatsnewinpublishing.com/95-subscriber-growth-in-less-than-3-years-how-a-news-startup-is-driving-reader-revenue-with-its-own-crm.

[63] https://english.atlatszo.hu/about-us-fundraising/.

Egypt, Ghana, Kenya, Namibia, Nigeria, Senegal, South Africa, Tanzania, Uganda and Zimbabwe).[64] Even if they do not focus on Russia itself as the source of false narratives, their exposure of disinformation in general helps to build public resilience to any activities that Russia may conduct.

Media Literacy Programs

Media literacy initiatives receive some of the broadest support as tools to combat disinformation. Since fact-checking cannot catch every falsehood, and many people never see fact checks at all, the most efficient way to fight falsehoods should be for people to recognize them by themselves. In schools, libraries and NGA forums, media literacy instructors are showing audiences how to verify information, judge if photos are authentic and assess news articles for bias.

There is no shortage of civil society groups, teachers and librarians who can be recruited to this cause. Course materials, including attractive online games, are freely available.[65] Plenty of money exists for media literacy efforts; at least three separate offices of just the US government fund media literacy projects abroad. Under such circumstances, media literacy projects have mushroomed. Libraries in the Czech Republic hold them for senior citizens. The French government's CLEMI agency runs programs in elementary and secondary schools.

---

[64] Duke Reporters' Lab database, https://reporterslab.org/fact-checking/#.
[65] See Cherilyn Ireton and Julie Posetti, *Journalism, 'Fake News' & Disinformation: Handbook for Journalism Education and Training* (Paris: UNESCO, 2018), http://unesdoc.unesco.org/images/0026/002655/265552E.pdf; the extensive curricula and multimedia offered by Stony Brook University School of Journalism in the United States, https://www.centerfornewsliteracy.org/; and The Bad News Game, https://getbadnews.com/.

Some results suggest media literacy programs are having an effect. High school students who went through a project in Ukraine in 2018 were twice as able to detect hate speech than a control group, 8 percent better at identifying fake news stories and 16 percent better at distinguishing fact from opinion.[66] Projects exposing the effects of false information can be quite engaging: the Slovak think tank GLOBSEC organized a project in which two popular video bloggers faked a feud, based entirely on rumors they claimed to have heard. Their spat was so realistic that it spiraled into six days of their fans denouncing each other and even posting death threats. Finally, the two posted a video showing it was all made up, and pointing out how easy it is for rumors to drive people to rage.[67]

Some people promote media literacy as the ultimate answer to disinformation. However, experts raise cautions about this belief. To begin with, media literacy efforts seem to thrive best in countries that have a strong sense of national identity, where much disinformation comes mainly from abroad and instructors are free to identify the sources by name. A slide shown to Finnish students asks bluntly, "Have you been hit by the Russian troll army?"[68] Many countries are more divided, their sense of national unity is weaker and much of their disinformation comes from internal sources. Media literacy classes can also have a boomerang effect. Citizens already disposed to mistrust mainstream media can become even more mistrustful, using their new media literacy skills to pounce on their occasional errors

---

[66] "Boosting Immunity to Disinformation: Ukrainian students better detect false information after teachers integrate media literacy into standard subjects," *IREX*, https://www.irex.org/sites/default/files/node/resource/evaluation-learn-to-discern-in-schools-ukraine.pdf.

[67] "Fighting hoaxes with Slovak YouTubers—case study," video, *GLOBSEC*, November 14, 2017, https://www.youtube.com/watch?v=RJdwJzM89jo.

[68] Eliza Mackintosh, "Finland is winning the war on fake news. What it's learned may be crucial to Western democracy," *CNN*, May 2019, https://edition.cnn.com/interactive/2019/05/europe/finland-fake-news-intl/.

and lack of balance. Those who spread disinformation can claim that media literacy programs themselves are a plot.[69]

Do either fact-checking or media literacy significantly move the needle in the fight against disinformation? Certainly it is good for people to be aware of false information. Truth, however, is not the controlling consideration for everyone. Some people share posts they find amusing with little concern as to whether they are true; they trust their friends not to build cathedrals around them, either. Even when people know a claim is false, the more they see it, the more comfortable they become with sharing it.[70]

It is possible that the coronavirus pandemic will change this situation for the better. People care more about news that concerns them personally, so they are likely to seek sources of reliable information related to protecting themselves personally from the disease.[71] However, this may not prevent them from sharing disinformation about slightly more distant topics, like how the disease originated.

---

[69] *RT* has mocked both fact-checking—a "controversial practice"—and media literacy activists, who it says are "more concerned with controlling the narrative" than encouraging people to think for themselves. Helen Buyniski, "Just (MSM-approved) facts, ma'am! Response to FB's political ad decision shows 'media literacy' was just cover for thought-police," *RT*, January 9, 2020, https://www.rt.com/usa/477861-facebook-factcheck-political-ad-targeting/.

[70] Daniel A. Effron and Medha Raj, "Misinformation and Morality: Encountering Fake-News Headlines Makes Them Seem Less Unethical to Publish and Share," *Psychological Science,* November 21, 2019, available from https://journals.sagepub.com/doi/abs/10.1177/0956797619887896.

[71] Harrison Mantas, "Fact-checkers fighting the COVID-19 infodemic drew a surge in readers," *Poynter,* June 9, 2020, https://www.poynter.org/fact-checking/2020/fact-checkers-fighting-the-covid-19-infodemic-drew-a-surge-in-readers/.

Funding

Money is essential if NGAs are to operate at scale. Democratic actors have deep pockets behind them. In addition to government grants, generous funding for anti-disinformation causes comes from tycoons, investment funds and foundations. In particular:

• George Soros' Open Societies Foundations (OSF) are the largest private sources that NGAs commonly turn to. The foundations budgeted $1.2 billion in overall spending for 2020, including $140.5 million for democracy programs, $16.2 million for freedom of information and digital access and $25.8 million for journalism, all of them increases from 2019.[72]

• The US Congress is pouring $300 million in FY 2020—a 40 percent increase over 2019—into the National Endowment for Democracy (NED) and its core grantees, including the International Republican Institute (IRI) and the National Democratic Institute (NDI). Although the money is from Congress, these organizations have nearly as much discretion in using it as privately run funds. NED alone makes more than 1,600 grants per year to non-government organizations working for democracy in more than 90 countries, with the average grant around $50,000. (Soros' OSF, NED, IRI and NDI all share the distinction of being on the Russian Federation's official list of "undesirable organizations,"[73] meaning they are officially forbidden from operating inside Russia.)

---

[72] https://www.opensocietyfoundations.org/.

[73] "Перечень иностранных и международных неправительственных организаций, деятельность которых признана нежелательной на территории Российской Федерации" ["List of foreign and international non-governmental organizations whose activities are deemed undesirable in the Russian Federation"], Ministry of Justice of the Russian Federation, accessed July 24, 2020, https://minjust.ru/ru/mobile/activity/nko/unwanted.

• Luminate, part of the Omidyar Group established by eBay founder Pierre Omidyar, funds civic and media initiatives to combat misinformation, authoritarianism and what it calls "insular, nationalist perspectives." Since its founding in 2018 Luminate has provided $350 million in funding to organizations in 17 countries.[74]

• In Europe, the independent European Endowment for Democracy, funded by the EU and 24 national governments, spends €16 million ($18 million, in July 2020) a year on democracy support projects. The EU's core European Instrument for Democracy & Human Rights budgeted €1.33 billion ($1.55 billion, in July 2020) for 2014–2020.[75] The EED also has Russian "undesirable organization" status.

• Self-exiled Russian billionaire Mikhail Khodorkovsky, based in London, spends between $5 million and $10 million a year on pro-democracy initiatives inside Russia.[76] These have included promoting independent election candidates, aiding arrested protesters, subsidizing flags and posters, and running public meetings on democracy issues.

Besides these foundations, there are dozens of others whose work includes promoting human rights and democratic societies. They include Germany's Friedrich Ebert, Konrad Adenauer and Heinrich Böll foundations, the Czech Republic's People in Need (also listed by Russia as an undesirable organization) and several Nordic foundations.

---

[74] "About Us," *Luminate*, accessed July 10, 2020, https://luminategroup.com/about.
[75] European Commission, "The Multiannual Financial Framework: The External Action Financing Instruments," news release, December 11, 2013, https://ec.europa.eu/commission/presscorner/detail/en/MEMO_13_1134; "Supporting People Striving for Democracy," EED Annual Report, 2018, https://www.democracyendowment.eu/en/component/attachments/attachments.html?id=289.
[76] Maria Logan (spokesperson for Mikhail Khodorkovsky), interview with author, January 9, 2020.

Recognizing that free media is an indispensable element of the democratic process, many funders have concentrated attention on independent newspapers, websites, broadcasters and fact-checking initiatives. They view media as natural allies and the fastest, most credible way to bring information to the public. "[T]he West should aim to overwhelm the Kremlin with renewed investment in local media and media-literacy education while simultaneously defending, and promoting, freedom of speech and the liberal democracy that protects it," says Anton Barbashin, editorial director at the Russian affairs journal *Riddle*.[77]

The funders' efforts have led to an extensive network of programs to train and protect journalists, often offered at no cost to news media in at-risk and developing countries. (Some worry there are so many opportunities that shrewd activists can become "professional trainees," spending most of their time at conferences.) The Open Information Partnership, started in 2019 with funding from the UK Foreign Office to combat false information, works with media organizations across Europe. Partners include Zinc Network—a London-based communications and implementing group— Bellingcat, the Atlantic Council and the Media Diversity Institute in Brussels.[78] BBC Media Action, a foundation legally independent from the larger *BBC*, partnered with the UK government to strengthen Ukraine's *Hromadske TV* as an independent source of news.[79]

US-funded journalism programs are also substantial. USAID spent $43 million on independent media in 2019, working through a variety

---

[77] Anton Barbashin, "Improving the Western strategy to combat Kremlin propaganda and disinformation," *Atlantic Council*, June 11, 2018, 6, https://www.atlanticcouncil.org/wp-content/uploads/2018/06/Improving_the_Western_Strategy.pdf.

[78] https://www.openinformationpartnership.org/.

[79] "Supporting independent news in Ukraine," *BBC Media Action*, accessed July 10, 2020, https://www.bbc.co.uk/mediaaction/where-we-work/europe-and-caucasus/ukraine/hromadske-tv.

of implementers.[80] Western journalism training often emphasizes the importance of media independence from government, reporting all sides of a story and holding rulers accountable. Russia has noticed Western programs and created journalism training projects of its own.[81] When Putin held a summit with African leaders in Sochi in 2019, Russian officials invited the heads of African news agencies and offered to create training programs for their staffs.

Several Western organizations have focused on the economics of media in at-risk countries, trying to help independent news outlets survive. Since 1995, the Media Development Investment Fund, based in New York and Prague, has plowed nearly $230 million in media ventures in 41 countries where independent information is threatened. (The fund began aiding Russian news companies in 1998. In 2016, the Russian Ministry of Justice declared it an "undesirable organization.")

All these funders of democracy and media causes, taken together, represent an enormous pool of money. NGAs should be swimming in cash. They are not. Many difficulties stand in the way of using the funding efficiently. In the next chapter I discuss measures to improve this situation.

Social Platforms

Around the world, online social networks are one of the most powerful tools of citizen empowerment, giving voice to many who otherwise would not be heard. It is hard to imagine pro-democracy or

---

[80] "Agency Financial Report Fiscal Year 2019: Promoting a Path to Self-Reliance and Resilience," *USAID*, accessed July 10, 2020, https://www.usaid.gov/sites/default/files/documents/1868/USAIDFY2019AFR_508R.pdf.

[81] See, for example, the *SputnikPro* project, http://rs.gov.ru/en/news/47170.

humanitarian work without the facilities these platforms offer. The companies are also unparalleled accelerants for disinformation. They generally act quickly to block content that is clearly illegal or gruesome. They will hide or downrank material they view as dangerous, like crackpot coronavirus cures or anti-vaccine agitation. However, they are largely unable or unwilling to counter the torrents of pernicious political and social narratives on their sites. At least for public consumption, they profess to be confident that good information and decent behavior will eventually outshine the bad. Facebook's Mark Zuckerberg says he stands for "free expression, understanding its messiness, but believing that the long journey towards greater progress requires confronting [rather than censoring] ideas that challenge us."[82] If a value judgment absolutely must be made, the platforms are happiest when they can outsource it. When Google in 2018 felt a need to characterize the reliability of government-funded television networks posting content on YouTube, the company avoided any judgment of its own by providing a link to the entry for each network on Wikipedia. Facebook not only uses outside fact-checkers to verify information on its platform, but outsources to the International Fact-Checking Network the accrediting of fact-checkers. Even accredited fact-checkers can come under fire for supposed bias.[83]

The belief that good information must ultimately drive out the bad strikes many as magical thinking. Former US Ambassador Daniel Fried says the platforms are trying to live in a "post-national paradise. They don't care about political concerns. They're not interested in

---

[82] Tony Room, "Zuckerberg: Standing For Voice and Free Expression" (full text of Zuckerberg speech), *The Washington Post,* October 17, 2019, https://www.washingtonpost.com/technology/2019/10/17/zuckerberg-standing-voice-free-expression/.

[83] Anton Troianovski, "Fighting False News in Ukraine, Facebook Fact Checkers Tread a Blurry Line," *The New York Times,* July 26, 2020, https://www.nytimes.com/2020/07/26/world/europe/ukraine-facebook-fake-news.html.

war. But war is interested in them."[84] Though the companies insist they are technology providers, not publishers, journalism scholar Sarah Oates at the University of Maryland says they need to "adhere to national media models and standards in the United States or, indeed, in any country where there is a free media. If not, prominent social media companies become active agents in the destruction of democracy from both domestic and foreign influences."[85]

However, unless governments and publics manage to force new responsibilities on the platforms, their philosophies—whether grounded in idealism or profit—will continue to rule the day. With their mindsets rooted in technical precision, they feel comfortable in blocking only material that can be objectively defined. Thus, they regularly take down terrorist manifestos, posts from bots and other coordinated networks, and accounts that impersonate people or misrepresent where their owners are based. Facebook removed pages belonging to two major voices in the pro-Russian ecosystem, *SouthFront* and *News Front*, not on the basis of their content but only after determining in May 2020 that they used fake accounts to amplify their visibility.[86] Because of the platforms' focus on technical criteria, any content—even benign—risks removal if spread in a coordinated way that looks "inauthentic" to the networks' systems.

Recognizing this, Russian IOs have evolved to make their social network operations look more like the work of individuals than of an organized system. Russia has largely dropped the use of the most obvious bots, which the platforms have become adept at detecting. Facebook took down a stunning 2.19 billion accounts that violated its

[84] Daniel Fried, interview with author, September 12, 2019.

[85] Sarah Oates, "When Media Worlds Collide: Using Media Model Theory to Understand How Russia Spreads Disinformation in the United States," paper for the Annual Meeting of the American Political Science Association, August 24, 2018, 17, available from https://dx.doi.org/10.2139/ssrn.3238247.

[86] "April 2020 Coordinated Inauthentic Behavior Report," Facebook, May 5, 2020, https://about.fb.com/news/2020/05/april-cib-report/.

standards in just the first quarter of 2019.[87] Russian operators now program their fake accounts to post more randomly, simulating how real people behave online. According to a study by the Atlantic Council's Digital Forensics Research Lab, the Kremlin increasingly distributes false content through "burner accounts" used only once, and over little-known websites and minor social networks. From there, the messages are redistributed at high rates by pro-Russian websites in multiple languages or by human-curated troll accounts on social networks large and small. These accounts may have been created by Russian operators or rented from individuals who do not mind what is done under their name. The content is then retold and retranslated by many more individuals who may not be Russian-controlled at all, but are simply fans of pro-Russian, populist or conspiracy causes. (Some committed individuals post 300 times a day.) Soon the original narrative is circulating on multiple platforms in so many versions and languages that it is almost impossible to determine by algorithmic means that it came from one central operation.[88]

Additional complexity comes when Russian narratives are posted on social platforms that are not easily visible to governments and NGAs, such as closed or encrypted chat rooms on Facebook, Telegram and WhatsApp.

Overarching questions remain about how much responsibility the major social platforms feel over their impact on the world. They could not exist without free societies, or the presumption by users that they are generally healthy information spaces. (Otherwise users would not bother to log on.) Google and Facebook have made sure the top news

---

[87] "An Update on How We Are Doing At Enforcing Our Community Standards," Facebook, May 23, 2019, https://about.fb.com/news/2019/05/enforcing-our-community-standards-3/.
[88] *Operation Secondary Infektion* (Washington: DFR Lab, 2019), https://docs.wixstatic.com/ugd/9d177c_3e548ca15bb64a85ab936d76c95897c7.pdf.

stories displayed on their platforms come from reliable sources. But beyond that, the networks' algorithms are basically non-ideological. They are designed above all to implement the fundamental goals of a commercial social network: to identify the interests of each user, connect that user to others of the same inclinations, and send to all of them content and ads they will find appealing. Researchers complain that Facebook in particular releases insufficient data to understand how false content moves on its platform, leaving open the possibility that the volume and speed with which it spreads are greater than any outsider knows.

A study for NATO found that "a core issue is lack of willingness of the social media platforms to engage in constructive dialogue [...] technologies are blackboxed to an extent that sustainable public scrutiny, oversight and regulation demands the cooperation of platforms."[89] At the very least, platforms could engage more constructively with civil society. An NGA group in Europe's East says it must spread word of hate sites and bots to hundreds of activists, who all submit reports to Facebook; reports from just a few people are not noticed. Understandably, platforms may not want to give thousands of groups, some of which are of doubtful authenticity, direct lines to its staff. However, this is the best way to make sure that legitimate complaints are heard while there is still time to blunt the effects of objectionable content.

With US authorities reluctant to regulate the platforms, most of the pressure on them in the United States has come from media and civil society. In Europe, other than a few measures by individual governments such as Germany's NetzDG law, most effort has been concentrated in the EU. In its cautious tradition, the EU began by convincing the platforms to sign, in 2018, a self-regulatory Code of

---

[89] Samantha Bradshaw, Lisa-Maria Neudert, and Philip N. Howard, *Government responses to malicious use of social media* (Riga: NATO Stratcom Centre of Excellence, 2018), 12, https://www.stratcomcoe.org/download/file/fid/79655.

Practice on Disinformation. The code largely enshrined best practices that the platforms were already implementing. However, European officials are losing patience with the platforms. They talk increasingly of the need for them to be more transparent and to face liability for harmful posts. It is not clear whether the EU has a way to regulate these behemoths while also maintaining a sense of reasonable expectations; to some extent, the platforms have created monsters that even they cannot control.

Some have called for modification of Section 230 of the US Communications Decency Act, which absolves owners of online sites of responsibility for whatever people post there. Such a step by the US Congress would greatly aid regulators worldwide, who see the United States as largely oblivious to the effect social platforms have on the rest of the world. However, US traditions of free speech in the "public square" strongly favor the spirit of Section 230, which also protects the operators of thousands of other sites, including those of mainstream media. Such proposals would force the tech companies, which have long been reluctant to pass judgment on free speech or truthfulness, to take up quasi-judicial roles that the world might live to regret. (Judging by their past behavior, the platforms would outsource these new responsibilities to a brace of subcontractors, adding another layer of controversy over whom they select.)

Many commentators also have called on the platforms to open to the public the algorithms that determine who sees what content. "We already see the Trump campaign preparing the ground for the 2020 election with claims that democracy is rigged because Google algorithms are designed to be biased against 'conservatives,'" Peter Pomerantsev wrote in 2019. "And the problem is, without the necessary algorithmic transparency, who's to say that this isn't so? The black box of the tech companies has to be broken open and public oversight enforced."[90] However, critics of the platforms may underestimate how easy it would be to draw quick conclusions about the algorithms if the platforms were somehow forced to reveal these trade secrets. Anyone looking for simple lines of code that allow or block disinformation will be disappointed. More likely, the algorithms consist of reams of constantly changing code, interlocked with scores of other programs and replete with years of patchwork modifications aimed at fixing one narrow problem or another. Their publication would generate its own industry of kibitzing and conspiracy theories over exactly how the code works.

Others have suggested the platform problem be tackled as a consumer protection issue. Platforms would be required to verify the identities of account holders, require clear labeling of who is behind ads and "promoted content," and make certain that everyone who engages with false content sees follow-ups when fact-checks come through. This would be equally effective against disinformation that is created within a country or that comes from abroad.

Such rules work better inside free countries than authoritarian ones. Rigorous checks on the identities of account holders could frighten people in repressive countries from posting anti-government comments. Repressive regimes could also force platforms to post material from faux fact-checking services to throw doubt on stories that were true. A practical problem also exists. In Argentina, foreigners who buy cellphone SIM cards are required to send photos of themselves, their passports and themselves holding their passports. These are then reviewed for a day or two before the ability to activate the SIM is granted. With 2.5 billion monthly Facebook users and 145

---

[90] Peter Pomerantsev, "The Death of the Neutral Public Sphere," *The American Interest*, September 18, 2019, https://www.the-american-interest.com/2019/09/18/the-death-of-the-neutral-public-sphere/.

million on Twitter, the complexity of verifying the identity of every social network user becomes obvious.[91]

If pressure on the platforms to police content becomes unbearable, their favored solution in democratic countries may ultimately turn out to be legislation like the NetzDG law. This German legislation levies its draconian fines only if platforms fail repeatedly to take down illegal content that is pointed out to them; the platforms may well accept the tradeoff of hauling down almost anything that is questioned in return for avoiding massive penalties.[92] Such laws would require a large infrastructure to receive complaints and delete posts, but if the platforms delete anything questionable they are at least protected from penalties. The law also gives the platforms a limited right to hire outside companies to review the complaints, in line with their tradition of outsourcing value judgments. Complying with such legislation promulgated by authoritarian regimes would be much more problematic, since content that would obviously be legal under Western free speech concepts could violate these regimes' laws. The platforms have often deferred to authoritarian regimes already in blocking content that in a free country would be considered legitimate political speech.

---

[91] Statistics from "Facebook Reports Fourth Quarter and Full Year 2019 Results," Facebook, January 29, 2020, https://www.prnewswire.com/news-releases/facebook-reports-fourth-quarter-and-full-year-2019-results-300995616.html, and "Q1 2019 Earnings Report," Twitter, April 28, 2020, https://s22.q4cdn.com/826641620/files/doc_financials/2019/q1/Q1-2019-Slide-Presentation.pdf.

[92] This could also be the platforms' favored approach to dealing with public pressure like the growing boycott of Facebook by large advertisers over hate speech on the platform. See Alex Barker, "Third of top brands likely to suspend social media spending, survey finds," *Financial Times*, June 30, 2020, https://www.ft.com/content/aa723316-67e6-41a3-9f37-e9c6b8855edb?utm_campaign=meetedgar&utm_medium=social&utm_source=meetedgar.com.

In their fight against sophisticated disinformation networks, platforms also need to decide how close they want to be to each other and to governments. Platforms tend to focus on their own sites and businesses. They share information inconsistently with each other. Sometimes it takes experts like those at the Atlantic Council's Digital Forensics Research Lab and the Stanford Internet Observatory to show engineers at each platform how activity on their sites fits into a broader disinformation mosaic. Clint Watts, a disinformation specialist and former FBI agent, says platforms should recognize the value of "intelligence-led social media defense" that would help them focus on the techniques and actors doing the most harm.[93] This implies, however, that platforms will choose to work primarily with the intelligence agencies of democratic countries, with whom they are most likely to agree on what "the most harm" consists of. Intelligence agencies of authoritarian countries will have quite different ideas of who the most pernicious actors are.

It is also important to realize that much disinformation circulates on small social platforms that receive little attention from governments and NGAs. Hostile actors are adept at detecting attempts by major platforms to shut them down, and quickly directing their adherents to other networks, websites and even text-messaging systems to remain in touch. Even far more successful efforts to purge disinformation from the major platforms would not solve this problem.

Governments, local NGAs, journalists, fact-checkers and media literacy activists are important building blocks of a successful campaign against Russian IOs. Platforms may ultimately be an ally, if only to stave off additional regulation. In the next chapter, I discuss

---

[93] Clint Watts, "Advanced Persistent Manipulators, Part Two: Intelligence-led Social Media Defense," *Alliance for Securing Democracy*, April 24, 2019, https://securingdemocracy.gmfus.org/advanced-persistent-manipulators-part-two-intelligence-led-social-media-defense/.

how all these actors can work together better, creating a whole that is far more powerful than the parts.

Chapter II: Making Responses More Effective

As we have seen, many important actors exist in the democratic world to counter information operations by Russia and its allies. However, all of them have significant limitations.

Governments have plenty of funding, but only some consider Russian IOs a priority problem. Even those governments that are committed to the effort suffer from internal confusion, slow decision-making and low public credibility. Legal and censorship measures are difficult for governments to apply and can backfire. Western international broadcasters have large audiences but respond only to their own sense of direction. Local NGAs are enthusiastic and courageous, but little match for well-funded opponents. Journalists, fact-checkers and media literacy trainers do excellent work, but their reach is limited. Social platforms are unpredictable allies.

Given all the drawbacks of each actor, the prospects of effective action against Russian IOs seem dim at first glance. An effective strategy would have to be:

- independent of a single government or coordinating body
- based on local, authentic actors
- nourished by plentiful money and training
- ready always to respond creatively to hostile messaging

Is such a strategy possible? Yes, because the components for it already exist. They have been growing organically in the past couple of decades, many of them noticeable individually but rarely appreciated in their entirety. Combining them to implement this strategy depends less on additional conceptualizing than on additional scale and imagination. The theme of this chapter is how best to combine and strengthen these forces.

The Question of Coordination

Many of those looking for strategies against Russian IOs long for a central bunker filled with government officials to direct a minute-by-minute "whole of society" response. However, central direction is rarely a plus in today's fast-moving, atomized world of information. Even if it were, governments are not the best leaders. Russian IOs benefit from the multiple actors they deploy; democratic countries can do even better by taking maximum advantage of the entrepreneurship and spontaneity they have long used to dominate the media landscape. "By definition, the West can't be united," says Kathleen Hicks, senior vice president of the Center for Strategic & International Studies. "The competitive advantage lies in the private sector, allies and partners."[1]

A dispersed approach is possible because the cause of freedom does not require a presidium. Arguments for freedom and decency do not need to be built in a test tube like disinformation, with a new formula for each opportunistic moment. Writing a false story takes leadership; true stories write themselves. At the annual summits of the International Fact Checking Network, or at training sessions for NGA activists, no time is needed to explain to attendees what their mission is. Conversation turns immediately to specific techniques for what

---

[1] Kathleen Hicks, interview with author, October 16, 2019.

everyone wants to do better: expose disinformation, fight corruption, advance democratic ideals and battle extremism.

Some specialists have advocated major new coalitions against disinformation, bringing together governments, NGAs, social platforms and media. A 2018 proposal from the Atlantic Council said the United States and the EU should establish such a coalition, which would be loosely organized under "a voluntary code of conduct outlining principles and some agreed procedures for dealing with disinformation."[2] Such proposals, however, require government energy and commitment that is in short supply, and they cement the idea of governments as the leading actors in the anti-disinformation effort. It is hard to imagine a balanced give-and-take between governments on the one hand, with all their authority and money, and a collection of small NGAs in desperate need of grants on the other. Many journalists who consider themselves objective would not want to sit at a table with government at all. A code of conduct presents a problem as well. Civil society groups differ markedly on how transparent they want their activities to be. They also disagree on whether their main task should be to promote objective information and reasoned discussion, or to trade punches with disinformation sources. Any code of conduct can have the effect of excluding those who do not sign on. In the context of a coalition with funding to dispense, non-signers could find themselves ineligible for grants, just as fact-checking groups that do not subscribe to the International Fact-Checking Network's Code of Principles cannot obtain funding from Facebook.

More important than broad new coalitions would be major financing, by a few well-coordinated sources, of a limited number of large-scale projects that could serve as the model to the entire pro-democracy

---

[2] Daniel Fried and Alina Polyakova, *Democratic Defense Against Disinformation* (Washington: Atlantic Council, March 5, 2018), https://www.atlanticcouncil.org/in-depth-research-reports/report/democratic-defense-against-disinformation/.

community. Examples might be a full-time radio station in an at-risk country, or a center capable of sophisticated social network monitoring and the speedy creation of videos and memes.

When governments are not always at the head of the table, it becomes easier for other pro-democracy actors to step out of their traditional roles and contribute to the effort in new ways. In information conflicts, private actors can do almost anything governments can. Podcasts can be made by professionals in a government studio or by 20-year-olds lounging with iPhones at home. Russian military moves can be exposed by government satellites or by journalists mining clues on Facebook. Governments that fear retaliation if they call out Russia by name can fund NGAs willing to take on that role. This can even be done quietly by lower-level officials if their political superiors are averse to angering Russia. A few European governments have encouraged organizations from other countries to assist their local NGAs in a manner that leaves the home government officially uninvolved.

Making Government More Efficient

Slowness and bureaucracy remain major problems for governments, but they do not have to be paralyzing. Governments have been hiring outside "implementers" to carry out programs quickly, creatively and with local expertise. These implementers include for-profit companies with pro-democracy principles, large NGOs, foundations, advertising agencies and universities. They work for a fixed period and then can be rehired or not depending on their performance and the funding agency's needs.

The British government hired an outside implementer to create its 2019 "Don't Feed the Beast" advertising campaign against online disinformation. Lea Gabrielle, head of the State Department's Global

Engagement Center (GEC), described the benefits of private advertising firms at a congressional hearing in 2019:

> Congress provided the GEC with an important tool to meet this need—the ability to hire private sector advertising and marketing firms. We know what story we want to tell. It is crucial to have local communications professionals help us tailor that story to local audiences. They understand the market, and they understand how to message to the market in the most appealing fashion.[3]

Implementers' tasks go well beyond advertising. The US Defense Department has used implementers to run news sites with an anti-extremist bent in locations including Africa, Southeastern Europe and Central Asia.[4] The California-based Democracy Council implements, on behalf of the Global Engagement Center, a project called the Information Access Fund (IAF). The fund's goals include analyzing foreign IOs and supporting local media capable of refuting disinformation. In 2019, as part of the IAF project, the council publicly sought a subcontractor to run a project worth up to $300,000 that would "enable Ukrainian students, notably military cadets and reserve officer students, to educate Ukrainian society about the manipulation of social media by Russian propagandists." According to the project announcement, the goals might involve an initiative by cadets and reserve officers that "motivates or empowers community influencers to become involved in countering Russian disinformation

---

[3] *United States Efforts to Counter Russian Disinformation and Malign Influence,* July 10, 2019 (testimony of Lea Gabrielle), https://docs.house.gov/meetings/AP/AP04/20190710/109748/HHRG-116-AP04-Wstate-GabrielleL-20190710.pdf.

[4] See Adam Mazmanian, "DOD shutters two 'influence' websites covering Africa," *FCW,* February 13, 2015, https://fcw.com/articles/2015/02/13/african-web-sites.aspx. At least one such site continued to operate in 2020, with an anti-extremist and anti-Russia tone. It is identified on its "About" page as a US Central Command product: https://central.asia-news.com/?locale=en_GB.

and propaganda."[5] Such programs can almost certainly be carried out by implementers more efficiently than by government officials. Some countries are also happy for implementers to be the public face of a project, so that the funding government remains less visible. When an implementer organized a recent training session for NGA activists, an official from the government that paid for it was invited to speak. The official declined, leaving the session to take place with some participants uncertain about where the funding had come from.

The degree of government control over implementers' work can vary greatly. Some contracts call for very specific actions and constant reporting; others allow more latitude. Contract language or local embassies may constrain or influence the list of NGAs that implementers can invite to training programs and what the discussions must consist of. A trainer who taught skills to NGA activists in Europe's East said his instructions—at least as he interpreted them—allowed him to talk about Russian disinformation, but not to conduct large-group discussions about the veracity of statements by US officials.

Strengthening NGAs

In many senses, local NGAs are superb vehicles for pro-democracy messaging. However, it is important to be clear-eyed about their shortcomings.

The greatest problem local NGAs face is impact. Many of them are small. They struggle to attract audiences at a time when disinformation outlets are generously funded and loaded with sensational, highly shareable content. Wojciech Przybylski, the chairperson of Poland's Res Publica Foundation, says moderate, pro-

---

[5] "RFP Countering Russian Propaganda in Ukraine," Democracy Council, November 25, 2019, https://demcouncil.org/?p=2877.

democracy voices represent the silent majority in many countries.[6] Yet, whether an NGA's goal is to expose disinformation, promote positive narratives or simply restore civil conversation, it needs resources to make an impression. Surprisingly, many NGA activists interviewed for this study did not list money as their top requirement. Bohumil Kartous, a spokesperson for elves in the Czech Republic, said taking money, especially from foreign donors, opens NGAs to accusations they are agents of foreign interests. "The whole idea of the elves is that we do this voluntarily," he said. "It's your decision to do it; it's your time and energy. You do it for your country, not for money."[7] Other NGAs acknowledge that a few full-time employees would help with organization, recruitment and technology. (The head of one group compared keeping its programs staffed and organized to caring for a Tamagotchi.)

Money will play a significant role if NGAs are to operate at scale. NGAs that are proud to be small volunteer organizations must understand that if they want to make a difference, they will need greater resources to reach significant audiences. It is time-consuming and expensive just to constantly monitor social networks for new disinformation narratives. To have impact, NGAs need the ability to run multiple websites and fire off graphics and video day and night. An effective anti-disinformation effort should have the equivalent of a 24-hour war room, since hostile operators can launch new campaigns at any hour and multiply them in minutes through chains of websites and fake accounts.

Ironically, local laws sometimes bar non-profits from money-making activity. Funders may also limit such efforts. A senior member of an Estonian NGA said an EU grant his organization received required it to become self-supporting in two years but prohibited it from posting YouTube advertising that would have helped achieve that goal. Some

---

[6] Wojciech Przybylski, interview with author, November 5, 2019.
[7] Bohumil Kartous, interview with author, May 9, 2020.

NGAs are wary of taking ads from advertising networks since it is hard to predict the ads that will automatically show up. Disinformation operators do not lose sleep over such things, but pro-democracy groups and their funders may worry over the taste, political content or commercial implications of ads that appear on their sites. A more palatable funding option for NGAs is crowdsourcing through contribution buttons on their websites or Kickstarter-type campaigns. Successful crowdsourcing, however, requires being known to begin with. A small or new NGA often must depend on grants from foreign or local sources until it builds up visibility.

NGAs also may be desperately short of training in social network analysis and online persuasion. This includes quick production of clever graphics and video. The Global Engagement Center said in 2019 that it was training civil society actors in 14 European countries to respond to disinformation "in locally relevant ways."[8]

A further complication for NGAs is that in some countries, they do not face a simple democracy-versus-authoritarianism equation. In Latin America, a political center can be difficult to find between leftist and rightist views of democracy. Russia plays on this split; in Argentina, for example, it has tried to make common cause with both leftist Peronistas and Catholic conservatives. NGAs must navigate between the extremes, trying to find some measure of support for true facts and rational dialogue.

Finally, NGAs often face difficulty operating outside of an elite, urban environment, where most of their activists come from. Peter Pomerantsev, the London-based expert on disinformation, puts it bluntly: "They think ordinary people are morons, which is good for Putin."[9] Disinformation thrives particularly in rural areas, where

---

[8] *United States Efforts to Counter Russian Disinformation and Malign Influence* (testimony of Lea Gabrielle).

[9] Peter Pomerantsev, interview with author, October 31, 2019.

people—especially older ones—believe their way of life is threatened by a stream of liberal positions emanating from urban politicians. Urban activists sometimes underestimate how much time rural voters spend with social posts and email chain letters that reinforce antidemocratic views. Socially liberal activists also need to be able to relate to citizens who are wary of Russia and support democracy, while at the same time having conservative views on social issues like abortion.

Improving Funding

The last chapter pointed out the striking amount of money available from government and private sources to fund resistance to Russian IOs. Yet, the flow of money to those who need it is a fraught process. NGAs find they must devote overwhelming amounts of time to chasing the next grant. "Getting grants and dealing with bureaucracy is a huge waste of time," says Agnieszka Romaszewski-Guzy, the leader of *Belsat,* which creates pro-democracy television content for Belarus. "It's a trek through purgatory."[10]

These are some of the reasons that the allocation of money to projects is not simple:

• *Thinking small.* Many grants are for projects to produce very limited products, like a handful of videos, a few conferences or training sessions, or a book. Large foundations give some six-figure grants, but many local democracy-oriented NGAs receive grants from foreign funders of less than $50,000 in a year. They may spend months competing for sums closer to $10,000. Funders are properly wary of giving more money to NGAs than they can absorb, but small grants

---

[10] Agnieszka Romaszewski-Guzy, interview with author, November 5, 2019.

provide little incentive to think big. They result in patchworks of small projects with limited impact.

• *Application and reporting burdens.* Funders, reasonably, want to be sure their money is well spent. NGAs sometimes seek funding for projects that are vaguely conceived and unsupported by testing. However, the paperwork involved to request grants can be daunting for small organizations. A point of diminishing returns exists where the complexity of obtaining funds reduces enthusiasm for new projects. "Working with national and international grant projects requires significant work and resources for accounting, documentation, correspondence and other formalities beyond the analytical work," says Adam Lelonek, a Polish analyst of information threats. He estimated smaller NGAs can spend as much as 80 percent of their time dealing with grant mechanics.[11] Donors must also design their evaluation processes to focus what the end goal of the project is. The most important metric for a media literacy project, for instance, should not be how many people attended training sessions, but whether their ability to identify fake news measurably increased.

• *Short funding timeframes.* Many grants are quite short-term, lasting only about a year. For risk-averse funders, such terms give them an easy escape if things do not work out well. If the project happens to work, however, the NGA involved faces a crisis. Funders' priorities shift constantly, meaning the source of the original money may not be interested in handing out more. At least there may be a gap before new funding begins. The result is an inability for NGAs to plan. "How long will a funder be invested in a country or region?" asks Angela Sirbu, who oversees Eurasia projects for Internews, a media and media-literacy NGA. "We try to take a lot of time to educate donors, to understand their agendas, to underscore the importance of flexibility."[12]

---

[11] Adam Lelonek, personal communication with author, March 25, 2020.
[12] Angela Sirbu, interview with author, March 6, 2020.

Even if funders understand the need for long-term support, their own internal bureaucracies may make that difficult. One major foundation gives multi-year grants, but all the money must come from the budget for the year in which the grant is made. Real breakthrough projects for NGAs might be big-ticket items like opening radio and television stations to compete with broadcasters controlled by governments and oligarchs. This is impossible with short-term grants. The unpredictability of donors requires NGAs to devote constant effort to finding new sources of money. Internews, which spends about $20 million a year in grants and projects, lists hundreds of donors and supporters on its website.[13]

• *Donor agendas.* Some donors combine their general support for democracy with specific agendas or methodologies. It is dangerous for outside funders to believe they know better what will work in a country than do local, authentic NGAs. Funders may also try to turn local NGAs toward agendas that reflect the funders' broad social concerns, rather than subjects where activists are currently being successful. An independent news site with a strong following for its political and corruption reporting, in order to stabilize its finances, may accept aid from a foundation that prioritizes LGBT rights, empowering women or climate concerns. The site must then begin generating content on these subjects to maintain the financing. Meritorious as these topics are, readers may feel the outlet has inexplicably turned away from the subjects that attracted them to begin with.

• *Disregard for underlying costs.* Funders usually grant money for projects aimed at specific results, not for the administrative overhead it costs NGAs to run offices, apply for grants and fill out paperwork. "For organizations like us, the key would really be core funding, unattached to a specific project," says Jeremy Druker of Prague-based

---

[13] "Donors and Supporters," *Internews*, accessed July 15, 2020, https://internews.org/current-donors.

Transitions, a media training organization that depends on grants for more than three-quarters of its income. "Of course, we are appreciative of all the project grants we've received over the years, but they have provided precious little for organizational development, for capacity building to let us grow."[14] Clearly, funders would prefer not to fill their websites with tales of how they paid an NGA's electric bill or the salary of a full-time grant writer. Such investments, however, are essential to turning small groups of activists into sustainable organizations.

• *Due diligence concerns.* Donors are wary of those they grant funds to. They fear that through lack of due diligence, they will wind up in bed with swindlers, people with questionable political connections or big talkers who fail to produce results. Funding organizations worry that some opponents of Russian IOs could be pathological Russophobes. Grant applicants could also overstate their own accomplishments or go after the wrong targets. In 2019, the Global Engagement Center had to cut off funding to a group hired to fight Iranian propaganda after it started attacking Americans it considered too soft on Iran.[15] Funding from the US Embassy in Armenia and the EU helped create an Armenian site, *Medmedia.am*, that in 2020 refused to delete non-staff posts claiming coronavirus vaccines were dangerous.[16] Activists could also have impeccable anti-Kremlin credentials, but espouse views in other areas that make them

---

[14] Jeremy Druker, personal communication with author, September 9, 2019.

[15] Alex Marquardt, "State Department suspends funding of anti-Iran group which targeted journalists and activists," *CNN*, June 5, 2019, https://www.cnn.com/2019/06/05/politics/us-suspends-funding-anti-iran-group/index.html.

[16] Tatev Hovhannisyan, "Revealed: US-funded website spreading COVID misinformation in Armenia," *openDemocracy*, May 28, 2020, https://www.opendemocracy.net/en/5050/us-money-armenia-misinformation-covid-vaccines/ and "US Envoy: A Unified Effort Is Going To Make A Difference in Fighting COVID" (interview with US Ambassador Lynne Tracy), *Radio Free Europe/Radio Liberty*, June 4, 2020, https://www.youtube.com/watch?v=hGkFfzFw2LI&feature=youtu.be&t=1123.

inappropriate recipients of aid. Western governments are still haunted by their hiring after World War II of people reliable in their anti-Soviet stances but with Nazi pasts that made it scandalous for them to hold government jobs. All these fears can lead to the slow approval of funds and extra reporting burdens after grants are made.

• *Lack of donor coordination.* Many donor foundations are generally aware of each other's work. Sometimes they collaborate on projects. However, there is no mechanism for donors to compare the totality of their programs, decide what causes deserve the most support, and jointly channel their funding to specific grantees. One reason is that the funding priorities of donors change rapidly. Another is that each donor has its own bureaucracy, meaning it is difficult to make solid promises at donor meetings. Finally, some donors would rather take full credit for a variety of small projects—and be able to direct them precisely—rather than send money to something larger that they do not fully control. In 2020, Luminate Group proposed creating an International Fund for Public Service Media, to be funded at $100 million or more by traditional donors and social platforms, to concentrate money and efforts on critically important independent media projects.[17] Such an undertaking could support the kind of large, long-term projects the pro-democracy movement needs.

Doing Better on Social Networks

For ten years, *Sputnik's* Armenian Service had been building diaspora audiences through techniques used before by Kremlin influencers. *Sputnik* employees created Facebook pages and groups featuring sports, recipes and women. Bit by bit, they used these assets to promote *Sputnik* as a reliable media brand and draw readers to pro-Russian content. The project was exposed in 2019 by the Atlantic

---

[17] "International Fund for Public Interest Media," *Luminate Group,* accessed July 15, 2020, https://luminategroup.com/ifpim.

Council's Digital Forensic Research (DFR) Lab in a textbook example of using sophisticated analysis to uncover a disinformation network. After being shown the DFR research, the lab reported, Facebook "made the independent decision to remove most of the assets."[18]

Analysis of hostile information campaigns is one of the capabilities NGAs need most. Russian IOs like the Armenia project may be prepared carefully for years, using hard-to-detect techniques honed by experience in multiple locations. Many small NGAs, with little ability to grasp such strategies, may focus on a few obvious disinformation websites and miss entire networks bringing pro-Russian messages to carefully selected audience segments. (The big Russian disinformation actors that receive the lion's share of Western attention, such as *RT* and *Sputnik*, help distract the anti-disinformation community from far more insidious Russian IOs.)

Some governments have those specialists and tools. The Global Engagement Center has about 25 data scientists,[19] a quite small team but capable of targeted projects. Ahead of the 2018 referendum on North Macedonia's name change, which Russia hoped would go down in defeat, representatives of the Global Engagement Center traveled to Skopje to help the government secure a "yes" vote:

> While in country from July 24 to August 17, the GEC worked with the communication teams within the Office of the Prime Minister. As part of this effort, the GEC delivered two major reports to the North Macedonian government. Other completed tasks included providing the host nation with a snapshot of the social media environment, data on media outlets, training on data analysis tools, and building awareness on the disinformation

---

[18] "Inauthentic *Sputnik*-Linked Pages Target the Armenian Diaspora," DFR Lab post, *Medium*, September 5, 2019, https://medium.com/dfrlab/inauthentic-sputnik-linked-pages-target-the-armenian-diaspora-3e4ed8923525.

[19] "Briefing on Disinformation and Propaganda Related to COVID-19."

tactics of our adversaries. We actually provided a people-on-the-ground [sic] there to support with insight reports, giving demographic and microtargeting information, really using data scientists to support that effort.[20]

The workings and findings of government systems are largely classified. NGAs need their own ability to track false narratives back to their sources, identify key influencers and understand how their own messages travel. Such work may require studying millions of tweets and Facebook posts to analyze the functioning of hashtags, memes and buzzwords—a task that can require many hours of effort even for experts with cutting-edge software. It is hardly a question of pressing a button and drawing a map of a hostile network, says Camille François, chief innovation officer at Graphika, a major New York–based social media analysis company. "The work is extraordinarily time-consuming. The only button we press is the one on the espresso machine."[21] The work is worth doing: when activists can document inauthentic networks, social platforms will usually take them down. However, few NGAs, no matter how dedicated, can do this work themselves.

To meet NGAs' need for software and knowhow, a series of initiatives have sprung up:

• A significant effort is based in Lithuania. The NGA Debunk.eu, funded in part by Google, has created keyword-searching software designed to catch web content containing more than 600 propaganda "narratives" such as abuses of local citizens by NATO troops.[22]

---

[20] *United States Efforts to Counter Russian Disinformation and Malign Influence* (testimony of Lea Gabrielle).

[21] Camille François, interview with author, January 14, 2020.

[22] "Debunk.eu: Countering disinformation with AI," video, *Google,* February 14, 2020, https://youtu.be/u1MThnflDTA.

• The German Marshall Fund's Alliance for Securing Democracy operates the Hamilton 2.0 Dashboard, a publicly accessible tool to monitor Russian-funded broadcasting and social network operations.[23]

• The International Republican Institute's Beacon Project, which brings together political parties, think tanks and NGAs, has created "Versus," proprietary software that lets NGAs search through thousands of web sources, including mainstream media. It can isolate disinformation themes in 14 East European languages.[24]

• The Dutch-based firm Trollrensics provides software designed to surface networks of troll activity.[25]

• The Observatory on Social Media at Indiana University offers a series of free programs to analyze Twitter activity. They include Hoaxy, which graphs the spread of a given narrative or hashtag; Botometer, which analyzes accounts to determine which appear to be bots; and Botslayer, which exposes the functioning of bot networks and other coordinated Twitter activity in real time.[26]

• The Global Engagement Center and the UK government have joined to encourage creation of additional software by private companies.[27]

---

[23] https://securingdemocracy.gmfus.org/hamilton-dashboard/.
[24] https://www.iribeaconproject.org/.
[25] https://www.trollrensics.com/.
[26] https://osome.iuni.iu.edu/tools/.
[27] In 2019 Semantic Visions, a Czech company, won a $250,000 grant from the two governments to finance a platform that delivers "real-time detection of adversarial propaganda and disinformation." See Cabinet Office, "Semantic Visions wins $250,000 Tech Challenge to Combat Disinformation, news release, March 11, 2019, https://www.wired-gov.net/wg/news.nsf/articles/Semantic+Visions+wins+$250000+Tech+Challenge+to+Combat+Disinformation+11032019112000?open.

• Professional social network monitoring companies like Graphika do *pro bono* work for human rights groups when they can. Also, a network of individual forensic enthusiasts tries to respond to calls for help on Twitter bearing the hashtags #digitalsherlocks and #OSINT.

All these efforts, however, fall short of what is needed. NGAs need not only effective software but also staffs to monitor the systems' findings and respond immediately. An effective resistance campaign would be able to detect new campaigns as soon as they start and quickly construct responses, including clever memes and video. When the campaign of French presidential candidate Emmanuel Macron was hacked in 2017, analysts in three countries were able to determine within hours that the leaked material was being broadly promoted online by the American alt-right. The news helped diminish the leaks' effect.[28]

The Potential of 'Backshops'

A decisive way to multiply the power of local NGAs would be to create regional social network "backshops" to be a force multiplier for local NGAs' efforts. Many companies already use social media analysis centers run by strategic communications agencies to monitor and protect their brands' reputations. Such backshops for NGAs would help stand guard over pro-democracy messaging and counter communications by adversaries.

Backshops could provide the kind of information the Global Engagement Center gave Macedonian officials during the 2018 referendum: analysis of the social network environment and

---

[28] Jean-Baptiste Jeangène Vilmer, *The "Macron Leaks" Operation: A Post-Mortem* (Washington: Atlantic Council/IRSEM, June 2019), 39, https://www.atlanticcouncil.org/wp-content/uploads/2019/06/The_Macron_Leaks_Operation-A_Post-Mortem.pdf.

recommendations on which groups to target. Small groups of activists using open-source analytical tools do not compare to professional-level systems with full-time, experienced operators. Sophisticated systems can analyze not only the different communities of discussion around a topic, but the sentiments and anger level of each community and other topics that community members are interested in. This is invaluable for targeting additional content to each group. Backshop analysts could also look across national boundaries to see patterns in disinformation themes and tradecraft that are often missed by separate, nationally based groups. They could identify nodes in disinformation and hate networks that generate original content or serve as key relay points between network subgroups. Social platforms take more seriously dossiers on inauthentic activity drawn up by professional monitoring centers than they do reports from small, less experienced NGAs.

Backshops can also move from monitoring to offense. Their staffs could include behavioral strategists to determine the best tactics against disinformation. If backshops can identify key sources of disinformation, they can dog them with posts and tweets identifying them as frauds or trolls. Centers can help "flood the zone" in at-risk countries by arranging help from across borders. Friendly activists elsewhere, familiar with local languages and issues, can have a multiplier effect by retweeting locally produced content or doing posts of their own. This has already been done clandestinely; American right-wing activists pretended to be French to influence that nation's 2017 elections.[29] However, it can be done overtly as well, with pro-democracy activists abroad expressing solidarity with like-minded citizens in the target country and describing their own struggles. Ukrainian students in 2015 recorded YouTube videos urging their

---

[29] Ryan Broderick, "Trump Supporters Online Are Pretending To Be French To Manipulate France's Election," *Buzzfeed*, January 24, 2017, https://www.buzzfeednews.com/article/ryanhatesthis/inside-the-private-chat-rooms-trump-supporters-are-using-to#.tfQGYyveA.

Russian counterparts not to believe Kremlin propaganda about Ukraine.[30] Voices from the Czech Republic, where NATO has broad support, might be effective in Slovakia, where more people see Russia as a friend. Such efforts can even cross continents. Brian Whitmore of CEPA writes:

> The United States should turn Moscow's narrative about U.S. support for "color revolutions" in places like Georgia and Ukraine on its head. Like Venezuela, Georgia and Ukraine experienced genuine, massive, and organic popular uprisings against corrupt, unpopular, Moscow-backed regimes. As in Venezuela, the United States was on the side of the people. As a result, the Georgian and Ukrainian people remain deeply grateful for American support. Get Georgians and Ukrainians to tell that story to the people of Latin America![31]

A backshop could operate its own set of accounts to further reinforce the messages. If NGAs are intimidated from working or forced out of their countries, the backshops could maintain the flow of social network content until new arrangements are made.

Who should run such backshops? Rand Waltzman of the RAND Corporation says a center for cognitive security—his term for a more elaborate kind of backshop—"should be nonprofit and housed in a nonprofit, nongovernmental organization that has international credibility and close ties with government, industry, academia, think tanks, and public interest groups internationally." Waltzman proposes initial funding from the US government but worries, rightly,

---

[30] See, for example, Vitalya Lyashchuk, "Обращение студентов Украины к студентам России" [Ukrainian students' appeal to the students of Russia], February 10, 2015, https://www.youtube.com/watch?v=7uCK73eU--Q.

[31] Brian Whitmore, "The Latin American Front: Russian Propaganda in Venezuela and Western Responses," (Washington: Center for European Policy Analysis, February 2019), 7,
https://docs.wixstatic.com/ugd/644196_a56b7c0167314e15bed79392ef24495b.pdf/.

that this could create the impression the center is a government appendage, hurting its credibility.[32] Starting anything from the ground up as a government project is also a slow process. More effective would be to build centers on the basis of existing anti-disinformation hubs like the Atlantic Council's Digital Forensics Research Lab, the Stanford Internet Observatory, the German Marshall Fund and Debunk.eu. Each of these organizations already has funding sources and deep experience in analyzing hostile social media activity. Either they could collaborate in building jointly run centers, or they could individually decide to concentrate intensively on various parts of the world. (At present, they often disperse their efforts among many countries.) Their work could be supplemented by academic, commercial and government researchers.

The Problem of Security

NGAs face serious dangers from agents of Russia and hostile actors in their own countries—including corrupt officials inside their home governments. Actions against NGAs can range from online harassment and posting of members' persona information, which have forced out many people from these groups already, to infiltration of the groups' ranks and even physical attack. In the 1920s, the Soviet state ran "Operation Trust" to penetrate and destroy organizations trying to undermine Bolshevik rule. The operation is still studied for its deadly effectiveness, and Russian capabilities have only improved since then.

Many activists are highly courageous. A spokesperson for Lithuania's elves says that in operating online, "a lot of people are fine with using

---

[32] *Cyber-enabled Information Operations,* Hearing of the Subcommittee on Cybersecurity, Senate Armed Services Committee, April 27, 2017 (testimony of Rand Waltzman, 7–8), https://www.armed-services.senate.gov/imo/media/doc/Waltzman_04-27-17.pdf.

their own names. They feel there's nothing to be afraid of, that we're in our own country, that we're fighting for real values." Still, many NGAs take basic measures to protect against infiltration:

• One group organizes itself as a "network of networks," with people in the central circle knowing only one or two people in the next circle, and so on until people in the outermost circles have no idea who the central leaders are. This is a reasonable strategy for a sabotage organization, where it is important for a captured member not to be able to identify the whole network. However, it is awkward for activists who stand for democracy and transparency.

• Another activist says she relies on "face checks"—the concept that everyone knows everyone in the pro-democracy community and can vouch for each other's loyalty. This may work among small numbers of old friends but cannot support a growth strategy. Friends and colleagues can also change their perspectives. People move between anti-Kremlin and pro-Kremlin groups, sometimes with little clarity as to why. In 2019 Maria Baronova, a close associate of Mikhail Khodorkovsky in London with a long history in anti-Kremlin movements, took a senior job at *RT* in Moscow. She said that in both cases she was serving her country.[33]

• A group that actively seeks new members online requires applicants to fill out questionnaires about their beliefs and motives. Recruiters then study their social profiles to assess when their accounts were created and evaluate their friends and group memberships. The technique makes sense as far as it goes but cannot guard against an infiltrator using an online legend that has been built for years.

---

[33] Ilya Zhegulev, "I want to serve my country," *Meduza,* February 28, 2019, https://meduza.io/en/feature/2019/03/01/i-want-to-serve-my-country-that-s-always-been-my-main-motivation.

NGA members vary in their commitment to smart security practices. An activist in one group said she continually has trouble persuading people to do such simple things as changing their communications habits from email to the more secure Signal app.

Among Western governments and funders, a frequent response to concerns about security is that "we don't really have anything to hide." Democracy promotion, ideally, should not be clandestine task. However, in at-risk countries, NGAs do have some things to hide. Some conduct online activities under false names or brands, and do not want it known who is behind them. Others have been taught by outside trainers—or are developing themselves—new skills to spread their messages more effectively online. They are anxious that these techniques not fall into the hands of their opponents. Most importantly, NGA members may want their identities guarded to prevent harassment and physical attack.

Funders must be careful not to endanger those they help. Executives of most foundations interviewed for this study emphasized the public nature of their work, pointing to lists on their websites of the NGAs they support. However, in further conversation, they commonly acknowledged that some recipients of their funding prefer not to be publicly associated with foreign money. The funders do not include these recipients in their public materials and the NGAs make no reference to this funding. Still, some funders seemed to have a relaxed attitude toward security. One foundation executive interviewed for this study said, "The Russians can probably find out who we're supporting if they really want to, but it's probably not that big an issue for them."

While it is hard to keep anything secure from a determined adversary, funders should maintain appropriate security around meetings, documents, communications and transfer of funds. They should demand the same of subcontractors. The Institute for Statecraft, a

British organizing center for pro-democracy activists funded by £2.2 million ($2.76 million, in July 2020) in UK government funds, was hacked in 2018. Western officials said the hackers were linked to Russia.[34] Documents seized in the hack from the institute and its main program, the Integrity Initiative, have been repeatedly cited by *RT* and *Sputnik* as evidence that the British government is attempting to build clandestine "clusters" of pro-Western operatives throughout Europe.

Funders, who have no way to physically protect NGA members on the ground, must feel comfortable ethically with encouraging activities that could result in harm to activists or their families. The usual position of funders is that activists work voluntarily and are aware of the dangers around them. Still, foreign organizations need to have clear conversations with those they help to make sure all dangers are understood. They should also make clear whether they are willing, for instance, to evacuate and take care of a local activist who winds up in serious trouble.

Once an effective structure has been built to push back at Russian IOs, what messages will that structure send? I will soon turn to messaging to at-risk populations in general, and then to messages specifically aimed at Russia. First, however, comes the overarching question of whether efforts to counter Russian IOs risk becoming a propaganda campaign themselves. The next chapter explores whether fighting Russian information violence simply means doing the same things the Russians do, but from our side.

---

[34] James Lansdale, "Russia-linked hack 'bid to discredit' UK anti-disinformation campaign - Foreign Office," *BBC*, December 10, 2018, https://www.bbc.com/news/uk-46509956.

Chapter III: Of Truth and Propaganda

Is All Persuasion Propaganda?

Discussing hostile information operations and the right ways to respond inevitably leads to questions of truth and ethics. Russia and its allies spread tendentious, destructive information worldwide. Their operators have no compunction about making up facts, or shredding real ones to the point of simply being garnishes on fundamentally false narratives. Western strategists commonly say the antidote to information violence is "the truth." But is there only one truth? How can the West aggressively promote its positions without engaging in unethical behavior itself?

Facts are facts—who did what on what date. But it is easy to put facts together in such a way as to create multiple and contradictory views of an event, all of them technically fact-based. Even *RT* uses a good deal of facts to support its narratives. Is there a way to determine objectively which fact-based argument is the correct one, or is it always a question of where one stands? Friedrich Nietzsche said, "There are no facts, only opinions." Other philosophers, from Immanuel Kant to Roland Barthes to Noam Chomsky, have also said we see events primarily through our own experiences. Even our attempts to communicate through words may founder on different people's personal experiences with the words we choose.

"There is no objectivity," declares *RT* Chief Editor Margarita Simonyan. She says no international news network, including hers, is objective, because each reflects its home country's interests.[1] To her, this is completely natural. In the Russian view, there is no material difference between what Russia and the West do in the information realm (though Russians these days may think they do it better).

In an information war, the "truths" that are easiest to advance are small, provable facts: that a law contains certain provisions, or that the EU paid for this road. Other truths are true enough in the Western view, but far harder to prove: that NATO does not intend to attack Russia, or that immigration is generally good for a society. To populations prone to conspiracy theories and grievance, the dangers presented by NATO and immigrants may seem as true as the sun rising in the east. Conspiracy theorists do not mind being called conspiracy theorists; it is simply what they believe. Just exposing people to our truths will have no magical effect. On the information battlefield, success depends not on some epistemological scale that determines which truth is more valid, but on the throw-weight of the resources available to punch a narrative home.

"It's not enough just to show our truth and people will flock to it," says a consultant to the US intelligence community interviewed for this study. "We need to compete in a world full of dirty information tricks. There are plenty of examples in history where evil information operations overcame the truth. The question for us is, what are we willing to insert into the world's information space?" In the words of former State Department official Richard Stengel, "We no longer know what a free and fair marketplace of ideas even looks like."[2]

Few people would condemn an aggressive, fact-based government campaign for people not to text while driving. Is it different if the

---

[1] Alexander Gabuyev, "Нет никакой объективности" [There is no objectivity], *Kommersant*, April 7, 2012, https://www.kommersant.ru/doc/1911336.
[2] Richard Stengel, *Information Wars: How We Lost the Global Battle Against Disinformation and What We Can Do About It*, 291.

campaign promotes the values of free societies, and calls out those that trade in corruption and tyranny? To me, both campaigns are moral and acceptable. For others, however, any government effort to mold foreign citizens' political sentiments—even if the message simply supports democracy—feels creepy. People in democratic countries are quick to label such endeavors as propaganda or unsavory "psychological operations." These concerns are "indeed an old philosophical conundrum faced by PSYOPS practitioners since the First World War," wrote the late Philip M. Taylor, the British historian of propaganda. "To put it simply, is it better to persuade an adversary to lay down his weapon and to desert, defect or surrender than it is to blow his head off?"[3]

The task of spreading democratic ideas is additionally complex because it involves not just convincing people of certain facts, but replacing a whole framework of beliefs disposed to one-party rule and social intolerance. Trying to implant democratic concepts in such a framework is like planting roses in sand. Over time, the goal must be to create a whole new framework of beliefs that is friendly to citizens' participation in government and tolerant of different people.

For the sake of both honesty and effectiveness, democracy messaging cannot take the line that everything an audience has heard about free countries is wrong. (One-sided, black-and-white messages are the clearest indicators of real propaganda.) Instead, it must include recognition of democratic countries' failings—something that will ring true in the audience's original framework of beliefs—but then begin to point out how successful countries are always reinventing themselves, and the importance of freedom to that process.

If sensitivities about governments leading such campaigns are too great, pro-democracy persuasion can be conducted by NGAs—ideally

---

[3] Philip M. Taylor, *Munitions of the mind: A history of propaganda* (Manchester: Manchester University Press, 2003), 313.

ones that are funded by sources other than governments. Yet, if they undertake such work, NGAs will face the same questions governments might: given the state of Western democracy these days, is it something to campaign for at all?

Who Are We to Preach?

Playing in the background in discussions of whether the West should promote democracy is a strong school of opinion that today's information problems are largely the West's fault to begin with. Rather than trying to message other nations, the argument goes, the West should build societies at home that truly embody equality, justice and compassion. It is not enough, in this view, just to stand for democratic ideals. Instead, the United States and its allies must rebuild themselves to be worthy of those ideals. Then their messaging will be natural and convincing, with no need for anything approaching propaganda. In the words of the American Security Project, "Rather than creating a new message or 'communicating better,' America must change its behavior to meet its own standards, and spend more time learning how it is seen from the outside." The project's 2019 white paper suggests a significant pullback in US messaging efforts until American internal and external behavior improves:

> Until the US makes a concerted effort to change its behaviors, it is unclear that major efforts should be made to undertake public diplomacy efforts aside from those that remove the government itself as a messenger [such as people-to-people exchanges].[4]

---

[4] Matthew Wallin, *A New American Message: Fixing the Shortfalls in America's Message to the World* (Washington: American Security Project, December 2019), https://www.americansecurityproject.org/wp-content/uploads/2019/12/Ref-0233-A-New-American-Message.pdf.

In Western Europe, sensitivities about propaganda are even greater. German worries are stratospheric because of the legacy of the Third Reich. The French recall the propaganda of the collaborationist Vichy regime in World War II, the failure of French messaging in the Algerian war, and government control of domestic broadcasting under Charles de Gaulle. "The EU has many tools against Russia if it wants to use them—sanctions, financial system access, investigations—and all of them seem more natural to the diplomats here than information actions with any element of propaganda," says an EU civil servant. "There is a growing trend to say Russian disinformation is bad, but any kind of Western propagandistic tone is bad, too. Even people who support sanctions against Russia are concerned about public Russia-bashing."

Given such attitudes, major EU governments are unlikely to suddenly throw themselves into messaging that unabashedly casts democratic states as "the good guys." Within individual EU nations, many citizens, as in the US, are in a general state of despair over the challenges the world faces and what seems to be chaos in their own countries. "France's foreign policy and defense elite sees itself as a loser in globalization. Africa is all it has left," says Gregory Daho, a foreign policy specialist at the Sorbonne in Paris. "Why would France conduct an information war? To show France has nice poetry? Victor Hugo? France has no international strategy. To have a good information war you need a positive view of yourself. France doesn't know what it wants to replace Russian disinformation with."[5]

Certainly, the message from Western nations will be far more powerful the more they exemplify their own exhortations. However, it is dangerous to extend the argument to the point where democratic countries put messaging efforts on the shelf:

---

[5] Gregory Daho, interview with author, May 28, 2019.

• The West's message is not only about democracy. It is equally about factual information and effective government. The coronavirus pandemic could eventually prove to be a powerful moment for true information, as people learn that virus denial and conspiracy theories were wrong. Increasingly, audiences are paying attention to mainstream media for reliable information about the disease.[6] Retribution could be swift for corrupt regimes that felt false information would be an asset in the crisis. François Heisbourg of the International Institute for Strategic Studies says, "The settling of accounts could be brutal in those countries in which improvidence or incompetence is seen as having wasted precious lives."[7] Public anger over Belarusian President Alyaksandr Lukashenka's failure to act against the coronavirus intensified the nationwide demonstrations against his rule after a disputed election in August 2020.

• As for democracy itself, the world does not depend on perfection in the West to understand its value. Western words and actions can give a tremendous boost to the world's democratic forces; Trump's indifference toward democracy abroad has deprived democracy advocates of a powerful ally. But in Venezuela, Iraq or Lebanon, the pluses and minuses of major Western states are not of critical importance. Activists fight for fair, equal societies where people have a voice not because they love how democracy works in the US or France[8], but because they love how popular rule can work in Venezuela, Iran or Lebanon. In the past several years, movements for democracy, and against dictatorship and corruption, have been

---

[6] *Reuters Institute Digital News Report* (Oxford: Reuters Institute for the Study of Journalism, 2020), https://reutersinstitute.politics.ox.ac.uk/sites/default/files/2020-06/DNR_2020_FINAL.pdf.

[7] François Heisbourg, "From Wuhan to the World: How the Pandemic Will Reshape Geopolitcs," *IISS Blog,* May 11, 2020, https://www.iiss.org/blogs/survival-blog/2020/05/from-wuhan-to-the-world.

[8] Democracy activists in many countries have condemned racial injustice in the United States.

growing worldwide, even as authoritarians have made progress too.[9] The result has been a certain amount of international chaos, where all sides are sometimes tempted to descend into demagoguery. The coronavirus has served as a pretext for governments with authoritarian tendencies to crack down further on speech and gatherings, but even authoritarians will eventually face citizens' judgments about their competence in handling the outbreak.

• America's image in the world still has resilience. The image has certainly suffered from the Trump administration and racial unrest, but the country is still widely envied for its personal liberty, scholarly institutions, entrepreneurship and enormous international charity. (When Trump suspended US government funding of the World Health Organization in 2020, the largest funder remaining was not any other country, but the Bill & Melinda Gates Foundation of the United States.[10]) The scholar-diplomat Joseph Nye notes that when protesters surged into streets around the world to denounce American intervention in Vietnam, they sang not "The Internationale" but "We Shall Overcome."[11] World views of the United States have been significantly more positive than of Trump himself.[12]

---

[9] For recent examples, see Pankaj Mishra, "Democracy Is on the March, Not in Retreat," *Bloomberg News,* November 2, 2019, https://www.bnnbloomberg.ca/democracy-is-on-the-march-not-in-retreat-1.1341836. See also Thomas Kent, "The Case for Democratic Optimism," *The American Interest,* March 2, 2018, https://www.the-american-interest.com/2018/03/02/case-democratic-optimism/.

[10] "Voluntary contributions by fund and by contributor, 2018," World Health Organization, May 9, 2019, https://www.who.int/about/finances-accountability/reports/A72_INF5-en.pdf?ua=1.

[11] Joseph Nye, "Soft Power," *The Atlantic,* November 2007, https://www.theatlantic.com/magazine/archive/2007/11/soft-power/306313/.

[12] At the start of 2020, a Pew survey of people in more than 30 countries found that 29 percent of respondents had confidence in Trump and 54 percent had a positive view of the United States. Richard Wike et al., "Trump Ratings Remain Low Around Globe, While Views of U.S. Stay Mostly Favorable" (Washington: Pew Research

• If one waits for the West to repair itself, opinions will always differ on when that repair is complete. US liberalism and conservatism have diverged so far from each other that it is difficult to imagine when they might agree that America has been mended.

• Even if everyone could agree that the West has come to embody the proper values, it is dicey to assume this will automatically shine through to the world's population. Unless the West learns to speak up for itself, almost anything, including a sudden rise in Western virtue, can be turned on its head by experienced opponents.

• Engagement with other countries is not just about enticing people to admire us or back our positions. It has a much broader purpose. As public diplomacy scholar Nicholas Cull explains:

> Public diplomacy is about advancing foreign policy, and that foreign policy may not necessarily concern the image of an actor: it may be directed at engineering improvement of the international environment, or empowering local voices within a target state or states. Once liberated from a narrow obsession with national image, foreign public engagement holds the potential to address a wide range of global issues. It is one of the few tools available to an international actor wishing to engage the international public, who hold the fate of the earth in their hands as never before. More than this, with public diplomacy now aimed at shared issues and using networks, old models of success are redundant. Some governments still have a narrow idea of success in international affairs. They understand the value of networks and relationships, but look for a unilateral advantage at the end of the process. This is untenable. One cannot win one's

---

Center, January 8, 2020), 3, https://www.pewresearch.org/global/2020/01/08/trump-ratings-remain-low-around-globe-while-views-of-u-s-stay-mostly-favorable/.

relationships. Relationships have to be based on mutual interest. The desire to win one's relationships is a symptom of psychosis.[13]

From this standpoint, it may be unfair for public diplomacy *not* to campaign for democracy anywhere it can take root.

• However great the failings of Western societies, the universe is not righted by letting the duplicity and destructiveness of Russian IOs reign unchallenged.

Fearing the Slippery Slope

The most common anxiety of those who oppose pro-democracy "propaganda," either by governments or NGAs, is that it will wind up racing Russia's messaging to the moral bottom. Aggressive democracy campaigners, in this view, would inevitably wind up competing with Moscow and its allies to spin facts dishonestly and even create disinformation. Many already worry about the term "strategic communications," a common phrase in public relations and military circles that is now enshrined in the names of the EU's Stratcom East task force and the NATO Strategic Communications Center of Excellence in Riga. In the view of ethicists Mervyn Frost and Nicholas Michelson of King's College London:

> What distinguishes an act of strategic communications from other kinds of communications, such as an academic paper in a journal, is that we assume the academic paper is in accordance with and seeks to uphold the fundamental values of academic practice, especially those to do with truth-telling and building

---

[13] Nicholas J. Cull, "The Tightrope to Tomorrow: Reputational Security, Collective Vision and the Future of Public Diplomacy," *The Hague Journal of Diplomacy*, 14 (2019), 7–8, https://nsiteam.com/social/wp-content/uploads/2019/06/Cull-Conclusion_HJD_014_01-02.pdf.

sound arguments, whereas, the former does not always do these things. An identifying feature of strategic communications is that it seeks a way around at least some of these ethical constraints. In academic papers we do not expect, accept, or tolerate tampering with the evidence, leaving out relevant counterexamples, ad hominem arguments, attempts to gild the lily, plagiarism, 'spinning' the facts, and so on. […] In contrast, we understand that such tools are the stock in trade of strategic communications—that it involves priming the audience, framing events, and "spinning the narrative" to suit the purposes of the user.[14]

In this study, I draw a line between messaging with honest and deceptive content. Honest messaging can acknowledge the failings of democratic societies while still arguing vigorously that they are ultimately the best form of government. Journalists have learned to be wary of "false balance"—the idea that, say, every reference to global warming in an article must be balanced by a climate-change denier saying the whole concept is hoax. Similarly, civics classes in democratic countries can reasonably advance the idea that democracy is a good thing without spending an equal amount of time tearing it down. There is no reason that honest advocacy for democratic values must inevitably turn into disinformation, any more than civics teachers must inevitably lie to make their points.

---

[14] Mervyn Frost and Nicholas Michelson, "Strategic communications in international relations: practical traps and ethical puzzles," *Defence Strategic Communication* 2 (Spring 2017), 16, https://stratcomcoe.org/download/file/fid/75915.

Chapter IV: Communicating to Threatened Populations

Messages and Vehicles

As president of *Radio Free Europe/Radio Liberty*, I met frequently with US lawmakers eager to counteract Russian IOs. On more than one occasion, I heard the same suggestion: Why not create a Russian-language version of *House of Cards*—making it into a story of intrigues and corruption in the Kremlin—and put it out to Russian viewers?

The cost of such a plan put it immediately out of the question. Netflix reportedly paid $100 million for two 13-episode seasons of *House of Cards.*[1] That is 80 percent of *RFE/RL's* annual budget. There was no sign that Congress was prepared to get into the movie business with appropriations of that size. But the idea also reflected the off-the-cuff nature of many proposals to advance democratic causes. The first question about such a plan would be what exactly is the United States trying to accomplish in Russia? How would a series like this help? Second, the suggestion conflated a creative idea with the means to convey it. If we thought a grim portrayal of Kremlin politics would

---

[1] Rebecca Greenfield, "The Economics of Netflix's $100 Million New Show," *The Atlantic,* February 1, 2013,
https://www.theatlantic.com/technology/archive/2013/02/economics-netflixs-100-million-new-show/318706/.

advance US goals, why not make a serial podcast, with cliffhanger endings, at a fraction of the cost of television? Why not a graphic novel distributed online as a PDF? How about a video game, where players could take on the roles of Kremlin powerbrokers and rack up piles of Rolexes?

This chapter looks at tactics to counter disinformation and advance democracy through news and entertainment media in at-risk countries. (The next looks specifically at strategies for audiences in Russia). I begin with a review of strategies to suppress or oppose IOs by Russia and its allies. Then I consider the messages pro-democracy forces might send. Only then do I come to the means through which pro-democracy content might be distributed. The appropriate platforms can vary widely depending on who is backing the project, the budget available and the media consumption habits of the target audience.

The Capitol Hill advocates of a Russian *House of Cards* proceeded from the idea that this megaseries would somehow be produced at government expense. NGAs may be in a far better position than government entities to identify effective strategies, craft messages to support them and find quick, effective ways to bring them to the public.

Defense: Fighting Adversary Media

Russian IOs are not ideologically picky. They can support local leaders or foment resistance to them, depending on their utility to Moscow. Russian messaging can skew right or left, aligning itself with whatever philosophy is ascendant in the population it seeks to influence. One constant, however, is that Moscow paints the world as divided into good and evil camps. In Europe, the narrative usually is a populist one where the good camp consists of ordinary people, working hard for a living and unashamed of their patriotism, their values and their borders. The evil camp consists of politically correct liberals beholden to national and EU elites, divorced from the common man and eager to "replace" him with impoverished immigrants (whose arrival they encourage by bombing their homelands). In EU nations, Russian IOs play on resentments toward other members—for example, feelings in Italy that their country is being exploited and humiliated by France and Germany. For countries formerly in the Soviet orbit, these messages are supplemented by manipulated memories of an egalitarian, virtuous Soviet past.

In communication to African and Latin American populations, the evil camp is Western powers, aided by local lackeys, trying to impose their will as if colonialism still existed. Local populations are in the good camp with their ally, Russia, with its genuine history of support for anti-colonialism and national liberation. (Soviet goals were not always altruistic, but the Kremlin's support was a fact.) In addition, according to Armando Chaguaceda of the Universidad de Guanajuato in Mexico, Kremlin media present Russia "as an alternative of order and development in line with Latin American interests, as opposed to an imperialistic and decadent West."[2]

These are all simple narratives. If one accepts their basic premises, they explain world politics completely. Nothing happens by chance; every event can be fitted into this framework of injustice, conspiracy and aggression. By extension, the elimination of a few evil forces will solve the world's woes.

As with most simplistic theories, these claims cannot bear much scrutiny. Their authors, however, do not count on defending them

---

[2] Armando Chaguaceda, "El Oso va a Occidente" [The Bear Heads West], *Foreign Affairs Latinoamérica*, Vol. 18, No. 3, July–September 2018, 75, https://www.academia.edu/38165496/El_oso_va_a_Occidente._La_agenda_rusa_en_Latinoam%C3%A9rica.

with logic. Their approach is simply to repeat them constantly, while drowning out dissenting voices. Assertions become more believable the more they are inserted into people's minds—what psychologists call the illusory truth effect. An Iraqi prime minister once told US Gen. Paul Funk, "General, you Americans […] you say one thing, put it in the information space, and then expect everybody to fall in. The Russians say disinformation a thousand times on every network in every domain every day."[3]

Killing the Messenger

In line with this saturation policy, Russia and its allies generate enormous amounts of false and misleading content. Trying to respond to every canard can exhaust not only democracy advocates but also the audience. News consumers can take only so many "don't believe this" warnings. For these reasons, it is essential to choose the battles one fights with Russian information warfare. Opponents of Russian IOs must opt to address only the highest-profile falsehoods, expose them in real time, and keep coming back to them repeatedly, noting the source of the false information each time. The point is not to just to deny specific falsehoods again and again, but to "kill the messenger"—a counter-brand strategy to undermine the sources that put them into circulation. The goal is for everything these sources produce in the future to be met with skepticism. One might, for example, highlight *RT* and *Sputnik* as the homes of conspiracy theories that are not only bizarre but inconsistent. In 2020, these

---

[3] Sydney J. Freedberg Jr., "'Desperate Need For Speed' As Army Takes On Chinese, Russian, ISIS Info Ops," *Breaking Defense*, August 21, 2019, https://breakingdefense.com/2019/08/desperate-need-for-speed-as-army-takes-on-chinese-russians-isis-trolls/.

organs simultaneously described the coronavirus as an apocalyptic threat and a hoax.[4]

An example of a fast reaction against a Russian messenger occurred in Estonia in 2018. Urve Eslas, an Estonian specialist in combating disinformation, described it as follows:

> On 13 March, Estonian media reported on an incident within the Estonian Defense Forces: a conscript had shot himself in the shoulder, he said, to "get a cool scar." According to the investigation, as reported by the media, the conscript—who had served as a driver at the Kuperjanov Infantry Battalion (a unit of the Estonian Land Forces)—stole a cartridge for his AK4 rifle and, when no one was near, pulled the trigger. According to the medical report, the conscript lost a lot of blood, but no critical organs were injured and he is recovering under medical supervision. Military police discovered no evidence that the shooting was caused by anything other than what the soldier claimed: the conscript was well trained, his relationships with his comrades were good, and he had earlier told his friends that he wanted a bullet scar. On 15 March, Estonian *Sputnik*, a branch of the Kremlin-financed media channel, sent an inquiry to the Estonian Defense Forces asking it to confirm the channel's supposed information that the conscript was a Russian speaker, that he was shot during an escape attempt sparked by tensions on base between Estonians and Russians, and that military doctors deny medical care to conscripts who do not speak Estonian. Instead of answering *Sputnik* directly, the Force sent the channel's inquiry to the Estonian media to publicize *Sputnik's* attempt to inflame conflict between ethnic Estonians and Russians and to

---

[4] "Disinformation Can Kill," *EUvsDisinfo*, March 26, 2020, https://euvsdisinfo.eu/disinformation-can-kill/.

neutralize any disinformation that *Sputnik* might try to spread. The neutralization was successful; *Sputnik* never wrote the story.[5]

The incident is an excellent example of not only shooting down a story, but the messenger too.

A fast response to high-profile disinformation narratives is also essential. In 2017, a rumor appeared in Lithuania that German soldiers on exercises there had raped a teenager. (The claim echoed the "Lisa case," a Russia-promoted claim in 2016 that Arab immigrants had raped a German girl in Berlin). Lithuania and NATO were ready. They had expected an IO attack against the German forces and reacted immediately, with a declaration by Czech Gen. Petr Pavel, head of the NATO Military Committee, that the claim was false and the work of Russians. He added that more such operations were expected, a good way to immunize Lithuanians against whatever the Russians might try next.[6]

Governments and responsible media, however, have a built-in speed problem. Their principles prevent them from reporting what they have not verified. Audiences are rarely satisfied to "wait and see"; they look for any explanation of events, however fanciful. Russian information professionals recognize that information "voids" around major events are dangerous, and they believe in filling them as soon as possible with something that serves their national interest.[7] When

---

[5] Urve Eslas, "Estonian Forces Neutralize Disinfo Attack," *Center for European Policy Analysis*, April 10, 2018, http://infowar.cepa.org/Briefs/Est/Estonia-Neutralizes-Sputniks-Disinformation-Attack.

[6] Teri Schultz, "Why the 'fake rape' story against German NATO forces fell flat in Lithuania," *Deutsche Welle*, February 23, 2017, https://www.dw.com/en/why-the-fake-rape-story-against-german-nato-forces-fell-flat-in-lithuania/a-37694870.

[7] Sergei Rogachev and Anna Vilovatykh, "Информационное обеспечение внешнеполитической деятельности в условиях цифровой реальности" [Informational security for foreign political activity in the conditions of digital

a Ukrainian airplane crashed in Tehran in January 2020, Western media outlets were careful to avoid speculation on the cause until the following day, when they could quote authoritative sources as saying Iran had shot it down. Western journalists pride themselves on such self-restraint. In contrast, the Russian *Federal News Agency* produced on the day of the crash an elaborate narrative, based on "too-suspicious coincidences," suggesting the plane could have been shot down by a US drone. (The "coincidences" included the proximity of American bases to Iran and a "not excluded" possibility that the US sent a drone to shoot down an Iranian plane but downed the Ukrainian jet by mistake.[8])

This problem of speed has long been critical in confronting disinformation. As Jonathan Swift put it, "Falsehood flies, and the truth comes limping after it." The best answer is for news media and governments to acknowledge baseless information that is circulating, while stressing that the real facts are, for the moment, unknowable. The days of professional news media being proud of refusing to touch dodgy stories "with a 10-foot pole" must end; when false stories gain traction on the internet, they must be dragged into the light and exposed, even if the full true story is not yet known. Journalists sometimes speak of handling such issues with a "truth sandwich": a good strategy. Instead of starting by reporting the questionable claim (which can put the claim into the headline) and then trying to knock it down, a story would start by saying the facts are unknowable. It would then cite a couple of examples of speculation (the more bizarre and contradictory the better) and finish up with the best estimate of when the truth might be known.

---

reality], *Problemy Natsionalnoi Strategii,* No. 6 (57) 2019, https://riss.ru/analitycs/65672/.

[8] "Непопулярная версия: американский БПЛА сбил украинский 'Боинг-737' в небе над Ираном" [An unpopular version: An American drone shot down the Ukrainian Boeing 737 in the sky over Iran], *Federalnoe Agentstvo Novostei,* January 8, 2020, https://riafan.ru/1240427-nepopulyarnaya-versiya-amerikanskii-bpla-sbil-ukrainskii-boing-737-v-nebe-nad-iranom.

The same applies to handling damaging hacks. Media may think the high road is to ignore them, but internet readers will not. When thousands of emails from Emmanuel Macron's presidential campaign were hacked in 2017, authorities quickly denounced the theft and media made it a top story. French media reported that some of the emails released were "probably false." Instead of focusing on what the emails said, as the hackers would have wanted, the media turned the story into a whodunit about the perpetrators—who was trying to sink Macron?[9] The French have also learned to seed databases of sensitive documents and emails with content that, when leaked or hacked, looks ridiculous, throwing doubt on the veracity of everything else the hackers have published.[10]

Democratic governments must not compound their speed problems further by a slow production of responses once they know the facts. If slowness is inevitable because of institutional sluggishness and approval processes, NGAs can do the exposing. Lithuania's government is often quick to expose disinformation, but the country also has a full, vertically integrated mechanism alongside government to identify and respond to hostile narratives. False tales identified by Debunk.eu's software are passed to subject-matter experts in elf groups, who research them and quickly send their findings to journalists. (Some elves are believed to be government employees, who function in their elf roles without the constraints of official clearance.) Should NGAs want to go beyond journalistic channels, the kinds of videos made by the UK's Foreign Office about the Skripal case can be created in just a few hours by anyone with basic video software. The US government created equally simple videos in its war against the Islamic State.[11] For greatest effect, social media posts that debunk

---

[9] Jean-Baptiste Jeangène Vilmer, *The "Macron Leaks" Operation*, 37–38.
[10] Jean-Baptiste Jeangène Vilmer, *The "Macron Leaks" Operation*, 35.
[11] For an example, see the video in Joby Warrick, "How a U.S. team uses Facebook, guerrilla marketing to peel off potential ISIS recruits," *The Washington Post*, February 6, 2017, https://www.washingtonpost.com/world/national-security/bait-

disinformation should carry the same hashtags as the original false claims.

Another issue arises with interview requests from media outlets run by Russia and its allies. These media often seek to interview public officials, including from Western countries, to make themselves look more objective. Some believe officials should refuse, even if they are being given an opportunity to counteract Russian claims. "We should refuse to have dealings with the Kremlin's lie-machines—the 'TV station' RT, and the 'news agency' Sputnik," argues Edward Lucas of the Center for European Policy Analysis. "No reputable commentator, politician or official should lend them credibility by responding to their requests for comment. Let these propagandists stew in their own swamp of cranks and conspiracy theorists."[12] The European Values think tank published in 2017 an indictment of "useful idiots" in the United States and Europe who it said add to RT's legitimacy even when their appearances on its air are "motivated by the desire to offset some of RT's more toxic and hyperbolic narratives." European Values published a list of 2,300 Westerners who had appeared on RT programs.[13]

Lucas and Pomerantsev have argued as well that reporters for such Russian outlets "should not enjoy the social and professional privileges—access to press conferences, media credentials—enjoyed

---

and-flip-us-team-uses-facebook-guerrilla-marketing-to-peel-off-potential-isis-recruits/2017/02/03/431e19ba-e4e4-11e6-a547-5fb9411d332c_story.html.

[12] Edward Lucas, "How the West should punish Putin," *CapX*, October 31, 2016, https://capx.co/playing-russia-at-its-own-game/.

[13] Monika L. Richter, *The Kremlin's Platform for 'Useful Idiots' in the West: An Overview of RT's Editorial Strategy and Evidence of Impact* (Prague: European Values, September 18, 2017), https://www.europeanvalues.net/wp-content/uploads/2017/09/Overview-of-RTs-Editorial-Strategy-and-Evidence-of-Impact-1.pdf.

by real journalists."[14] France, Canada and the UK are among countries that have denied coverage accreditation to *RT* and *Sputnik* reporters.

However, it is a fact that these outlets have their audiences, and it is impossible to enforce a boycott of them by anyone they might approach for a comment. In addition, the refusal of many Russian officials to give interviews to the *Voice of America* and *Radio Free Europe/Radio Liberty* because they are "foreign agents" does not speak well of press freedom in Russia. I would propose a middle course: issuing written statements in response to questions from Russian media. This prevents them from claiming that a Western institution "refused to comment," but avoids on-screen interviews in which Western spokesmen are seen to be engaging with *RT* employees as if they were normal journalists. If *RT* uses the statement in a distorted way, the Western institution can go directly after *RT*'s honesty by publishing comparisons of the statement it made and how *RT* reported it. (Some Westerners are confident they can control on-screen interviews, even winning the day. However, given the skills of *RT* and *Sputnik* in video editing and controlling the context in which people are quoted, this is a very uncertain tactic.)

Block or Not?

Many countries have legislation on their books allowing their governments to control foreign broadcasting on their territories.[15] Some have used this to take Russian media off the air. Lithuania, Moldova, Ecuador and Bolivia have cut off television programs from Russia at various times. Ukraine has jammed Russian radio and TV

---

[14] Edward Lucas and Peter Pomerantsev, *Winning the Information War Redux* (Washington: Center for European Policy Analysis, April 2017), 39, https://docs.wixstatic.com/ugd/644196_264a764d8fc04714a883355f4ac682b9.pdf.
[15] *Limits on Freedom of Expression* (Washington: Library of Congress, June 2019), https://www.loc.gov/law/help/freedom-expression/limits-expression.pdf.

transmissions, cut off access to Russian social networks and blocked the Russian-language search engine Yandex.

However, censorship is not efficient. While Ukraine has blocked television programs from Russia, local media with pro-Russian sympathies continue to purvey their narratives. Despite occasional government blockages, about 50 Russian TV channels are available in the Baltic republics. Content blocked on the air will inevitably pop up somewhere on the internet. The more governments make content "forbidden fruit," the more people will look for it.

Another problem is that whenever democratic countries block foreign voices, they can be seen to be endorsing Moscow's line that, in the name of "information sovereignty," governments should be entitled to control what their citizens see. This undermines the West's ability to criticize Russia for its own repression of information. As Peter Pomerantsev argues:

> [Censorship] plays right into the Kremlin's desire to normalize censorship, to put governments in charge of deciding what is harmful, and pushes us towards its desired end state of "sovereign internets." In the US such legislation is less likely due to the First Amendment, but the language that we use to define the Russian operations, words like "interference" and "meddling," play into the equivalency of a Trump or Putin: these subjective, value free terms suggest that any type of information flowing across borders is "meddling," that there is no difference between journalism by Deutsche Welle and a Kremlin troll farm.[16]

---

[16] Peter Pomerantsev, "Peter Pomerantsev on information wars, Trump, Putin, and regulations," *Coda*, October 16, 2019, https://codastory.com/disinformation/disinfo-newsletter/pomerantsev-information-wars-trump-putin-regulations/.

Given all these considerations, I believe governments should not block Russian media. Corina Rebegea of the Center for European Policy Analysis suggests a reasonable step short of censorship: making sure that channels that convey disinformation are at least not included in "must carry" packages governments impose on cable companies. That way, people wanting to subscribe to them will have to pay extra, diminishing audience size.[17]

An exception to this principle could apply when a country produces radio and television content designed for Russian audiences. In such cases, it is reasonable to insist on reciprocal access. No Western broadcaster can distribute Russian-language programs on cable to Russian audiences. *Radio Free Europe/Radio Liberty* lost all its local radio frequencies in Russian cities after Putin came to power. Despite that, *RT* is on cable systems in localities across the US. *Sputnik* is allowed to have AM and FM radio signals in Washington, DC, and expanded in 2020 to Kansas City.

Some countries have gone further than blocking Russian programming by taking direct action against Russian correspondents. Estonia closed *Sputnik*'s Tallinn bureau at the start of 2020, saying it was complying with EU economic sanctions. In 2019, Lithuania barred for five years the editor-in-chief of *Sputnik's* local branch as a threat to national security. Ukraine charged the local head of the *RIA Novosti* news agency with treason in 2018 (he was later freed in a prisoner exchange). These actions risk giving legitimacy to the actions of authoritarian governments that arrest, expel and harass journalists worldwide. Unless it can be demonstrated that a journalist is engaged in covert work or is an imminent danger to public safety, unpleasant and even misleading media coverage is just one of those things that democratic governments must put up with.

---

[17] Corina Rebegea, interview with author, April 20, 2019.

Choking off the Money

NGAs have been active in efforts to discredit and dry up financial support for websites controlled by Russian and conspiratorial forces. Many such sites were created just to make money, not out of deep ideological conviction. The NGAs' reasonable position is that undermining democracy should not be a profitable undertaking.

New York–based NewsGuard is one of several rating services that use human editors to create "nutrition warnings" for news sites.[18] When a reader opts into its service and clicks on an *RT* story, NewsGuard pops up a warning that says, "Proceed with caution: this website generally fails to maintain basic standards of accuracy and accountability." NewsGuard generally gives high ratings to mainstream Western news sources, while issuing warnings about Russian media. *RT* calls NewsGuard "something akin to a bundled anti-virus feature, only this time the virus targets your brain."[19]

More threatening to disinformation outlets than rating services, which many readers may never opt into, are projects to deprive the outlets of revenue. According to the Global Disinformation Index (GDI), disinformation sites haul in nearly a quarter-billion dollars a year by posting ads they receive from commercial advertising networks.[20] A GDI study said 70 percent of disinformation sites display advertising from Google, while others receive ads from the

---

[18] https://newsguardtech.com.

[19] "No need to install: Microsoft has controversial fake news filter NewsGuard built into mobile browser," *RT,* Jan. 23, 2019, https://www.rt.com/news/449530-newsguard-edge-browser-media-integrated/.

[20] *The Quarter-Billion Dollar Question: How is Disinformation Gaming Ad Tech?* (Global Disinformation Index, September 2019), 4, https://disinformationindex.org/wp-content/uploads/2019/09/GDI_Ad-tech_Report_Screen_AW16.pdf.

AppNexus, Amazon, Criteo and Taboola networks.[21] *RT* and *Sputnik* are among those that make money from US ad networks.

GDI is creating a worldwide listing of disinformation sites, which it says it identifies through human ratings and artificial intelligence. Ideally, ad networks would refuse to provide ads to sites on the list. "We've seen early indications that give us hope, but it continues to be an uphill battle," says Danny Rogers, a co-founder of GDI. "Not only are these issues fraught with issues of political speech, etc., but they are also so entrenched in such lucrative business models that I fear we have a serious headwind before any of this gets adopted in a large scale way. […] In short, while I recognize the challenges, I'm very hopeful Google and other platforms will indeed adopt our methodologies and collaborate with us to deplatform hate and disinformation actors from their networks."[22]

GDI's supporters include the UK Foreign Office, Luminate and the Knight Foundation, a major US funder of journalism projects.[23]

Defunding campaigns in can exist at the level of a single country. Several nations have defunding groups working under the name "Sleeping Giants."[24] An effort in the Czech Republic has convinced some large banks and other companies to stop advertising on disinformation sites.[25] The Slovak Konšpirátori.sk project seeks to choke off revenue to 160 sites identified by its human reviewers as containing "materials of charlatan nature, magical preparations that are obviously fraudulent to an expert, websites featuring deceptive or

---

[21] *"The Quarter-Billion Dollar Question: How is Disinformation Gaming Ad Tech?"* 6, Global Disinformation Index.

[22] Danny Rogers, personal communication with author, April 2, 2020.

[23] "About Us," *Global Disinformation Index*, accessed July 24, 2020, https://disinformationindex.org/about/.

[24] For the US group, see https://www.facebook.com/slpnggiants/?ref=page_internal.

[25] https://www.nelez.cz/.

fake news, imaginary or profoundly twisted events that are in clear contradiction to the facts, conspiracy theories, vulgarisms, calls to violence, spreading false alarms, defaming minorities or races, as well as websites that do not respect basic principles of journalistic ethics."

Addressing web advertisers, Konšpirátori.sk says:

> The content networks, such as Google Display Network, pay to websites using their advertisement system about 70% of the price of advertising, purchased by you through these networks. This is how you become a direct financial supporter of the websites providing content that is far from representing ethical and balanced news. Your brand thus becomes associated with the content that may seriously damage your reputation and, moreover, you are directly funding the creation of such content. Using our database, you or your agency are able to easily prevent this, avoiding any association of your brand with controversial content or its creation. We think that it is the social responsibility of each company to take into consideration who is financially benefiting from that company's marketing activities.[26]

Ján Urbančík, the founder of Konšpirátori.sk, notes that some 4,000 Slovak companies now refuse to advertise on sites on Konšpirátori's index. Some sites he has listed have sued the project for devastating their revenues. His response is that the list simply represents the opinion of the project team, and as opinion it should be protected as free speech. He notes the list does not force anyone to stop advertising; that is a voluntary decision by an advertiser. The site does not make specific allegations as to what content led to a site's inclusion on the list.

---

[26] "Why is it that the content ad networks fail to protect the advertisers?" in "Reasons behind creating this initiative," *Konšpirátori.sk*, accessed July 24, 2020, https://www.konspiratori.sk/en/why-this-initiative.php#2.

Urbančík said he has no idea how many sites may have closed as a result of his work, but he is proud of one that decided to clean up its shady content and as a result was removed from his list.[27]

To some advertisers, business is business, and they are fine with advertising their products on any site where they will be seen. "Even Nazis brush their teeth," says Danny Rogers of GDI. He believes only public heat will force some companies to stop advertising anywhere they can attract eyeballs.[28] Focusing that heat requires constant effort, since new disinformation sites are always springing up.

The information landscape is also replete with "propaganda mercenaries" who specialize in shaping social media images and campaigns.[29] To the extent that these companies are assisting IOs by Russia and its allies, their role needs to be revealed. Some of these actors—though not all—are large public relations and consulting firms that may be concerned about their image.

While condemning and defunding disinformation sites is a valuable strategy, it is also important to have a positive strategy of directing audiences to reliable outlets. NewsGuard gives "green" ratings to media its raters consider trustworthy. Estonia's Propastop plans a "white list" of dependable news sources.

---

[27] Ján Urbančík, personal communication with author, March 25, 2020.

[28] Danny Rogers, interview with author, June 5, 2019.

[29] For a description of some of these operations, see Samantha Bradshaw and Phillip N. Howard, *The Global Disinformation Order: 2019 Global Inventory of Organised Social Media Manipulation"* (Oxford: Oxford Internet Institute, September 26, 2019), https://comprop.oii.ox.ac.uk/wp-content/uploads/sites/93/2019/09/CyberTroop-Report19.pdf.

Degrading Tech Support

One way to affect disinformation outlets has received relatively little attention. Most websites depend on privately run technology companies to register their URLs, protect them from cyberattacks and provide computing power. These service providers can be compelled by sanctions to stop serving a site, or they can make their own decision that a site's content is something they do not wish to support. After the US message board 8chan was widely criticized in 2019 for hosting statements by mass shooters, a variety of support companies refused to work with them, knocking the site off the web.[30] In January 2020, the Iranian *Fars News Agency* said its Farsnews.com address had been blocked by its server company because of US Treasury Department sanctions.[31] A US company pulled the security certificate it had issued to the Russian-registered USAReally.com site in 2019. If a site lacks a valid security certificate, browsers may block it or warn visitors it is insecure.[32]

This situation opens the way for NGAs to try to influence those who provide technical support to disinformation sites. In many cases, the sites targeted can come back online by technical legerdemain or by finding less picky support providers. However, even forcing a site off the web briefly can open a useful public debate about the site's content and who stands behind it.

---

[30] Kate Conger and Nathaniel Popper, "Behind the Scenes, 8chan Scrambles to Get Back Online," *The New York Times,* August 5, 2019, https://www.nytimes.com/2019/08/05/technology/8chan-website-online.html.

[31] Maryann Sinaiee, "Iranian News Agency Targeted by US Sanction Resorts to Hacking To Get Domain Back," *Radio Free Europe/Radio Liberty,* January 25, 2020, https://en.radiofarda.com/a/iranian-news-agency-targeted-by-us-sanction-resorts-to-hacking-to-get-domain-back-/30396680.html.

[32] Tim Johnson, "Security certificate yanked from Russia-backed website, hurting ability to divide voters," *McClatchy DC,* January 2, 2019, https://www.mcclatchydc.com/news/policy/technology/cyber-security/article223832790.html.

'Taking us for fools'

Another tactic against hostile outlets is to expose them as manipulators of the local audience. This is the "killing the messenger" tactic discussed earlier, with the more emotional overlay that "they take us for fools." Especially in countries with strong reserves of nationalism, it may make sense to reveal Russian IO operators as foreign puppeteers trying to divide the country and rewrite history— abetted by local citizens who make money serving foreign manipulators. In the words of Keir Giles of Chatham House:

> To combat the particular challenge of how human psychology is exploited by social media disinformation, governments' responses should be as interesting as the fake news they are countering. Simple explanations that a particular piece of news is false are not sufficient to engage target audiences. Countermeasures should focus not on fact-checking but on the deceit—emphasizing that people were conned—and, like the original disinformation, should appeal to readers' emotions rather than their rationality, in order to be effective.[33]

Analyst Rand Waltzman of the RAND Corp. also endorses such tactics. He writes:

> One way that a [counter-]disinformation warrior might turn "an attacker's energy against him rather than directly opposing it" is to turn the target's fear and anger back on the attacker. Using the same tools as the attacker, the disinformation warrior might be able to accomplish this. Show the target that they are being taken for fools and deceived and for what purpose and that they should

---

[33] Keir Giles, "Countering Russian Information Operations in the Age of Social Media," *Council on Foreign Relations*, November 21, 2017, https://www.cfr.org/report/countering-russian-information-operations-age-social-media.

be outraged. This wouldn't be accomplished by calm rational fact-based argument. It would be accomplished using the same type of emotional appeal and manipulation used by the attacker, but in reverse.[34]

Latin American and African audiences, with a long history of being exploited by outsiders, may be sensitive to revelations of Russian covert IOs targeting their countries on social networks. Certainly Western countries and cultures massively influence media on those continents, but at least that impact is overt.

One tactic to evoke justifiable anger against hostile IOs is to "cross their channels"—to transport messages meant for one audience to another that will find them offensive. For instance, one might have translated for US audiences in 2020 racist references in the Russian media to American blacks protesting police brutality.[35] African audiences could be made aware of assertions in Russian media that white farmers deserve credit for all of South Africa's agricultural success, and that "black racism" against whites may be pushing the country toward civil war.[36] In May 2015, Russian television broadcast to domestic audiences a documentary about the Soviet invasion of Czechoslovakia that cast Soviet troops as "helping" Czechs save themselves from a pro-Western coup. Czech public television exposed the Russian narrative by rebroadcasting the program in full to its

[34] Rand Waltzman, personal communication with author, October 3, 2019.
[35] See Dmitry Steshin, "14 добрых и дельных советов американскому Майдану" [14 friendly and useful suggestions for the American Maidan], *Komsomolskaya Pravda,* May 30, 2020, https://www.kp.ru/daily/27136.5/4227260/.
[36] Dmitri Pavlenko, "Правящая партия ЮАР готовится отнять землю у белых фермеров" [RSA ruling party prepares to seize land from white farmers], *Tsargrad TV,* December 22, 2017, https://tsargrad.tv/articles/unizhenie-belyh-chjornyj-peredel-prevratit-juar-v-novoe-zimbabve_102121. Regarding this and other examples of Russian media disparaging black governments, see Sergey Sukhanin, "The Kremlin's Controversial 'Soft Power' in Africa (Part Two)," *Eurasia Daily Monitor,* December 10, 2019, https://jamestown.org/program/the-kremlins-controversial-soft-power-in-africa-part-two/.

viewers with subtitles. As expected, it angered Czechs and Slovaks. In the words of a Global Engagement Center analysis of the incident, "In general, when we expose the disinformer's misdeeds and their most absurd, offensive false claims and actions, we set the frame and tend to win. But, if we allow the disinformer's false claims to set the topic of conversation and are constantly trying to respond to them, we are on the defensive and tend to lose."[37]

Offense: Pro-Democracy Narratives

Communication on behalf of democracy will never succeed if it consists solely of blocking, disparaging or defunding hostile outlets. It is also unrealistic to expect that transparency alone—*mea culpas* about Western shortcomings—will make democratic countries more attractive simply because of their honesty. The Center for Strategic & International Studies says "the ability of the United States to 'own up' to any instances of corruption or political miscalculation denies Russia and other adversaries the opportunity to use such information as an attack on the U.S. systems' norms, values, and narrative."[38] Unfortunately, experience shows this is not the case. Russian IOs dance endlessly on admissions of US and other Western deficiencies as proof of their claims the West is rotten overall. To succeed, democratic forces must outflank destructive narratives with their own strong, positive messages that appeal to the intellect, common sense and emotions of the audience.

---

[37] "Three Ways to Counter Disinformation," *GEC Counter-Disinformation Dispatches #2*, Global Engagement Center, February 11, 2020 https://commons.america.gov/article?id=69&site=content.america.gov.
[38] *By Other Means, Part II: U.S. Priorities in the Gray Zone*, 35.

Some Strategic Considerations

Given the complexity of democratic ideas and the imperfect record of Western countries in delivering on them, the challenges of selling democracy are considerable. These strategies and considerations will be useful:

• *Have clear goals for each nation.* Discussions between local NGAs and foreign funders may be contentious on this point, but for effective action there must be a common view of the desired outcome. Tomáš Valášek of Carnegie Europe worries that the EU mixes the fundamental requirements for democracy in East European states, such as an independent judiciary and rule of law, with a "values agenda" that, for example, pressures countries to legalize abortion or welcome immigrants. In the fight over the values agenda, Valášek says, the importance of rule of law could be lost.[39] The same applies in the opposite direction. Some US aid to Africa is constrained by a values requirement that it not be used for abortion. Those interested in democratic and economic development need to define and prioritize their most important concerns. One does not necessarily have to downplay the social values that exist in developed democratic countries or accept hateful ideologies as the price for democratic institutions. However, replicating in detail all the social attitudes of developed Western societies need not be a precondition for cooperation.

Similar questions arise regarding foreign policy. Does "success" in pro-democracy campaigning mean Moldova and Bosnia-

---

[39] Tomáš Valášek, "How Not to Lose Friends and Alienate People," *Carnegie Europe,* March 1, 2018, https://carnegieeurope.eu/strategiceurope/75677. EU rhetoric has described members' "obligations under EU law" to accept refugees as one and the same as the overall concept of "orderly and structured society governed by rule of law." See Lorne Cook and Samuel Petrequin, "Legal opinion: Poland, Hungary, Czechs broke EU migrant law," *The Associated Press,* October 31, 2019, https://apnews.com/353b99a01ae949958d730b59737ee0a2.

Herzegovina must seek EU membership and join NATO? Or would it be enough for them to build strong democratic institutions, even if that leads to their populations' deciding to be neutral in the competition between Russia and the West? (Moldova's Constitution says the country should be permanently neutral.) In Latin America, how essential is it that a government oppose the Nicolás Maduro regime in Venezuela? Russian IOs pick targets based on such litmus tests.[40] Making a point of such issues can undermine the claim of pro-democracy forces to be concerned primarily with altruistic goals of spreading representative government and rule of law.

• *Calibrate the Russian connection.* Russian and local actors have many common beliefs but they cannot always be responded to together. In formerly Soviet bloc countries, the economic and political interests tied to Russia are obvious. Pro-democracy messaging in this region will logically include many references to Moscow and its behavior. However, local populist parties often build their arguments on local issues; they cannot be opposed simply by calling them Russian lackeys. In Georgia, right-wing and xenophobic forces flourish, serving Russian interests by enhancing instability but without provable Russian direction. This is even truer in Western Europe. No Russian instructions were needed for France's Front National or Germany's Alternative für Deutschland to agitate for limits on immigration. *RT* and *Sputnik* provide covering fire for populist parties, but many citizens are unaware—or do not care—that these media outlets are Russia-controlled. In much of Africa and Latin America, Russia is such a distant power that trying to connect it to local actors is a stretch without hard evidence. In 2017, fewer than a

---

[40] Postings by unidentified social media accounts believed to be under Russian control spiked during protests in the fall of 2019, in Chile, Bolivia, Ecuador, Peru and Colombia—countries where opposition was strong to the government in Venezuela. Lara Jakes, "As Protests in South America Surged, So Did Russian Trolls on Twitter, U.S. Finds," *The New York Times,* January 20, 2020, https://www.nytimes.com/2020/01/19/us/politics/south-america-russian-twitter.html.

third of Africans and a quarter of Latin Americans thought Russia was a major threat to their countries.[41] "The most conspicuous fact about Russia in Africa is that it is absent from discussions," says Albert Kofi Owusu, general manager of the Ghana News Agency.[42] In a 2017 survey, nearly a third of Africans and a fifth of Latin Americans interviewed offered no response as to whether Putin could be counted on to do the right thing in world affairs.[43] The idea of Russia having any influence in Latin America or Africa may make Westerners' blood boil, but it does not drive passions on those continents. Countries there recognize the value of good relations with the United States and the EU but appreciate the advantages of being simultaneously courted by Russia, China and rising powers like the United Arab Emirates and Turkey. A little Russian aid or a mutually beneficial contract can be welcome. Governments and peoples feel they have the right to associate with, and derive advantage from, whomever they want.

• *Give people choices.* Citizens like agency and a feeling they are respected. These feelings are enhanced when they are not urged to support a specific candidate or party but given a choice of alternatives. When the political system offers more than a binary choice, pro-democracy activists will find the greatest success if they can point to multiple candidates or parties that all would be acceptable in power, campaigning only against the most dangerous.

• *Stay on message.* Jed Willard, director of global engagement at the FDR Foundation at Harvard, emphasizes the importance of selecting positive pro-democracy messages and repeating them incessantly.

---

[41] Margaret Vice, *Publics Worldwide Unfavorable Toward Putin, Russia,* (Washington: Pew Research Center, 2017), 2, https://www.pewresearch.org/global/wp-content/uploads/sites/2/2017/08/Pew-Research-Center_2017.08.16_Views-of-Russia-Report.pdf.
[42] Albert Kofi Owusu, interview with author, November 23, 2019.
[43] Vice, "Publics Worldwide Unfavorable Toward Putin, Russia," 16–20.

"Refute fabrications but for every refutation make sure you have multiple reassertions of your own positive narrative," he says.[44]

• *Build diverse support.* Attractive as democratic government is, it is not the top issue on everyone's mind. It can, however, be combined with many other issues. Democracy and anti-disinformation activists should seek the strength that comes from intersectionality with other causes, like economic equality, women's and workers' rights, public safety, climate activism, anti-extremism and press freedom.[45] Invidious comparisons can be made to Russia's record in each area; the disastrous 2019 forest fires in Siberia, which hastened global warming further by pouring black carbon on Arctic ice,[46] would have been a good topic to join with environmental groups in spotlighting. However, bringing Russia into every argument is not essential. "The important thing is to encourage Western unity on climate change and anything to improve society, rather than necessarily always using anti-Russian plays," says Estonian analyst Dmitri Teperik.[47]

Protests in Slovakia over the murder of anti-corruption journalist Ján Kuciak and his fiancée in 2018, which brought 70,000 people into the streets, unified supporters of press freedom, democracy and the fight against corruption. They helped motivate voters to elect a pro-democracy president, Zuzana Čaputová. In 2020, the country's populist-oriented ruling party was defeated in elections and the new

[44] "Russian Information Operations in East Europe," (comments by Jed Willard), video, Harriman Institute, Columbia University, April 2, 2020, https://www.facebook.com/TheHarrimanInstitute/videos/593326268194157/.

[45] In Ghana, the fact-checking organization Dubawa Ghana linked up with the Alliance for African Women Initiative to fight disinformation on the coronavirus. Harrison Mantas, "Fact-checkers use new tools of engagement to fight fast-moving hoaxes," *Poynter*, June 10, 2020, https://www.poynter.org/fact-checking/2020/fact-checkers-use-new-tools-of-engagement-to-fight-fast-moving-hoaxes/.

[46] Greenpeace International, "Massive forest fires in Siberia is a climate emergency," news release, August 5, 2019, https://www.greenpeace.org/international/press-release/23660/massive-forest-fires-iSn-siberia-is-a-climate-emergency/.

[47] Dmitri Teperik, interview with author, July 18, 2019.

government pledged itself to a pro-NATO and -EU course. In France, activists against Russian influence meet regularly with civil society groups focused on domestic hate crimes and extremism.

Maria Stephan of the United States Institute of Peace says nonviolent "people power" movements are most successful if there is large, diverse and sustained participation by "lots of different people who have different sources of power, skills and the like that are able to sustain their participation over time."[48] Local NGAs may also be freer now to design programs that they think will work best; Michael Silberman, global director of the training group Mobilisation Lab, says there was a "shift of power conversation" in 2020 in which outside funders of many grassroots causes, unable to travel frequently to oversee local programs because of the pandemic, began to leave more decision-making in local actors' hands.[49]

• *Keep it local.* People know best the conditions in their own countries. While it is important to explain the liberties that developed Western democracies enjoy, the most effective messaging conveys how such freedoms could improve conditions in the target country. That means exposing the drag that corruption and repression, including at the most local level, puts on commerce and society. A story about corruption in a local market can have more impact than one about an oligarch stealing millions in the national capital. People often feel big-time corruption is inevitable, but local venality hurts them directly. While *Radio Free Europe/Radio Liberty* devotes much of its Russia coverage to events in Moscow, audiences have grown for its localized websites for the North Caucasus, Tatar-Bashkir, Siberian, and St.

---

[48] "Maria Stephan on What We Get Wrong About Protest Movements," *On Peace*, podcast, United States Institute of Peace, December 19, 2019, https://www.usip.org/publications/2019/12/maria-stephan-what-we-get-wrong-about-protest-movements.

[49] "People Power in a Pandemic" (comments by Michael Silberman), video, United States Institute of Peace, May 19, 2020, https://www.youtube.com/watch?v=YOwmydRwxDo.

Petersburg–Kaliningrad regions. These services deal with local events that residents can verify for themselves, adding to the overall credibility of *RFE/RL*. In campaigning for common-sense measures to halt the spread of the coronavirus, it is far more effective to use the voices of local doctors and nurses than to cite far-away scientific authorities.

• *All about the timing.* "There's truth, but there's also the right time for truth," says a former State Department spokeswoman interviewed for this book. As every journalist knows, a news story attracts the most readers in two situations: when it is more compelling than anything else that day, or when it adds an important angle to something already occupying the public's attention. NGAs must be careful not to publish investigative revelations in news cycles where audiences are preoccupied with other matters. Unless there is a danger of being scooped, it is worth saving up information for when it will have more impact. During the delay, new information may come to hand that will make it the story even more effective when finally published.

• *Attack or soothe?* A strategy choice with excellent arguments on both sides is whether to attack IOs by Russia and its allies with the same aggressiveness they resort to, or instead work to create more thoughtful and rational public dialogue that should be less prone to conspiracy theories and extremism.

Hostile IOs usually seek to ratchet up anger and anxiety toward liberal governments, immigrants, social minorities and the wealthy. Being moderate may not feel like much of a strategy when hostile IOs are gaining ground. Mainstream US liberals have long made a virtue of moderation and thoughtful dialogue. Yet, in 2020, many believed that blocking the reelection of Donald Trump was of existential importance to the country. Several Democratic groups adopted aggressive practices on social networks that were more in the spirit typical of right-wing messaging. (One producer said "we punch them in the mouth with the truth.")[50]

The competing argument, in favor of moderation, is to try to move conversations onto a more responsible track where facts might mean more and polarization can be blunted. Speaking at the 2016 Democratic convention about domestic right-wingers, Michelle Obama declared, "Our motto is, when they go low, we go high." Anna Fotyga, a former Polish foreign minister and the European Parliament's rapporteur on disinformation, says, "I am in favor of disputes based on arguments, not emotions."[51]

Emblematic of the more soothing approach is the "I Am Here" movement, an initiative in Europe and North America to encourage more level-headed conversations on social networks.[52] The Swedish founder of the campaign, Mina Dennert, says activists patrol the internet looking for groups and comment boards where hate speech is prominent. This can include comment sites of news outlets that do not moderate their audiences' posts. Activists point these locations out to each other, and then try to submerge angry comments with more moderate posts of their own. "We don't answer trolls," Dennert says. "We 'like' each other's comments to increase their visibility in algorithms and create a healthier conversation. If trolls discuss our comments, it helps to push them up further." Sometimes just two or three people can change the tone of conversation. At times it may take 100, she says. Dennert notes that the Swedish group has 75,000 members and the German group 45,000; groups are active in eight other countries. "I Am Here" activists also try to flood networks with messages supporting people who are being harassed on the internet.

---

[50] Nick Corasaniti, "How Immigrant Twin Brothers Are Beating Trump's Team on Facebook," *The New York Times*, May 18, 2020, https://www.nytimes.com/2020/05/18/us/politics/occupy-democrats-facebook.html.

[51] Anna Fotyga, interview with author, June 25, 2019.

[52] https://www.jagarhar.se/kolumnen/the-iamhere-network/.

A civil society initiative in Slovakia deploys another "soothing" technique, trying to deprogram, over social media, individual people who post conspiracy theories and pro-Russian messages. According to one person involved in the effort, they begin by agreeing with what the person says, then gradually point out information to the contrary. They also try to move the conversation from public pages and chat groups to direct messaging, where they have more privacy for the interaction.

An international broadcasting version of such soothing tactics has been attempts by *Radio Free Europe/Radio Liberty* to encourage dialogue among Serb, Croats and Muslims in the Balkans, and between moderate and more radical Muslims in Central Asia.

Soothing techniques have their downsides. Some targets of deprogramming remain hostile. Trolls have gone after individual "I Am Here" members, exposing their personal information and forcing them to stop working. Dennert worries that her initiative does little to stop the enormous tides of hate on social networks. "Our organization is very small compared to all the hate. I'm not very optimistic," she says. She also notes that extremists can still advance dangerous, discriminatory policies without using the kinds of incendiary speech that the groups are alert to. The "I Am Here" movement has merit nonetheless, she says, if only to give moderate activists the sense they are doing something, and to support victims of harassment.[53]

Is it better to attack or soothe? At present, the question is unanswerable because testing has been inadequate. Though each approach has its adherents as a matter of personal preference, it is essential to experiment scientifically to see which generates more engagement and produces greater shifts of opinion. Social networks offer excellent laboratories to compare the effects of each approach.

---

[53] Mina Dennert, interview with author, December 16, 2019.

The answer may be different depending on the country and audience segment being targeted.

Once democracy advocates have settled on their goals and strategies, the time comes to select messages.

Promoting Democracy

"Unless your campaign contains a big idea, it will pass like a ship in the night," advertising icon David Ogilvy used to say. Ogilvy also said one cannot bore people into buying a product.

Big ideas must be big enough to capture people's imaginations but small enough to fit on a bumper sticker. Unfortunately, democracy is not as simple to promote as a Ford truck. People have long grasped the idea of individual freedom, economic opportunity and choosing their own leaders. The genie of democracy is out of the bottle; the very idea that countries should have elections—hardly a given in human history—is now practically universal. Yet, people struggle with how traditional Western democracy is supposed to guarantee freedom and prosperity, especially given the elitism and incompetence of more than a few democratic governments. Loyalty to a strong leader, and intolerance for other people, are easy and comfortable emotions.

Democracy is more complicated. Its meandering lawmaking processes often lead to unsatisfying compromises. It requires tolerance for speech and publications that seem disturbing or even unpatriotic. It asks citizens to actively participate in national life rather than just let someone else run the country while gaming the system to one's own advantage. Free journalists are crucial guardians of a democracy's integrity, but they may so thoroughly expose leaders' venality and ineptitude as to shake public confidence in the whole democratic project.

Former US Defense Secretary James Mattis once said of his days in military uniform, "I had many privileged glimpses into the human condition, but I never once saw human beings flee the freedom of speech; I never saw families on the run from the free practice of religion in the public square; and as a young Marine, I never picked anybody out of a raft on the ocean desperate to escape a free press."[54] That may have been his experience, but large numbers of people these days vilify speech that offends them, disparage others' religions and assert that no media are truly free and independent. Some would readily trade free speech or the freedom to travel in return for prosperity, security of the preservation of traditional values.[55] It is also true that some of the most revered leaders of democracies were the least democratic, remembered not so much for respecting public opinion but for fighting it in favor of personal beliefs that proved to be right. Democracy requires citizens to believe that, in the long run, despite all the corruption and chaos of the system, it will deliver prosperity and security more effectively than any other form of rule.

On occasion, democratic countries have produced their own highly effective bumper sticker-sized messages. Sometimes they have not included the word "democracy" at all—a word that has lost much of its effect from being constantly mocked by dictators (when they are not claiming to be democrats themselves, in their own way). Franklin D. Roosevelt's Four Freedoms and Ronald Reagan's "Mr. Gorbachev, tear down this wall!" come to mind as ringing cries for liberty. The potential for such communication continues to exist, built around:

• The pervasive corruption in authoritarian states
• The right of people to choose their own leaders

---

[54] James Mattis, address to IRI Freedom Dinner, May 15, 2018, https://www.youtube.com/watch?v=YsnyeGt7kng.

[55] *Voices of Central and Eastern Europe* (Bratislava: Globsec, June 23, 2020), 24, https://www.globsec.org/wp-content/uploads/2020/06/Voices-of-Central-and-Eastern-Europe_read-version.pdf.

• Freedom of speech

However, in recent decades, such pro-democracy messaging has faltered. One reason is a lack of Western leaders with stature great enough to compel attention to their words. Another is the tendency of democracy advocates, critical of their own societies, to affix so many asterisks to such messages as to drain them of any impact. Simplicity, to some, is simplistic; Western faith in a democratic society has been replaced by, in the words of R.R. Reno, "a negative piety, which gives priority to critique and self-questioning over conviction."[56] Thus, critics believe any exposure of the corruption of authoritarian states must be balanced by acknowledging corruption in democratic societies. Pride in democratic elections must be balanced by acknowledgement that money can swing US campaigns, and that democratic elections in Europe can put Nazi sympathizers into parliament.

All these downsides of democratic societies exist, just as freedom of speech allows the pornography industry to thrive. However, democratic countries must be willing to believe, and say out loud, that their systems, *on balance,* are better than the authoritarian alternative.[57] Authoritarian societies are actually more corrupt. Western elections are objectively better than Russia's rigged ones. Free speech is, overall, a bigger deal than pornography.

---

[56] R.R. Reno, *Return of the Strong Gods* (Washington: Regnery Gateway, 2019), 65.
[57] Many people do believe this. In almost all Latin American countries, most people believe democracy is the best form of government—although the overall percentage of citizens believing that declined from 68 percent in 2004 to 58 percent in 2018–2019. Elizabeth J. Zechmeister and Noam Lupu (Eds.), *Pulse of Democracy* (Nashville: LAPOP, 2019), 13, https://www.vanderbilt.edu/lapop/ab2018/2018-19_AmericasBarometer_Regional_Report_10.13.19.pdf. Most East Europeans also favor multiparty democracy with regular elections, though large majorities are dissatisfied with how government works in their countries. *Voices of Central and Eastern Europe,* 12–14.

The FDR Foundation's Jed Willard points out that positive narratives about democracy need not all center on the present. "Positive narratives are about the future we want," he says—not just about how things are today.[58] In most cases, the futures that people want do not involve authoritarian rulers, police surveillance and restrictions on personal liberty. Democratic structures guard against them.

Campaigns for democracy are much more powerful if they call out specific authoritarian states, such as Russia, both as a source of disinformation and a poor example of how to run a country. Many governments may not have the stomach for this, but NGAs do. In some countries, as we have seen, Russian IOs intertwine themselves with locally popular causes, such as conservative social values or resistance to immigration. If they are so inclined, NGAs have the local experience to draw a distinction between fundamental civil and political rights, on one hand, and the liberal social values that Russian IOs claim are inseparable from democracy. This does not always come easily to liberal-minded civil society activists. They may see, for instance, a woman's right to vote and to be safe from domestic violence as absolutely on the same level as her right to an abortion. But this connection is not obvious to everyone; some people may favor the first two but not the third. In Europe's East and Latin America, the message to emphasize may not be that abortion is legal in Western nations and therefore should be locally. Rather, it might be that all points of view on the subject are heartfelt and deserve respect, and that democracy allows open discussion with the final decision made by popular will.

Economic Prosperity

Pro-democracy communication should have a natural advantage when it comes to economic prosperity. The countries with the highest

---

[58] "Russian Information Operations in East Europe" (comments by Jed Willard).

standard of living are all democracies. Corruption distorts markets, while business benefits from freedom of information and rule of law. (The America for Bulgaria Foundation, a major funder of social and business initiatives for that country, smartly classifies its aid to independent media as a program to help Bulgarian business.) The prosperity of Western countries is obvious to everyone; clearly, they must be doing something right. The trick is to convince citizens within prosperous countries that opportunities for further growth still exist, and citizens in emerging democracies that the West's prosperity can embrace them as well.

Anti-democratic IOs strive constantly to paint the most prosperous Western states as infinitely exploitative, not only toward Latin America and Africa but newer members of the EU. All these regions have made great economic strides in recent years, but rising expectations create a demand for ever more. Poverty is still a major fact of life in Latin America and Africa. New EU members in Central and Eastern Europe see a steady migration of their populations to the West, many of them skilled professionals and young people.

The EU has been an enormous force for prosperity in its new member states but has failed to convey to citizens the scale of what it has done. With the EU wary of "propaganda" and recipient governments often happy to take credit for projects themselves, the EU's contributions are often little appreciated.

Serbia, for instance, is one of the biggest recipients of EU funds in the world, amounting to some €200 million ($233 million, in July 2020) per year for bridges, highways, medical care, air quality and other programs.[59] Yet, citizens commonly believe that Russia is their biggest benefactor. Russia is very good at optics, and Serbia's leadership may hope to obtain even more from the EU by reminding Brussels it has

---

[59] "EU Assistance to Serbia," The Delegation of the European Union to the Republic of Serbia, http://europa.rs/eu-assistance-to-serbia/?lang=en.

other friends. When Russia airlifted coronavirus supplies to Serbia in April 2020, the occasion was designed for maximum media effect, complete with a welcoming ceremony with Serbian and Russian flags arrayed in front of a Russian IL-76 transport. Serbian women in national costume greeted the Russian crew with traditional bread and salt.[60]

EU officials are frustrated over the gratitude Moscow can reap with one-off gestures when Brussels does so much for its members and partners. The bloc should react more effectively to authoritarian states swooping in to claim credit in areas where it has made huge investments. "You have to think more in a PR logic," says Péter Krekó, the director of the Political Capital think tank in Budapest. "If you don't sell your messages or your measures it's almost as though they are non-existent."[61] However, many questions remain about what successful "PR logic" might look like. EU Vice President Věra Jourová says, "We see propaganda amplified now against the EU. We will never fight with the same weapons, I believe. We will not use any kind of dirty propaganda against those who produce these news [sic]. We have to fight by providing the people with trustworthy information and the facts and figures which are easy to verify."[62] To reach broad populations, these facts must appear somewhere beyond EU websites.

EU publicity efforts must be skillful, however. The bloc was slow in delivering coronavirus aid to Italy, where anti-EU feelings have long

---

[60] "Četiri aviona sa medicinskom pomoći i lekarima iz Rusije sleteli u Batajnicu" [Four planes with medical aid and doctors from Russia land in Batajnica], *N1,* April 3, 2020, http://rs.n1info.com/Vesti/a585344/Avioni-sa-medicinskom-pomoci-i-lekarima-iz-Rusije-sleteli-u-Batajnicu.html.

[61] "COVID-19 Infodemic: Push and Pull Factors," video, GLOBSEC, May 28, 2020, https://www.facebook.com/GLOBSECforum/videos/274110043780526.

[62] "Coronavirus: an unprecedented challenge to democracy?" (video interview with Věra Jourová), *Euronews,* April 9, 2020, https://www.euronews.com/2020/04/09/coronavirus-an-unprecedented-challenge-to-democracy.

been strong. Then, after finally sending aid in, the EU posted a graphic on social networks that announced, "France and Germany combined have donated to Italy more masks than China."[63] Commenters roasted the EU, saying that if it were such a reliable friend it would have made aid from China unnecessary to begin with.

A poll in Italy after China and Russia delivered supplies found that 53 percent of Italians considered China a friendly country, 32 percent considered Russia friendly, 45 percent considered Germany an enemy and 38 percent considered France an enemy.[64] Jourová said she was shocked at the findings. "One reason for [the results] is that in the European Union we take helping each other for granted," she said. "Another that our member states too easily roll out the red carpet and communicate about dubious help from outside, while forgetting to apply the same standards about [aid from the] EU."[65] Major democratic countries and blocs must make sure their contributions to partner countries are well known in good times so they will be remembered in bad. It is ironic that US-financed *RFE/RL* carries (at its own expense) large amounts of material about the EU to the countries of Europe's East, while the EU has invested in no broadcasting operation of its own.

---

[63] European Commission (@EU_Commission), "In the face of adversity, the people of Europe are showing how strong we can be together," Twitter, March 26, 2020, 2:29 p.m., https://twitter.com/EU_Commission/status/1243243613724782592/photo/1.

[64] Massimilliano Lenzi, "Libertà superflua per 2 italiani su 3" [For 2 Italians out of 3, freedom is superfluous], *Il Tempo*, April 18, 2020, https://www.iltempo.it/cronache/2020/04/18/news/coronavirus-app-tracciamento-liberta-spostamenti-italiani-sondaggio-covid19-1316880/.

[65] European Union, "Speech of Vice President Věra Jourová on countering disinformation amid COVID-19 'From pandemic to infodemic,' " news release, June 4, 2020, https://ec.europa.eu/commission/presscorner/detail/en/SPEECH_20_1000.

Talking About History

The interpretation of historical events remains a battleground in many countries. Russian IOs and their allies have consistently distorted the Soviet era by suppressing the terror and penury it inflicted on Soviet-controlled populations. This has led to modern-day disputes like the highly emotional clashes between Russia and Poland over the Soviet role in World War II and the 2019 debate in Bulgaria over efforts to soften the image of Soviet-era dictator Todor Zhivkov. NGAs need to be aware of how hostile forces distort history and be ready to counter them.

In Lithuania, in 2019, elves and their allies revolted against Russian claims that the Molotov-Ribbentrop pact, which led to the Soviet takeover of the Baltic States, was just an understandable act of defensive *realpolitik* by Russia. Elves posted on *RT's* Facebook page denunciations of the deal with the Nazis, accompanied by a mock commemorative logo for the pact with an entwined swastika and hammer and sickle.

Researchers in Ukraine have found that rather than "top-down" approaches in which video narrators or other authority figures promote a certain version of history, "bottom-up" content in which ordinary people talk about what they experienced is more effective. Another finding is that rather than trying to counter beliefs that people were more equal or united in Soviet times, a "future-oriented" approach works better: such as citing Soviet-era restrictions on personal freedom that most people, even Soviet nostalgics, would oppose on their lives today.[66]

---

[66] "From 'Memory Wars' to a Common Future: Overcoming Polarisation in Ukraine," Arena Project, London School of Economics and Political Science, July 2020, https://www.lse.ac.uk/iga/assets/documents/Arena-LSE-From-Memory-Wars-to-a-Common-Future-Overcoming-Polarisation-in-Ukraine.pdf. For a test

The Power of Religion

In the Cold War, the United States made religious faith and freedom a key part of its messaging to countries behind the Iron Curtain. The goal was not only to encourage believers' resistance to "godless Communism" but to portray America as a pious and moral nation. The *Voice of America,* which had a director of religious programming, poured content into Communist countries that mixed religion with anti-Communist politics. A 1951 Christmas message to Eastern Europe by the archbishop of Baltimore conveys the tone:

> These feasts have special meaning for everyone throughout the Christian world, but they have special meaning for you, dear friends in Hungary and Czechoslovakia who languish under a tyrant's rule. Take courage from the example of St. Stephen, who gave his life in its very prime rather than deny Christ.[67]

Since the Cold War, the religious ground has shifted dramatically in the United States and Western Europe. Faith has become a smaller part of life, especially among elites. Whereas, Russia has seized on religious imagery and messaging, bringing its government and the Russian Orthodox Church into close alignment and making common cause with conservative, even reactionary, religious activists in the "near-abroad." While this church-state alliance gains strength, pro-democracy activists and Western evangelical movements may shy away from working together. Liberal activists oppose evangelical positions on issues like abortion. Some evangelicals insist their allegiance is to God, not to any political system on earth. However, there is a long tradition of Christians resisting oppressive regimes in

---

"bottom-up" video made by the researchers, see
https://www.facebook.com/watch/?v=3269954663048742.
[67] Department of State, Press Release No. 94, Feb. 4, 1952, quoted in Jonathan P. Herzog, *The Spiritual-Industrial Complex* (Oxford: Oxford University Press, 2011), 128.

Latin America and Africa, as well as in Eastern Europe under Soviet rule.[68]

The goals of NGAs and religious groups overlap significantly in their opposition to violence and ethnic hatred. NGAs need not compromise with religious groups over issues of human dignity or belief in science.[69] But NGAs should look for areas of intersectionality where possible. The resources of religious activists are significant: churches form large networks in every country and are often backed up by missionaries from abroad. In addition, religious broadcasters blanket the world. US-based *Transworld Radio* operates in 230 languages— nearly four times as many as the US government's international broadcasters—and *Vatican Radio* offers 35.

Russia's Weakness

A byproduct of Western alarm about Russia has been to inflate its strength in the minds of at-risk populations. Western spokespeople and media tend to paint Russia as endlessly powerful, with only occasional references to how far above its weight it is trying to punch. With pro-Russian actors also promoting the Kremlin's strength, the effect is to convince people that Russia is indeed an economic and military colossus.

---

[68] By some accounts, European missionaries—particularly evangelistic Protestants— have been a crucial catalyst for democracy since the 1600s. See Robert D. Woodberry, "The Missionary Roots of Liberal Democracy," *American Political Science Review*, Vol. 106, No. 2 (May 2012), https://doi:10.1017/S0003055412000093.

[69] See, for example, "Moldova's Orthodox Church Lashes Out At 'Anti-Christ Plot' To Develop Virus Vaccine," *Radio Free Europe/Radio Liberty*, May 20, 2020, https://www.rferl.org/a/moldova-s-orthodox-church-lashes-out-at-anti-christ-plot-to-develop-virus-vaccine/30624250.html.

Hungary offers a good example. Researchers there found that two-thirds of Hungarians think Russia's military expenditures top those of the United States and China, and that half believe Russia is one of the top six importers of Hungarian goods. In fact, Moscow's defense spending is far lower than Washington's or Beijing's; and in 2018, Russia was the 20th-largest importer of Hungarian products. (Thirteen EU countries imported more from Hungary than Russia did.)[70]

Russia adds to perceptions that it has limitless resources through narrow, high-profile actions, such as its showy deployments of bombers to Venezuela in 2008 and 2018.

Yet, at the same time, Russian IOs often do not succeed. Despite efforts by Russia and its allies, recent elections in Slovakia, Romania, Bolivia and Poland have arguably strengthened pro-democracy tendencies—or at least created parliamentary space that could yield more progressive and inclusive policies. Other ventures in Madagascar and Sudan have failed as well.

Western messaging can address the image of Russian omnipotence with facts about Russia's propaganda failures and its small overall footprint on the world stage. In Africa and Latin America, Russia practically disappeared in the 1990s and could do so again as its economic problems mount and China's importance grows. Another factor is the Kremlin's mismanagement and authoritarianism at home. Plenty of authoritative sources spotlight Russia's internal failings, including official Russian statistics. This line of messaging benefits from people's tendency to believe preconceived notions, since most people grew up knowing about political repression in and economic frailty of the Soviet Union.

---

[70] Krekó, Molnár, and Rácz, *"Mystification and Demystification of Putin's Russia."* Export data for 2018 from https://globaledge.msu.edu/countries/hungary/tradestats.

One might also invite citizens of at-risk countries to imagine living in Russia themselves. Citizens could consider all the organizations, public discourse, internet postings and political activity—while ubiquitous in their own countries—that would be illegal in Russia; the same goes for their ability to change their political leaders. If a country has a large evangelical population, messaging could highlight how such sects are barred from operating under Russian law.

Conveying the Narratives

Once the best themes have been chosen for pro-democracy communication, how should they be spread? In today's marketplace of ideas, buyers cannot be counted on to buy what is good for them; they look for brightly wrapped goods that require the least effort to use. Arguments for democracy must be conveyed in an attractive and accessible manner.

I look now at some of the vehicles available to convey pro-democracy messaging. As with almost all the strategies in this book, they can be used at various scales either by governments or NGAs.

Entertainment

Wrapping democracy messages in entertainment content is the most frequently proposed strategy for winning the information war. Hollywood carried American and Western values to the world for many decades, and still does. (It is interesting that American private entrepreneurs dominated world culture for decades without the US government ever having had a Department of Culture.) Many speak now of a "Hollywood 2.0"—the use of new platforms and techniques by private actors for pro-democracy messaging.

Russia certainly believes in using entertainment for political purposes, including big-budget productions. Spy dramas and World War II movies have long painted Russia's security services and military in heroic roles. To counter the HBO blockbuster *Chernobyl,* Russia's NTV network planned to air its own series about the disaster, in which the explosion is touched off by a CIA saboteur.

Moscow also generates plenty of humor and satire for Russian-speaking audiences to advance its positions (some dub it "hahaganda"). Typical is the sarcastic humor of *Mezhdunarodnaya Pilorama* (*International Sawmill*), hosted by Tigran Keosayan, husband of *RT* chief editor Margarita Simonyan. At the start of one show, as upbeat music plays and the audience laughs along, Keosayan says, "While the West chokes on the sewage sludge of lies and those in Ukraine eat up the last of gas with no oil, *International Sawmill* will protect you from the dirt of Russophobia with the snowfall of humor and the blizzard of satire."[71] The Russian government also quietly funded a quirky YouTube satire site, *Spasibo, Eva* (*Thanks, Eva*) until the undercover support was revealed by the hacking group Anonymous.[72]

Why do democratic countries not go on an entertainment offensive? In many ways their entertainment strength is already overpowering. The pull of Western films and television remains enormous around the world. Few people outside the former Soviet bloc can name Russian films or actors; Bollywood and Turkish TV dramas have bigger followings. As disenchantment inside Western societies has become more widespread, movies have turned more cynical, replete

---

[71] "Ru media uses humor to justify aggressive politics," video, Ukraine Crisis Media Center video, March 11, 2019, https://www.youtube.com/watch?v=h1tbxlyV9GE&feature=youtu.be.

[72] "How the Kremlin Bankrolled An Online Comedy Channel," *Radio Free Europe/Radio Liberty,* November 17, 2019, https://www.rferl.org/a/how-the-kremlin-bankrolled-an-online-comedy-channel/30273568.html.

with flawed heroes, social injustice and perfidious people in authority. Still, Western concepts of justice and decency are recognizable even in those movies—in the sense that they are what the imperfect heroes are departing from.

As for a sudden stream of big-budget movies conceived to advance democracy, the likelihood is approximately zero. Even in past decades, Hollywood was focused on profits rather than ideology, although some productions promoted democratic and patriotic sentiments. Most films had the effect of boosting the United States to foreign audiences not through their political messages, but by showing slices of a prosperous America. Foreign viewers' eyes were not just on the stars, but on the automobiles, homes and luxury goods that surrounded them.

A British intelligence officer who contributed thoughts to this study said governments today need a "wartime-scale" budget to pay for films promoting democratic values. Productions created with that goal, however, would likely be met with derision from critics and claims they were "psychological warfare."

Even during the Cold War there was suspicion of entertainment products with an obvious political overlay. In 1981, after Poland's Communist leadership imposed martial law in a desperate attempt to stop the Solidarity movement, the US government enlisted Bob Hope, Frank Sinatra and a host of other celebrities for a $500,000 international television spectacular called "Let Poland Be Poland." Despite broad Western sympathy for Solidarity, the whole undertaking was widely mocked as propaganda.[73]

---

[73] Arthur Unger, " 'Let Poland Be Poland' - is the program really that bad? Closer look at an international special finds some unpredicted meaning," *The Christian Science Monitor*, February 5, 1982, https://www.csmonitor.com/1982/0205/020500.html.

A second drawback to embedding messages in entertainment is cost. As with the proposed Kremlin version of *House of Cards,* movies and TV series are expensive. It is highly unlikely we will see a surge in productions like *Chernobyl* and *Occupied,* the 2015 Norwegian TV series about a Russian invasion of Norway. Western studios seek to recoup their investments by selling their productions to as many countries as possible, including Russia and other authoritarian states. These markets are not looking for democracy-themed productions. "We can't compete where we can't compete," Agnieszka Romaszewski-Guzy of *Belsat* says of high-budget entertainment productions.[74] She believes it is better to focus programming on politics, history and telling people about their own communities.

Fortunately, there are many entertainment options that governments and NGAs can carry out for far less than big-studio shows. Some good television programming can be created inexpensively in lower-cost countries. Romaszewski-Guzy notes that *Belsat*'s animated TV comedy *Ministerstvo Pravdy (Ministry of Truth)*, produced in Poland, costs less than $4,000 a show to produce. The talk show *Vecherny Shpiel (Evening Stiletto)* costs about $2,000 per episode.[75] In Moldova, a US Embassy project to create television content to challenge Russian channels budgeted $15,000 to $50,000 for five to ten episodes of an entertainment series and $1,000 an hour to dub foreign content into Romanian.[76]

Online videos and podcasts can cost as little as nothing if people volunteer their time and have some basic technical skills. GLOBSEC, the Slovak NGA, ran an inexpensive "Music Versus Hoaxes" contest

---

[74] Agnieszka Romaszewski-Guzy, interview with author, November 5, 2019.
[75] Agnieszka Romaszewski-Guzy, interview with author.
[76] "Notice of Funding Opportunity: PAS-CHISINAU-FY18-08," US Embassy Chisnau, April 15, 2018, https://s3-us-west-2.amazonaws.com/instrumentl/grantsgov/303573.pdf.

in the four Visegrad countries and the Balkans, encouraging young people write music opposing fake news.[77]

Useful messages can also be conveyed through video games. Making a game in Ukraine can cost as little as $20,000. Messages can be posted within video games as paid advertisements, or for free on message boards attached to game and movie downloading sites. The Prague Civil Society Center, a large NGA, holds Gamechanger workshops where civil society activists are paired with programmers and designers to create games intended to make their players engage with social issues.[78] Depending on a country's broadcasting laws, low-power radio may be an inexpensive way to distribute locally focused messages and entertainment.[79]

Many believe comedy and satire are a particularly effective way to combat IOs by Russia and its allies—or at least to antagonize authoritarian leaders. They point to the cancellation, shortly after Putin came to power, of *Kukli* (*Dolls*), a puppet satire that savaged Russian political leaders. Lithuanian comic Andrius Tapinas hosted a *Daily Show*–type program in Russian in 2017–2018, satirizing political events and figures in Russia, Belarus, Ukraine and other formerly Soviet countries. The US-funded *Current Time* network carried several of the shows for viewers in Russia and elsewhere. In Slovakia, GLOBSEC worked with online comedian Ján Gordulič to create a "Hoax of the Week" section of his show that makes fun of disinformation and hate speech. Other Instagram and Facebook

---

[77] Rebeka Kosečeková, " 'Hudbou proti hoaxom' bojujú v novej kampani aj Sajfa či Gogo" [Saijfa and Gogo join the new 'music against hoaxes' campaign], *Mediálne,* December 6, 2018, https://medialne.trend.sk/marketing/hudbou-proti-hoaxom-bojuju-novej-kampani-aj-sajfa-gogo.

[78] "It's a gamechanger: Gamification for civil society," *Prague Civil Society Centre,* accessed July 26, 2020, https://praguecivilsociety.org/gamification-for-civil-society/.

[79] For details of this technology, see https://grassrootsradio.eu.

accounts in Slovakia satirize conspiracy theories daily, using popular memes.[80]

However, satire is always dicey. The *BBC* launched *Tonight with Vladimir Putin* in 2019, an awkward attempt at humor with a Putin avatar interviewing British celebrities. The most effective way to deploy satire is sometimes just to amplify authentic local satirists who are already doing it. In the Cold War, US officials collected political jokes from within the Soviet bloc and publicized them worldwide as examples of how citizens living under Communist regimes were mocking their own authorities. In Russia today, fans of American late-night comedians subtitle clips and post them on social networks. Many of the clips take sharp aim at US leaders, but they at least convey the freedom with which politicians can be skewered on national TV. There are many examples of anti-regime satire within Russia now that could be translated and rebroadcast to populations elsewhere.

Social Platforms

Governments and NGAs can execute many strategies on social platforms. Ideally, NGAs will be aided by the backshops discussed previously.

Already pro-democracy forces are building bridges to online influencers. The $300,000 Ukraine-focused project undertaken by the Democracy Council for the GEC, discussed earlier, was aimed in part at "motivating community influencers" to push back against Russian IOs. In September 2018, the State Department's Bureau of Educational and Cultural Affairs sponsored an "Influencers' Forum"

---

[80] Miroslava German Sirotnikova, "Disinformation Nation: The Slovaks fighting in defence of facts," *Balkan Insight*, June 7, 2019, https://balkaninsight.com/2019/06/07/disinformation-nation-the-slovaks-fighting-in-defence-of-facts/.

in Thessaloniki, Greece, to teach "frontline tactics to push back against disinformation." It was held under the banner of the Digital Communicators Network, established by the State Department in 2016.[81]

Working directly with individual influencers has its downsides for governments. Encouraging influencers to carry out a specific strategy can take a good deal of face time, which government officials do not have. (Some influencers will advocate for causes in return for money, but no official interviewed for this study spoke of using such persons.) Governments may also want to maintain some distance from influencers who pride themselves on their independence. A better strategy is for governments to work through NGAs, which themselves are influencers by nature and know others in their territory.

Democracy advocates need to become as fluent as their adversaries in leveraging the power of social networks. "If we keep throwing flowers while they flood us with bots and trolls, it's not sustainable," said an East European specialist in social messaging. The activist said NGAs should identify and take advantage of how social media algorithms work. In some extreme situations, the activist said, it might make sense to use bots to increase the reach of posts. Many other tools are available, too:

• Activists or governments can buy search terms, assuring that anyone who looks for a given topic on a search engine sees certain pages first. (The search results may carry tags like "sponsored content," but they still push down less-desirable links.)

---

[81] Marie Royce, "A Strategy to Fight Digital Disinformation: Digital Communicators Network," State Department blog, February 19, 2020, Google cache copy: http://webcache.googleusercontent.com/search?q=cache:1o24NV95XMwJ:https://blogs.state.gov/stories/2018/09/20/en/strategy-fight-digital-disinformation-digital-communicators-network&client=firefox-b-1-d&hl=en&gl=us&strip=1&vwsrc=0.

• Content can be targeted to audience segments based on age, profession or political views. The US used such techniques to send anti-terrorism messages to young Muslims with jihadist interests.[82] If those searching for information can be enticed into visiting a website and accepting cookies, additional information can be made to show up as ads on other sites they visit.

• Social network feeds can be set up focused on food, hobbies and other special interests to attract people who do not care about politics. Political material can then be added in. (Jenna Abrams, a fake American created by the Internet Research Agency in St. Petersburg, acquired a wide following on Twitter for her dissections of Kim Kardashian's fashions. Once her numbers reached a high level, her tweets swung to the political, taking on a right-wing, anti-immigrant tone.)[83]

• Direct messages on Twitter to people interested in a subject are more likely than public tweets to receive their attention and lead to action.[84]

• Chat applications, used by many companies for customer service purposes, can be adapted for pro-democracy goals. The Brazilian fact-checking group Aos Fatos created a bot that went out looking for false information. The bot, Fátima (short for "Fact Machine"), searched Twitter for people posting discredited stories and responded to them with correct information. The bot gave priority to posters of false

---

[82] Warrick, "How a U.S. team uses Facebook, guerrilla marketing to peel off potential ISIS recruits."

[83] Ben Collins, "Jenna Abrams, Russia's Clown Troll Princess, Duped the Mainstream Media and the World," *Daily Beast,* November 3, 2017, https://www.thedailybeast.com/jenna-abrams-russias-clown-troll-princess-duped-the-mainstream-media-and-the-world.

[84] Alexander Coppock, Andrew Guess, et al., "When Treatments are Tweets: A Network Mobilization Experiment over Twitter," *Political Behavior,* 38 (2016), available from https://link.springer.com/article/10.1007/s11109-015-9308-6#page-1.

information who had many followers.[85] In Slovakia, Checkbot was created to help Facebook users identify misinformation and unreliable news sites.[86]

• Monitoring the topics people are talking about can help create messages that benefit from those interests. Most news sites have "trending topics" sections that suggest ideas for campaigns.

One of the best ways to achieve success on social networks is through memes—the images and quotes, often humorous or sarcastic, that people share obsessively. Dmitri Medvedev, when he was Russian prime minister, told Russian teachers in 2016 that there was no money for salary increases but "you hold on." Russian social networks exploded with memes inserting Medvedev's quote into other situations. One suggested diners tell waiters that they had no money to pay the check, but that the restaurant should "hold on there"; another showed pilots parachuting out of a crippled plane while advising the passengers left behind to "hold on."[87] Similar sarcasm occurred a year earlier in reaction to the regime's "Krym Nash" ("Crimea Is Ours") social media campaign.[88] The Lithuanian elves used a meme strategy against Adidas when they replaced the hammer

---

[85] Marie Von Hafften, "Ahead of Brazil's election, Twitter bot Fátima spreads fact-checked information," *Ijnet* (International Journalists' Network), October 5, 2018, https://ijnet.org/en/story/ahead-brazils-election-twitter-bot-f%C3%A1tima-spreads-fact-checked-information.

[86] Peter Dlhopolec, "Checkbot educates and warns. It never tells the truth," *The Slovak Spectator,* November 22, 2019, https://spectator.sme.sk/c/22266109/checkbot-educates-and-warns-it-never-tells-the-truth-bringing-world-to-the-classroom.html.

[87] "Денег нет, но вы держитесь" [There's no money, but you hold on there], *Meduza,* May 24, 2016, https://meduza.io/shapito/2016/05/24/deneg-net-no-vy-derzhites.

[88] " 'Krymnash' Meme Part of Russian Society's Return to Late Soviet Times," *Euromaidan Press,* June 10, 2015, http://euromaidanpress.com/2015/06/10/krymnash-meme-part-of-russian-societys-return-to-late-soviet-times/.

and sickle on its Soviet-nostalgia sportswear with a swastika. Fortunately, subjects for memes are not hard to find. Medvedev's comments to the schoolteachers were widely ridiculed as soon as he made them, making it obvious they would make good meme material.

The US military has considered the value of memes in information operations. In 2006, a Marine officer imagined a "Meme Warfare Center."[89] Others believe memes are inherently a destructive tool that democracies should avoid. Security writer Jacob Siegel says:

> Memes appear to function like the IEDs of information warfare. They are natural tools of an insurgency; great for blowing things up, but likely to sabotage the desired effects when handled by the larger actor in an asymmetric conflict… Meme wars seem to favor insurgencies because, by their nature, they weaken monopolies on narrative and empower challenges to centralized authority. A government could use memes to increase disorder within a system, but if the goal is to increase stability, it's the wrong tool for the job.[90]

This view assumes that democracy is always the larger, established actor, while anti-democratic forces are the insurgents. Considering the disruptive power currently directed at democracies worldwide, it is questionable whether democratic governments are the ones with "monopolies on narrative."

A tougher question is whether Siegel's "larger actors"—government departments of major democracies—have the capability to launch meme operations that respond to IO challengers with the same humor

---

[89] Michael B. Prosser, "Memetics—A Growth Industry in US Military Operations," (MA diss., Marine Corps University, 2006), https://apps.dtic.mil/dtic/tr/fulltext/u2/a507172.pdf.

[90] Jacob Siegel, "Is America Prepared for Meme Warfare?" *Vice*, January 31, 2017, https://www.vice.com/en_us/article/xyvwdk/meme-warfare.

and snark they use. Clint Watts writes this about US government social media efforts against Islamic militants: "Even the terrorists knew that the CTCC [Counterterrorism Communication Center] experiment wouldn't last long. State Department analysts manning official accounts couldn't win, boxed in as they were by bureaucrats, not allowed to think nimbly or respond quickly, heckled by the media and terrorists." One online persona tweeted back at the CTCC, "Your boss is going to fire you soon if these tweets don't improve."[91] Another issue is that of dignity—whether it looks childish for official government agencies to be flinging out memes. In 2020, State Department spokesperson Morgan Ortagus tweeted a photo of Iran's foreign minister meeting Syrian President Bashar al-Assad, with a clumsily inserted image of piles of money on a table between them. It was a far cry from the kind of communication traditionally expected from the State Department's official voice.[92]

Amid such challenges, governments have two options. One is to keep experimenting with social media combat, to eventually get better at it. Such efforts in full public view can be embarrassing (unless governments use accounts with false identities, which involves its own problems). The other option is to leave memetic warfare to NGAs, which in many ways are more appropriate to the task. They can quickly identify the kinds of memes that do best in their environment. They already know people who are skilled at making them.

---

[91] Clint Watts, *Messing with the Enemy*, 204.

[92] Morgan Ortagus (@statedeptspox), "Since 2012, the Iranian regime has provided more than $10 billion of the Iranian people's money to Assad. Wonder how much plundered cash the regime's chief apologist is delivering to Damascus today?" Twitter, April 20, 2020, 4:44 p.m., https://twitter.com/statedeptspox/status/1252337243357921281/photo/1.

International Broadcasting

International broadcasters run by democratic governments are another force multiplier for pro-democracy efforts. For audiences in many countries, their radio, television, web and social network content provide essential balance to government propaganda, often thanks to courageous investigative reporting. They may also be the primary source of news in regions and languages ignored by other media. However, as we have seen earlier, they operate with substantial budgetary constraints, and their editorial independence bars governments from using them for direct messaging. Content they create is determined by their own editors' concept of what is appropriate and professional. The broadcasters also suffer from domestic political winds. Since World War II, Congress has repeatedly reorganized US international broadcasting in various attempts to improve or redefine it, each time causing disruption to operations but little effect on the product. Boris Johnson's insistence on downsizing the *BBC* has added to the funding shortages that were already affecting its World Service output.

Discussion of the future of international broadcasting tends to split along two lines. Some believe the broadcasters have their mission exactly right, providing a steady baseline of reliable information in a world overwhelmed with fraudulent content. The *BBC* says its World Service and foreign-language news content reaches 394 million people weekly.[93] The five US networks financed through the US Agency for Global Media (USAGM) claim 350 million.[94] Presumably, these large audiences find the broadcasters' content valuable as is. The *Voice of*

---

[93] "BBC international audience soars to record high of 426m," *BBC*, June 18, 2019, https://www.bbc.co.uk/mediacentre/latestnews/2019/bbc-international-audience-record-high.
[94] "FY 2019 Performance and Accountability Report," US Agency for Global Media, November 2019, https://www.usagm.gov/wp-content/uploads/2019/11/USAGM-FY2019-PAR.pdf.

America said it set new audience records during the coronavirus pandemic as audiences looked for reliable information.[95] Other observers believe the broadcasters' soft power has proven unequal to the worldwide flood of hostile disinformation, including from Russia and its allies. In this view, the broadcasters need to be toughened in some way; and as government-funded entities, their content should be subject to more than their own staffs' judgment.[96] Given the strong political constituencies for both points of view, the broadcasters often try to split the difference in their public remarks, asserting they are fully independent and objective and, at the same time, a valuable tool of national strategy against disinformation.[97]

Any "toughening" of the broadcasters that turns them into appendages of government messaging raises substantial risks. Becoming government messengers would mean running news and programming choices through a filter to make sure they align with government positions, something audiences would quickly notice. The broadcasters' coverage already has a natural slant in favor of democracy and against dictatorships, much as most Western media go easier on free countries than on authoritarian ones. Trying to make

---

[95] Voice of America, "*Voice of America* experiences record audience numbers due to its robust global coverage of COVID-19," news release, April 7, 2020, https://www.usagm.gov/2020/04/07/voice-of-america-experiences-record-audience-numbers-due-to-its-robust-global-coverage-of-covid-19/.

[96] Republicans in the House of Representatives declared, in June 2020, that "the mandate of USAGM should be changed to focus on actively supporting democratic governance and exposing authoritarian regimes." "Strengthening America & Countering Global Threats," Republican Study Committee, 80.

[97] In its 2020 budget request, USAGM spoke of confronting "disinformation and propaganda by bringing more fact-based, accurate journalism to populations worldwide"—and simultaneously of working to "efficiently make an impact on behalf of the American taxpayer and United States national security and foreign policy objectives." See "FY 2021 Congressional Budget Justification," US Agency for Global Media, February 10, 2020, 1 and 16, https://www.usagm.gov/wp-content/uploads/2020/02/FINAL-USAGM-FY-2021-Congressional-Budget-Justification_2_9_2020.pdf.

their tone more argumentative could throw away their existing credibility for an experiment in that might well flop.

One tactic, however, could preserve the credibility of the networks' news coverage and still provide the stronger messaging some politicians seek. Namely, the networks would continue to self-produce their flagship news coverage, making it as objective and balanced as possible; but for other content, they would aggregate material from other sources. The *Voice of America*, whose job is "to tell America's story," would link more in its English-language service to content from other US media. This would allow its own journalists to concentrate on US stories with foreign angles that other US media do not cover. For broadcasters like *Radio Free Europe/Radio Liberty* and *Radio Free Asia*, whose mission is to give voice to democratic forces within the countries they serve, an aggregation strategy would focus on local NGAs. The networks would help develop text, audio and video material from civil society organizations, investigative journalists and fact-checkers, and help them reach broad audiences by incorporating the products into their own network programming. The *Voice of America* could do the same in regions, like Africa and Latin America, where its mission includes covering local news and development efforts as well as reporting about the United States. The central theme of this book is that pro-democracy messaging is best done by local actors. The explosion of independent reporting in most countries offers a rich source of material for USAGM's networks, and aiding free media is one of the agency's stated priorities.

Such an approach would provide some of the strong messaging some politicians want, but clearly separated from the broadcasters' own coverage. *Current Time*, the international Russian TV network operated by *RFE/RL* in cooperation with *VOA*, already commissions much of its programming from independent producers in the Russian-speaking world. USAGM's Persian-language television network, *VOA 365*, also acquires content from outside providers. One could even imagine turning over blocks of time or portions of webpages to local NGAs that were willing to be associated with a US-funded broadcaster. The structure would take a page from *Trans World Radio* (*TWR*), the gargantuan US-based Christian network that broadcasts over 2,000 transmitters worldwide. *TWR* produces some of its own programs, but also runs content created by dozens of other ministries with similar beliefs.[98]

One objection to such an approach would be that the broadcasters would lose control over their brands, since content on their platforms would come from multiple sources. However, the broadcasters might think of themselves less as brands and more as production houses for whole families of pro-democracy content. Modern audiences already think of content in a highly atomized way, as products in themselves rather than appendages of an overarching network. (Audiences search online for *Daily Show* clips by typing the name of the show, not the *Comedy Central* network.) Although broadcasters must monitor what is produced under their roofs, audiences arguably can distinguish, say, between the *Voice of America*'s flagship news programs and a program or podcast clearly attributed to an NGA.

Another objection to such a new structure might be that NGA-created programming would be amateurish in quality. However, modern audiences clearly can forgive quality if the message is interesting enough. Thousands of people, many of them young or with strong political views, have built powerful YouTube followings with negligible production skills. "If productions by local groups are too professional and slick, they can even undermine your credibility and look too foreign," says Jerzy Pomianowski, executive director of the European Endowment for Democracy. "You need to stay genuine. Yuri Dud [a Russian 30-something influencer] gets away with 70-

---

[98] https://www.twr.org/.

minute interviews, despite what they say about the time span people will watch things for on the web."[99]

In the absence of suddenly larger budgets, international broadcasters will be forced to redeploy their funding for the greatest effect. Aggregating content from NGAs will free some resources. Alina Polyakova, president of the Center for European Policy Analysis, recommends that USAGM "be tasked with conducting an audit of its existing programs and services to assess which are underperforming. It may not be a good use of resources to continue to fund traditional television broadcasting."[100] To date, USAGM has tried to do it all, stepping up digital operations while launching 24/7 television networks in Russian and Persian. Its plan to create a 24/7 Mandarin network appears to have been scaled back to a web and social media play. This will be more cost-effective, even if it is embarrassing that the United States cannot do more in this critically important language. A full-time television channel is expensive. Posting videos on YouTube is far simpler and can draw viewers for years.

Public Diplomacy

Public diplomacy includes direct messaging to foreign publics by government entities such as the State Department. During the Cold War, much of the job was simply to share with the rest of the world know what life was like in democratic countries. Modern communications make it possible for foreign publics to have as intimate a knowledge as they wish of events and attitudes in the West—including its shortcomings. Russia, meanwhile, has

---

[99] Jerzy Pomianowski, interview with author, June 25, 2019.
[100] *United States Efforts to Counter Russian Disinformation and Malign Influence*, July 10, 2019 (testimony of Alina Polyakova), https://docs.house.gov/meetings/AP/AP04/20190710/109748/HHRG-116-AP04-Wstate-PolyakovaA-20190710.pdf.

professionalized its own public diplomacy and soft power projects through such groups as the Gorchakov Fund and Creative Diplomacy. They hold conferences of young, politically minded foreigners, teach organizational skills to NGOs and promote "objective information" about Russia.[101]

In Cold War times, countering Russian IOs was a major public diplomacy goal. US public diplomacy in recent years has had some inspired moments in that effort. State published a fact sheet in 2014 to denounce Putin's "10 False Claims" about Ukraine, saying the world had not seen such startling Russian fiction "since Dostoyevsky wrote, 'The formula two plus two equals five is not without its attractions.' "[102] The department also posted a highly professional infographic about "Russia's Aggression in Ukraine."[103]

However, current US public diplomacy feels weak. One marquee effort is the State Department's Share America website, a mix of short news pieces that restate US foreign policy positions and ones that speak positively of the US and its leaders.[104] (A search of the site in March 2020 found 36 positive references to Ivanka Trump and no mentions of impeachment. To its credit, during the coronavirus outbreak it carried extensive coverage of US aid to other countries.) US public diplomacy efforts suffer from a restricted budget (about 4 percent of international affairs spending), a lack of skills to compete in a modern multimedia environment, and shell-shock among US officials caused by President Trump's mercurial positions, his

---

[101] See https://gorchakovfund.ru/en/ and https://www.facebook.com/picreadi.eng/.

[102] Department of State, "President Putin's Fiction: 10 False Claims about Ukraine," fact sheet, March 5, 2014, archived at https://www.liveleak.com/view?t=2b0_1394109329.

[103] Available at https://dos-cso.maps.arcgis.com/apps/Cascade/index.html?appid=8dad6c865bed491ead3190c7f fb2fafe, accessed July 15, 2020.

[104] https://share.america.gov/.

nastiness toward US allies and developing countries, and America's poor record on the coronavirus and race relations.

The hardest task for US public diplomacy toward Russia under the Trump administration has been to establish a consistent tone that will not fall victim to some sudden new twist in White House attitudes. For its part, the EU, as we have seen, faces public diplomacy limitations caused by disunity among its members and an aversion to "propaganda." Under these circumstances, the most effective pro-democracy communication will probably not come through government channels but by enhancing the strength of NGAs that suffer fewer inhibitions. A Bundestag official interviewed for this study said the German government had no taste for "propaganda" against Russia. He had no problem, however, with Germany supporting "independent media" in Europe's East—even though independent media have been active in exposing Russia-aligned disinformation and corruption.

If Western public diplomacy remains dispirited and disorganized, the best bet for governments is probably to invite more people to Western countries for exchange programs and education. These outflank Russian IOs by bringing influential foreign populations into contact with all aspects of democratic societies, not only those cherry-picked by critics. Visitors are still put off by some aspects of Western life but see them in the context of other things they admire. Governments might also recruit prominent Westerners, rather than government spokespeople, for their campaigns. Vasily Gatov of the USC Annenberg Center imagines a "dream team" of US innovators, entertainers and philanthropists, such as Elon Musk, George Clooney and Bill and Melinda Gates, to promote democratic messages.[105] During the Cold War, the US quietly subsidized the Congress for

---

[105] Vasily Gatov, "How to Talk with Russia," *The American Interest*, February 26, 2018, https://www.the-american-interest.com/2018/02/26/how-to-talk-with-russia/.

Cultural Freedom, which ran public conferences where the likes of Bertrand Russell, Arthur Koestler and Sidney Hook denounced Soviet Communism to US and European intellectuals.

Journalists

Journalists who specialize in opposing Russian IOs are a major pillar of the anti-disinformation cause. Other journalists, for reasons of objectivity, may be more reluctant to publicly embrace any side in the information wars. Still, the survival of their outlets depends on press freedom, making them strong potential allies so long as their ethical boundaries are respected.

Journalists are likely to be interested above all in clear evidence of Russian IOs in their own countries or other nations toward which they have affinity. It is important, however, how such evidence is offered. Journalistic professionals are rightly wary of information from activists with a political point of view, especially if they cannot verify it themselves. Effective democracy campaigners have learned to give reporters plenty of space, offering information in a low-key way. "We might show a newsroom some breadcrumbs that could lead them to do a story on disinformation by *RT* and *Sputnik*," says a researcher from a major training and analysis center. He says he is careful never to appear to be pressing for publication. Journalists do like genuine scoops, however. An activist from another NGA recommends setting up communications networks with trusted journalists on Facebook or the secure Signal app to give them fast breaks on new lines of disinformation.

As for news outlets that need Western resources, most funders emphasize that they just provide training and support to independent media and do not attempt to influence their editorial content. That said, these funders openly stand for free media, human rights and civil political discourse. They are unlikely to finance a news company, however independent, that advocates for undemocratic positions. (Most of these have their own sources of support in any case.) Sometimes it is quite clear that aid is designed specifically to counter Russian IOs. Global Engagement Center head Lea Gabrielle highlighted to Congress the success of US projects "supporting independent media in two vulnerable European countries to produce higher-quality reporting that exposes and educates their publics on Russian disinformation."[106] At the same hearing, Jim Kulikowski, the State Department's assistance coordinator for Europe, Eurasia and Central Asia, said USAID was working to give Balkan audiences information options other than *RT*, *Sputnik* and outlets influenced by local governments. He noted that "USAID-supported investigative journalists in Bosnia and Herzegovina broke news stories about weapons purchases and the presence of Russia-trained fighters in the Republika Srpska."[107]

Coverage of Russian IOs can be encouraged in quite general ways. A government or foundation might subsidize a publication or broadcaster to hire a reporter to write about a generic subject like disinformation. If Russian IOs are active in the publication's area of coverage, it is likely the reporter will write about them sooner or later, without the grantor needing to specify Russia as the target.

In some countries, journalists who normally compete have made an exception for fighting false content. In addition to the growing collaborations among fact-checking teams, the *BBC* and several other news and technology companies held a Trusted News Summit in 2019 that called for "a new industry collaboration" against misinformation. They proposed measures including an early warning system "so

---

[106] *United States Efforts to Counter Russian Disinformation and Malign Influence* (testimony of Lea Gabrielle).
[107] *United States Efforts to Counter Russian Disinformation and Malign Influence* (testimony of Jim Kulikowski).

organisations can alert each other rapidly when they discover disinformation which threatens human life or disrupts democracy during elections. The emphasis will be on moving quickly and collectively to undermine disinformation before it can take hold."[108] Such a system bringing together anti-disinformation activists might be more successful at the journalistic level than the EU's Rapid Alert System has proven for governments. Joining an effort like the Trusted News Summit under the aegis of the *BBC* would be acceptable to many US news organizations (*The Wall Street Journal* took part in the summit's initial session). However, they would be wary of the media-government collaborations against disinformation that have developed in Western Europe. In their view, government is something for journalists to hold to account, not to team up with. They would fear that any close interaction with government officials would be seized on as a sign that they had given up their editorial independence. Later in the book, I will discuss efforts, sometimes successful, by Russian cyber operators to disable news media computer systems or plant false information on their sites. US media outlets have taken advice from government authorities about that danger, but they are, nonetheless, unlikely to let government technicians roam freely through their systems to identify vulnerable points. Some have hired private consultants for that task.

In at-risk countries, one of the biggest problems for independent media is scale. Teams of reporters are expensive. It is hard for a website, even a good one, to win a lasting audience when there is so much competition. While some independent news operations are successful, like *Gazeta Wyborcza* in Poland and *Dennik N* in Slovakia, many more teeter, dependent on the next foreign grant or on

---

[108] "New collaboration steps up fight against disinformation," *BBC*, September 9, 2019, https://www.bbc.co.uk/mediacentre/latestnews/2019/disinformation?ns_linkname= corporate&ns_mchannel=social&ns_campaign=bbc_press_office&ns_source=twitte r.

government advertising that can be withheld as a form of intimidation. Shared distribution may be a useful approach to their problem, with several journalist groups collaborating on a website, podcast series or radio network. It would be more efficient for funders to support such joint undertakings instead of scattering small grants among many recipients with smaller audiences.

A significant way to help media in at-risk countries would be to subsidize their access to Western news agencies such as *The Associated Press, Reuters, Agence France-Presse,* Spain's *EFE,* Italy's *ANSA* and Germany's *DPA.* The major Western agencies have minimal distribution in many poorer nations. Media eager for their text, photo and video services are plentiful; but the news agencies, under financial pressure themselves, are wary of providing content to anyone for free. Therefore, many outlets, including small broadcasters and websites, wind up using content from such cheap or free sources as *RT, Sputnik,* and China's *Xinhua.* It would cost Western news agencies nothing out of pocket to offer their content to these outlets; they would simply have to give them access to their internet content portals. They fear that if they start handing out free access, other cash-strapped subscribers that still manage to make their monthly payments will start pressing for free service, too, undermining their pricing structure. Unless the agencies are willing to take some risks in the interest of reliable information, the only option would be for government or private funders to cover the cost of these services. The costs are not high. The agencies would likely provide service to some outlets for $500 to $1,000 a month.

Another source of financial assistance to independent media is training in using ad networks and e-commerce to boost their income. Other NGAs could use these moneymakers as well. Ads on a think tank's home page might look odd to some, but they offer the prospect of easy revenue.

National Elites

In many countries, elites are highly aware of Russian IOs and have created think tanks and other infrastructure to oppose them. This is not universal, however, even in states with political freedom. Russian IOs may simply not be big on politicians' radar in southern Europe, Africa and Latin America. Countries far from Russia that feel little heat from Russian operations are wary of being dragged into major foreign governments' conflicts with Moscow. They have not been enthusiastic about sanctioning Russia over its invasion of Ukraine. Latin America and Africa had long and bloody experience during the Cold War with coups and proxy wars that stemmed from the US-Soviet struggle and have nothing to gain from a new round.

These beliefs by elites often reflect widespread public attitudes. In Latin America, the United States evokes memories of coups and repression far more than does Russia, whatever the misdeeds of Moscow's leftist allies on the continent. In Africa, Russia has none of the colonial baggage that still bedevils Western powers. It is remembered favorably (at least by older generations) for its long opposition to South African apartheid. Latin American and African visitors had good impressions of the 2018 FIFA World Cup in Russia. Moscow can also make common cause with those African countries that, like the Russian Federation, are under US, EU and UN sanctions.

African and Latin American countries struggle with fake news and disinformation from domestic actors, so intense at times that people think any foreign component must be negligible. However, Russian efforts can be substantial.[109] In 2019, Facebook took down three networks of accounts with a half-million followers that it said were

---

[109] For a summary of Russian operations and intentions, see Luke Harding and Jason Burke, "Leaked documents reveal Russian effort to exert influence in Africa," *The Guardian*, June 11, 2019, https://www.theguardian.com/world/2019/jun/11/leaked-documents-reveal-russian-effort-to-exert-influence-in-africa.

linked to Yevgeny Prigozhin and targeted at Madagascar, the Central African Republic, Mozambique, the Democratic Republic of Congo, Ivory Coast and Cameroon.[110] The network, which was first identified by the Stanford Internet Observatory, posted positive content about Russian activities in Africa while criticizing the US and France.[111] Russian social media efforts often bolster weak or corrupt governments in states where Moscow seeks military agreements or access to natural resources. In the words of one Carnegie Endowment study:

> [Russia's] gains have been mostly in pariah states ostracized by the international community, such as Zimbabwe, and strategically less important ones, like the Central African Republic, from which other major powers have largely disengaged. Moscow has devoted relatively few resources to expanding its influence in Africa compared to other major external actors such as the European Union (EU), the United States, and China. But it has repeatedly demonstrated a knack for spreading narratives about Moscow's resurgence as a leading power and fostering the impression that its accomplishments on the continent have come at the expense of the United States and its allies.[112]

---

[110] By one account, Prigozhin in 2019 had economic interests in 39 African countries and political advisors in at least 20. Ilya Rozhdestvensky, Michael Rubin, and Roman Badanin, "Шеф и повар. Часть третья" [Master and chef. Part 3], *Proekt*, April 11, 2019, https://www.proekt.media/investigation/prigozhin-polittekhnologi/.

[111] Nathaniel Gleicher, "Removing More Coordinated Inauthentic Behavior From Russia," Facebook blog, October 30, 2019, https://about.fb.com/news/2019/10/removing-more-coordinated-inauthentic-behavior-from-russia/. For details, see Shelby Grossman, Daniel Bush, and Renée DiResta, "Evidence of Russia-Linked Influence Operations in Africa," Stanford Internet Observatory, October 29, 2019, https://fsi-live.s3.us-west-1.amazonaws.com/s3fs-public/29oct2019_sio_-_russia_linked_influence_operations_in_africa.final_.pdf.

[112] Andrew S. Weiss and Eugene Rumer, "Nuclear Enrichment: Russia's Ill-Fated Influence Campaign in South Africa," *Carnegie Endowment for International Peace,*

African nations will ultimately judge Russia on what advantages it concretely delivers to their people. "Where democratic norms are strong, Russia's power is weak," says Kimberly Marten, a professor of political science at Barnard College.[113] The sweet spots for the Kremlin are countries like Libya and the Central African Republic, with rich economic resources but stubborn armed conflicts. In these cases, the Kremlin can hope, by military, intelligence and information means, to help one side win and then profit from the resources. Moscow is less successful in more developed countries that have internal order and a sense of democratic governance. Russia's attempt to ram through a sweetheart nuclear deal with South Africa under former President Jacob Zuma collapsed after opposition from investigative journalists and civil society, aided by a Russian environmental NGA that leaked a crucial document. Russia's IOs are hardly invincible. Its efforts through social media, newspapers and billboards failed to elect a candidate important to Prigozhin's business interests in Madagascar in 2018. Disinformation by Russian operatives could not save Sudanese President Omar el-Bashir in 2019.

Russia's limited economic strength can rebound to the benefit of stronger African and Latin American governments. If such governments are unsettled by Russian IOs, they may succeed in forcing Moscow to back down if they make this a condition of economic cooperation. This presupposes that governments, journalists and academics in these countries are aware of the threat. Christopher Walker, vice president of the National Endowment for Democracy, notes the lack of experts on Russia in Latin America and Africa, and the need to make more people aware of the nature of its

---

December 16, 2019, https://carnegieendowment.org/2019/12/16/nuclear-enrichment-russia-s-ill-fated-influence-campaign-in-south-africa-pub-80597.
[113] Kimberly Marten, interview with author, October 3, 2019.

government.[114] A 2017 survey found 51 percent of people in six African countries believed the Russian government respects personal freedom; 30 percent of Latin Americans agreed.[115] "In Latin America, the political class is not aware of the level of the danger," says Armando Chaguaceda of the Universidad de Guanajuato in Mexico. "We need more forums with intellectuals from Europe and the US."[116]

[114] Christopher Walker, "What is 'Sharp Power?' " *Journal of Democracy*, July 2018, https://www.ned.org/wp-content/uploads/2018/07/what-is-sharp-power-christopher-walker-journal-of-democracy-july-2018.pdf.

[115] Margaret Vice, "Publics Worldwide Unfavorable Toward Putin, Russia," 2.

[116] Armando Chaguaceda, interview with author, April 2, 2019.

Chapter V: Communicating to Russia's Population

Why Message Russians?

I have pointed out that most of the struggle against Russian IOs has taken place on the territory of Western powers and at-risk countries. The Western focus has been on resilience at home to Russian operations, rather than an information offensive aimed at Russia's own citizens. This chapter proposes substantially stepped-up communication to Russia's population.

The West was proud during the Cold War of its massive radio broadcasting to Russia, an effort aimed directly at undermining the Soviet regime. Since then, however, Western sensibilities about engaging in "propaganda" have risen, along with a loss of confidence that the West has much to propagandize people about. Western governments also fear that messaging to Russians will not work—or that if it happens to, Russia will strike back with some brutal information, cyber or military assault. EU Vice President Věra Jourová says the EU does not want to transmit "propaganda" to Russia, but just "provide the proper facts and information to our citizens."[1] In short, we are deterred from a new messaging campaign to Russian citizens, by fear of Russia and by our own sensibilities.

---

[1] "Going viral: lessons from the COVID-19 crisis for fighting disinformation" (comments by Věra Jourová), video, European Policy Center, June 12, 2020,

It is also arguable that if the goal is to affect Russian policy, the easiest way to do so is not by communicating to Russia's population but by building resistance to Russian IOs elsewhere. Since Russia has very few allies, its information operators have a steep climb in every country whose society they wish to impact. The West's institutions and culture, by contrast, are familiar almost everywhere, giving democratic countries a natural advantage if they choose to use it.

Still, messaging directly to Russian citizens is a certain way to get Kremlin attention. Dmitri Teperik of Estonia's International Center for Defense and Security advocates for a "ruthless projection of truth" to the Russian people.[2] Yet, in recent years, the State Department considered a messaging campaign to Russian citizens highlighting the failings of the Putin regime. The project was killed on the grounds there was no need to intervene in Russian internal affairs. In 2020, US Cyber Command reportedly was preparing limited operations against individual Russian officials to warn them against interfering in the US presidential elections. The command was said to have ruled out any attempt to reach the overall Russian population because officials anticipated "limited success given Putin's control of the country, including much of the media."[3] (It is a sign of their independence from the rest of the government that *Radio Free Europe/Radio Liberty* and the *Voice of America* routinely broadcast in Russian about Russia's internal conditions.)

---

http://www.epc.eu/en/events/Going-viral-lessons-from-the-COVID-19-crisis-for~33df4c.

[2] Dmitri Teperik, "Does the West Dare to Open the Eastern Front of Information War?" ICDS Blog, June 8, 2020, https://icds.ee/does-the-west-dare-to-open-the-eastern-front-of-information-war/?fbclid=IwAR1-RP8We46yrziJuSSqt2NLvPRJsU_ZQU5h9ARgOyhRWYO38Tnq4LKMbLk.

[3] Ellen Nakashima, "U.S. Cybercom contemplates information warfare to counter Russian interference in 2020 election," *The Washington Post*, December 25, 2019, https://www.washingtonpost.com/national-security/us-cybercom-contemplates-information-warfare-to-counter-russian-interference-in-the-2020-election/2019/12/25/21bb246e-20e8-11ea-bed5-880264cc91a9_story.html.

Calculating the advisability of an information campaign aimed at Russia requires a consensus on several points: how much danger Russia actually presents, the goals in addressing Russian citizens, and the risks democratic countries are prepared to run.

A strong contingent of policymakers in democratic countries believes Moscow's threat is far from existential, given Russia's overall weakness. In this view, aggressive responses to Russian IOs, by information tools and otherwise, can only worsen the situation. Russian acts like the invasion of eastern Ukraine are hard to minimize, but most Russian activity is in the so-called "gray zone"—a fuzzy realm of information, political, intelligence and cyber jousting where the seriousness of an action is at least partially in the eye of the beholder. Was the social media onslaught by Russian assets in support of Catalan independence in 2017 an intolerable attack on Spanish sovereignty, or just routine fishing in the troubled waters of a NATO state? In 2020, Angela Merkel declared that a Russian cyberattack against the Bundestag was "outrageous"—but said she would still strive for good relations with Moscow.[4] Five months earlier, Germany expelled two Russian diplomats over the murder in Berlin of Chechen separatist Zelimkhan Khangoshvili, but it did not call for the kind of EU-wide response that the UK urged after the death of Sergei Skripal. If one's goal is to avoid conflict with Russia, almost any Russian action can be dismissed as being either just more of what Russia has always done (if perhaps with new tools) or an understandable move given Russia's historical insecurities. (This is often called the "Russlandversteher" or "Russia-understander" argument). Proposals for an aggressive response can be rejected on the grounds that the West must not give Russia a pretext to escalate to a new spiral in the conflict. In this way, those who hesitate to confront Moscow can

---

[4] "Merkel droht Russland wegen Hackerangriff mit Konsequenzen" [Merkel threatens Russia with consequences for hacking], *Frankfurter Allgemeine Zeitung,* May 13, 2020, https://www.faz.net/aktuell/politik/ausland/merkel-droht-russland-wegen-hackerangriff-mit-konsequenzen-16767763.html.

frame their reticence as a cunning strategy to deprive Russia of a "provocation" it can capitalize on.

Such rationalizing of inaction comes with high costs, such as allowing Russia to continue to hold conquered swaths of Ukraine and Georgia. According to a 2019 study by the US Center for Strategic & International Studies, "Hyper risk conscious U.S. decisionmakers— convinced that the long arc of history favors continued U.S. dominance—can see aggressive action against capable gray zone rivals like Russia and China as risky flirtation with uncontrolled and costly escalation." However, it added, "appeasement is tacit acknowledgement of rival gains… In the end, the deferred hazard of inaction presents attractive incentives for US decisionmakers to wait out the opposition. Unfortunately, irreversible strategic loss is a natural outcome."[5]

Those who favor stronger action by democratic countries, including in the information realm, argue that reluctance to provoke Russia only results in more aggression. "They want the world to play according to their pre-set objectives. If we try not to tease the bear, they win," says Anna Fotyga of the European Parliament. "Things are bad even without our being active in the information space, so there is nothing to fear if we're careful."[6] To this more assertive camp, there is no point in trying not to "antagonize" Russia, because it is already at war, deploying invasion, subversion and disinformation wherever it can. "The Russians didn't need a provocation from us to seize Crimea. The worst scenario is already here. The best way to stop them is with forceful action, not accommodation. Their strategy is about power,

---

[5] Nathan Freier, "The Darker Shade of Gray: A New War Unlike Any Other," *Center for Strategic & International Studies,* July 27, 2018, https://www.csis.org/analysis/darker-shade-gray-new-war-unlike-any-other.

[6] Anna Fotyga, interview with author.

and only power will hold them back," says Lithuanian European Parliament member Petras Auštrevičius.[7]

Opposing views of how to conduct the information conflict with Moscow have surfaced in many Western forums, including discussions at NATO. A French government study says:

> The French position, which is to limit NATO's role [in opposing Russian disinformation] to detection, analysis and response regarding its own activities (and not its disinformation and destabilization activities on the whole) is widely shared within the alliance. Cracks appear, however, among the allies over what the response should be, and over the idea of "beating Russia at its own game" by sowing doubt, including among Russian-speaking populations, about the activities and intentions of Moscow or by proposing a new reading of certain chapters of history. This position is, however, far from unanimous within the alliance, where differences also continue over the assessment of the threat, reflecting in part the differences in the allies' analysis of the role of Russia and the posture that NATO should adopt toward Moscow.[8]

Jean-Baptiste Jeangène Vilmer, an author of the study and director of the French Armed Forces' strategic research institute, says "information war" is a Russian term that overinflates what Moscow is up to. He says we are witnessing a militarization of information by the Kremlin for targeted political purposes, but it is hardly the kind of all-out conflict that war implies. Our response, in Vilmer's view, should

---

[7] Petras Auštrevičius, interview with author.

[8] Jean-Baptiste Jeangène Vilmer, Alexandre Escorcia et al., *Les Manipulations de l'Information* [*The Manipulation of Information*], 139 (Paris: CAPS-IRSEM, August 2018), https://www.diplomatie.gouv.fr/IMG/pdf/les_manipulations_de_l_information_2_cle04b2b6.pdf.

be like the "war on drugs"—a commitment to fighting a problem that is permanently with us, not a military-style conflict with a clear beginning and end.[9]

Goals of Messaging

An overarching question is what the West seeks to accomplish with its Russia policies. During the Cold War, its task was mainly to keep NATO strong and hope the Soviet Union's economic weakness would catch up with it. With a resurgence now in Russian military actions, accompanied by espionage and information violence, democratic countries must reevaluate whether this strategy is still valid. Can Russia still be waited out, or should we be working toward certain outcomes, with information weapons as part of the arsenal? These outcomes could include:

• An end to the Putin regime, and its replacement by a democratic government. The hope would be a rerun of the fall of the Soviet Union in 1991 with a better long-term result.

• A less dramatic change in Russia, perhaps with Putin still in charge, that would advance the rule of law, grant more internal freedoms and reduce adventurism abroad.

• A reduction in Russian IOs and other aggression abroad, irrespective of what happens internally in Russia. The West would "show its teeth" to demonstrate that Russia's own information environment is at risk unless it deescalates IOs outside its borders.

• Not trying to affect events in Russia but simply maintaining an open communication channel to its population, for use whenever it might be suddenly needed.

---

[9] Jean-Baptiste Jeangène Vilmer, interview with author, May 29, 2019.

It is hard to construct any information strategy against Russia without deciding which goal we want to pursue. Yet, Western government officials interviewed for this study were highly reluctant to make a choice. Although the end of the regime sounded good to all of them in principle, many doubted that any Western action can substantially affect Russia's internal situation. Many felt that even the mildest effort to nudge internal Russian dynamics could evoke a vicious response.

It is interesting that while Western officials debate how they might communicate to Russia, Russian officials feel their population is already the victim of a media onslaught that promotes the attitudes, technology, fashions, business practices and even the English slang of Western countries. The internet offers enormous amounts of material, much of it in Russian, promoting Western viewpoints and criticizing Russian authorities. In 2018, according to a report by the Russian Federation Council (upper chamber of parliament), "mass media controlled by Washington and its allies […] were fully utilized during the presidential election and campaign with the aim of illegitimate pressure from outside on the Russian Federation's organs of power and Russian society."[10] Kremlin authorities accused the Russian service of German broadcaster *Deutsche Welle* of trying to intensify the 2019 Moscow Duma election protests with a website headline reading "Muscovites, come out!"[11]

---

[10] "Доклад А.А. Климова на комиссии СФ по итогам работы мониторинговой группы за период с 30 мая по 12 сентября 2019 года" [Report of A.A. Klimov to the commissions of the Federation Council on the results of the work of the Monitoring Group from May 30 to September 12, 2019], Federation Council of the Russian Federation, October 8, 2019, http://council.gov.ru/media/files/cWoDECZrNAv9hKQ2ZOPkOpA6vPHLgAUG.pdf.

[11] The headline in Russian was "Москвичи, выходите!" See "Москва обратится к США и ФРГ из-за вмешательства во внутренние дела России" [Moscow will address the USA and Germany about interference in the internal affairs of Russia], *RIA-Novosti*, August 4, 2019, https://ria.ru/20190804/1557158646.html.

It is not clear whether Russian authorities truly feel threatened by pro-democracy communication, or if they are simply following the Cold War playbook of reacting vociferously to the slightest attempt to reach their citizens. The fact that Russian declarations today are often tied to claims of election interference suggest their worries may be for show, designed mainly as a riposte to charges of Russian intrusions into Western voting. If, on the other hand, they genuinely feel threatened by outside information efforts, then one or another of the goals laid about above might not be impossible.

Russia's Internal Situation

The underlying factors that could lead to cataclysmic change in Russia exist. Many Russians feel the Putin regime has failed to bring them the prosperity it promised, and the 2020 oil price crash and coronavirus pandemic portended greater economic strain. Half of Russians say they have only enough money for food and clothing.[12] Putin was forced, in 2019, to raise the pension age. The total size of the Russian economy is smaller than Brazil's. Successful private entrepreneurs face intimidation by corrupt officials and organized crime. Given this picture, it is not surprising that more than half of young Russians say they are interested in joining their compatriots who have already left the country. They cite as reasons Russia's economy, medical and educational services and "the political situation."[13] This puts further pressure on the country's population level of 146 million, a number that has been slowly declining since before the start of this century.

---

[12] Rosstat data cited in "Песков заявил, что в Кремле трезво оценивают уровень благосостояния россиян" [Peskov declares that the Kremlin is seriously assessing Russians' well-being], *TASS*, May 30, 2019, https://tass.com/politics/1060833.
[13] "Эмиграционные настроения" [Mood toward emigration], *Levada-Center*, November 26, 2019, https://www.levada.ru/2019/11/26/emigratsionnye-nastroeniya-4.

Polls show deepening frustration with domestic conditions and official repression. From 2017 to 2019, the number of Russians who believe the country needs "decisive comprehensive change" rose to 59 from 42 percent, and those afraid of mass repression (a term that evokes Stalinist times) rose to 39 from 21 percent.[14]

More significant than polling results is the increased willingness of citizens to turn their frustrations into public protests over issues ranging from Putin's legitimacy and police brutality to road taxes and construction projects. Protests over the 2019 Moscow Duma elections brought 50,000 people into the streets. In February 2020, a memorial march in the capital for slain Kremlin critic Boris Nemtsov attracted as many as 20,000. An online meeting to protest Putin's proposed constitutional amendments attracted 70,000 YouTube views in April 2020.[15] Protests over national political issues have tended to obscure the sharp growth of demonstrations and activism by NGAs elsewhere in the country, many of them on local topics. If during Soviet times citizens were mortally afraid of the security services, citizens now—especially young ones—have a strong sense of their right to speak their minds. Support groups have sprung up around protests, helping demonstrators communicate when authorities slow the internet, dispatching lawyers and food to those detained and posting the identities of police officers who have beaten demonstrators.[16] Local journalists have catalogued the protests in detail and rallied broad support for reporters, like Ivan Golunov, who have become government targets. (Golunov was released after a clumsy attempt to plant drugs on him in 2019.) The minor penalties handed down to

---

[14] "Страхи" [Fears], *Levada-Center,* October 29, 2019, https://www.levada.ru/2019/10/29/strahi-4/.

[15] Кампания НЕТ! "Онлайн-митинг «За жизнь»" [Online rally 'For Life'], YouTube video, 2:53:07, April 28, 2020, https://www.youtube.com/watch?v=gYDkz-tjn7E.

[16] For "doxing" of police officers, see https://bewareofthem.org/en/category/archive-en/lawenforcement-en/. This group is based outside Russia.

most arrested protesters are likely a calculation by authorities that a stronger reaction would bring even more opposition.

Despite all its popularity and police power, Putin's government has failed to fully control Russia's information space. About half of Russians trust state television.[17] Independent and anti-regime internet influencers have attracted large followings with their often-sarcastic assessments of Putin and his lieutenants. Authorities have used new laws against fake news and insulting state officials to sporadically harass many individuals, but the state's actions apparently have not had a large effect. Independent news media, whose investigative reporting often puts the regime in a bad light, have used the internet to build strong national visibility. (The hardline pro-regime *Federal News Agency* issues frequent lists of sites publishing the most "anti-Russian and fake news stories"; most of the sites it denounces are inside Russia.[18]) Most of the information Russians ingest still comes from government-approved sources, even if they do not fully trust it. Yet, authorities have been denuded of their control over information consumed by young Russians and the politically aware.

To be sure, Putin's government retains huge sources of strength. Along with command of major media, it directly or indirectly controls much of the economy. Authorities have managed to identify the most obvious sources of opposition, such as Alexei Navalny's anti-corruption movement, and harassed them intensely enough to prevent the creation of any strong, national center of anti-regime activity. (Still, Navalny's regular videos on official corruption enjoy 3.3 million YouTube subscribers.) The security apparatus is pervasive, perhaps unnecessarily so; there is no sign that most Russians believe overthrowing the government is possible or desirable. Even if Putin

---

[17] "Российский медиаландшафт-2020" [Russian media landscape 2020], *Levada-Center,* April 28, 2020, https://www.levada.ru/2020/04/28/rossijskij-medialandshaft-2020/.

[18] https://riafan.ru/category/reiting-antirossiiskikh-smi.

were to vanish from the scene, it is not sure that democracy would be the popular choice of rank-and-file Russians, especially after the chaos of the "democratic" Yeltsin years. In a 2019 survey, the label "very important" was attached by only 38 percent of Russians to free media (down by 8 percentage points since 2015), by 45 percent to free speech (down 2 percentage points) and by 40 percent to free elections with at least two competing parties (down 17 percentage points).[19]

Putin remains personally popular despite a spate of scandals over government corruption, incompetence and brutality.[20] A March 2020 poll found 56 percent of Russians feel positively toward him (though this represented an eight-point drop since October 2019).[21] The constitutional changes adopted in 2020 laid the groundwork for Putin to remain in power until 2036. Specialists are split over whether this showed that Putin believed his authority was so secure that he could count on ruling without challenge for more than a generation, or that he feared his support had peaked and he needed to take drastic action to maintain any influence after 2024.

Even approval of the constitutional proposals in July 2020 added new uncertainty to the political landscape. For many Russians, Putin *is* the state. Laying the groundwork for him to rule until 2036 could lead to instability on two fronts: desperation among Putin's opponents over the prospect of his remaining in power indefinitely, and fears among

---

[19] "Democratic Rights Popular Globally but Commitment to Them Not Always Strong," *Pew Research Center,* February 27, 2020, topline questionnaire, https://www.pewresearch.org/global/wp-content/uploads/sites/2/2020/02/PG_2020.02.27_global-democracy_TOPLINE.pdf.

[20] For one list, see Tony Wesolowsky and Robert Coalson, "Teflon Putin? Over 20 Years In Power, Scandals Don't Seem To Stick To The Russian President," *Radio Free Europe/Radio Liberty,* August 8, 2019, https://www.rferl.org/a/putin-20-years-power-corruption-scandals/30100279.html.

[21] "Отношение к Владимиру Путину" [Feelings about Vladimir Putin], *Levada-Center,* April 14, 2020, https://www.levada.ru/2020/04/14/otnoshenie-k-vladimiru-putinu-4/.

his supporters that an attempt to rule the Kremlin until he is 84 years old must fail at some point, with unpredictable consequences.

It is even questionable how many Putin supporters back him particularly deeply. Despite assertions by the president's allies that Russia's "deep people" will insist on a Putin-style regime even if someone else eventually leads it,[22] this is not a certainty. A 2019 article in a popular Moscow newspaper argued that Russians are well known for their "total indifference to the fate of power structures once they collapse." The author, Yevgeny Gontmakher of the pro-democracy Committee of National Initiatives, said:

> At [Joseph] Stalin's funeral there were widespread, apparently sincere tears, but just three years later people calmly accepted the revelations of his "cult of personality" and then the removal of the former leader's body from the mausoleum. […] So to think that the present system stands on a solid foundation of tens of millions of ordinary Russian people is a huge illusion. If this system gets into trouble as a result of some internal or external factors, no one "from the people" will offer it a hand.[23]

Aim for Major Change?

When an authoritarian regime is weakened by political and economic malaise and loses control of information, it is not difficult to imagine

---

[22] This was asserted most notably in 2019 by a top advisor to Putin. See Vladislav Surkov, "Владислав Сурков: Долгое государство Путина" [Vladislav Surkov: Putin's long state], *Nezavisimaya Gazeta*, February 11, 2019, http://www.ng.ru/ideas/2019-02-11/5_7503_surkov.html.

[23] Yevgeny Gontmakher, "Никто не подставит российской власти плечо в момент ее обрушения" [No one will offer the Russian authorities a hand at the moment of their collapse], *Moskovsky Komsomolets*, March 6, 2020, https://www.mk.ru/politics/2019/03/04/nikto-ne-podstavit-rossiyskoy-vlasti-plecho-v-moment-ee-obrusheniya.html.

a chain of events that can push it off a cliff. The trigger can be a government crackdown or, as in the case of Gorbachev, a sudden liberalization. It can be an event entirely outside the political sphere. Putin's government has faced severe public criticism over events that made it look hapless and incompetent, like the sinking of two navy submarines, forest fires in Siberia, a fatal explosion at a White Sea weapons test center and slipshod fire safety regulations that led to the deaths of scores of people at a shopping center in the city of Kemerovo. In 2020, Putin lost an oil price war with the United States and Saudi Arabia, saw his shaky accommodation with Turkey imperiled and miscalculated the impact of the coronavirus. Analyst Paul Goble believes Putin's failure to control the virus has dealt a mortal blow to the sense of omnipotence he has cultivated, making him far more vulnerable politically than before.[24] Some of his Kremlin colleagues may conclude that Russia—and they personally—have benefited as much as they can from Russia's current course, and changes are essential. If Gontmakher is right that Russians are unsentimental about their governments, even those who are satisfied with Putin as leader may not be moved to "offer a hand" in the face of mass demonstrations or a decision by plotters inside the Kremlin that he has become a liability.

The problem is that this is all fantastically speculative. While a coup or color revolution is not impossible in Russia, predicting it is. Almost every major political event in Russia, from the Bolshevik Revolution to Putin's ascent to the presidency, came as a surprise to the world public (though some were predicted within circles of specialists.) Events can be triggered by small groups of people, either in the streets or corridors of power. An information policy aimed at creating a palace coup or a sudden, intense public uprising cannot realistically be planned or managed because it depends on too many unknowable

---

[24] Paul Goble, "Pandemic has Changed Russians, But Can It Change Russia?" *Eurasia Daily Monitor,* April 21, 2020, https://jamestown.org/program/pandemic-has-changed-russians-but-can-it-change-russia.

factors. A Western information campaign blatantly aimed at triggering Putin's overthrow would be as likely to be exposed by independent Russian media as by the FSB. It would also just confirm the regime's long-standing allegations of a Western conspiracy aimed at regime change.

Aim for Slow Change?

An alternative goal for Western information efforts might be less dramatic change in Russia, even under Putin, that would advance the rule of law and internal freedoms. Ultimately this could lead to less adventurism abroad if Russia became more prosperous and its people had more of a voice about policy. These efforts would largely reinforce the themes already being championed by international broadcasting to Russia today—an emphasis on human rights, while celebrating stories of Russian charity, civil activism and entrepreneurship. A more concentrated overt campaign would vastly increase the volume and targeting of this content, while being transparent about where it comes from. Russian sources would be encouraged to create more such material themselves. Such a campaign would implicitly make note of government failures but in a context that spoke positively about Russians themselves; one example might be a story about how a rural doctor manages to serve her patients despite the poor equipment and transportation the state provides her.

Show our Teeth?

Some experts propose a "showing of teeth"—not aimed at bringing about immediate internal change but at demonstrating that the West can do IOs, too. The point would be to raise the potential cost to the Kremlin of further IOs abroad by demonstrating the vulnerability of the Russian information space, should the West decide to exploit it.

To truly impress Russian information operators, a demonstration operation would have to include everything they do: disruptive anti-government messaging with bots, false identities, cyber actions against Russian news media and outright disinformation. This raises ethical and practical questions that I will explore in the chapter on covert action. Even if Western actors acted by totally overt means, Russian authorities might still be taken aback by a demonstration of capability and will. The demonstration could be over something completely nonpolitical, like inventing a fashion idea or bit of slang to see if a messaging campaign can make it popular. Despite the innocuous subject, there would be a clear message to authorities that Russian citizens are no more immune to manipulation than those in the West.

One specialist fancied that a "teeth-showing" effort could be in the spirit of the so-called Doolittle bombing raid on Japan four months after Pearl Harbor. The 16 US bombers caused little damage on the ground but alarmed Japanese planners who, it was hoped, would turn their forces from offensive operations to defending their homeland. The situations are not exactly analogous, but the goal would be similar.

Keep a Line Open?

Another possible objective could be simply to maintain an open communication line to the Russian population, to be used in the event of a crisis inside Russia. Since major events in Russia happen by surprise, there will be no time at a crisis moment to create information brands from scratch. This was part of the mission of Western broadcasts to the Soviet Union during the Cold War. No one knew how the Soviet regime might end; the goal was just to hold on to audiences, gain whatever influence was possible and be prepared for future eventualities. Western countries invested in that strategy for four decades.

Today, Russian audiences with an inclination to seek out foreign perspectives are somewhat familiar with existing Western broadcasters. The *Voice of America* and *Radio Free Europe/Radio Liberty* claim to reach 7.7 percent of Russia's population.[25] At the same time, as independent news outlets, their output cannot be controlled by governments, civil society actors or anyone else; they respond only to the beliefs and principles of their editors. In addition, their staffs and distribution networks are subject to Russian harassment and blocking. To assure that other messaging capabilities exist, governments or other Western actors, including NGAs, can build new sites or social media accounts with almost any content, so long as they attract audiences and build a brand name. (Western broadcasters' content is heavily political, which appeals only to certain segments of Russians.)

Russia uses this tactic itself. It has created, alongside its marquee media properties like *RT* and *Sputnik*, lesser-known sites for foreign audiences like "In the Now."[26] Filled mainly with non-political clickbait, these sites seem to just be quietly gathering followers in anticipation of some future purpose.

Western governments and NGAs must make a decision among these goals if they wish to direct a strategically coherent information campaign at Russian citizens. Next comes the question of what the most effective content would consist of.

---

[25] "FY 2019 Performance and Accountability Report," US Agency for Global Media.
[26] https://www.facebook.com/inthenow/.

Tone and Segmentation of Content for Russian Audiences

Most of the content areas listed in the last chapter for pro-democracy messaging in general apply to content for Russian audiences as well. These include promoting the values of honest government, fair and open elections, free speech, rule of law, and an economic system that rewards hard work and entrepreneurship. Moreover, there is space for religious content. Other, more Russia-specific, content areas exist as well. The tone of the messages will depend on the larger strategic goals that are chosen. For instance, depending on the goal, messaging about women's issues could take a tough tone about the regime's indifference to women's concerns; celebrate women who break glass ceilings; promote a fashion trend as a test of influence; or be devoted to features and clickbait on subjects that attract female audiences. (That said, women's interest is hardly attracted mainly by traditional "women's issues"; women have been at the forefront of many democracy movements, often leading broad campaigns against disinformation and corruption.)

Messages must be segmented to appeal to different population groups. Outside analysts commonly see key Russian segments as those with pro-Western or democratic tendencies, those who strongly support Putin, and a silent majority who are patriotic and fear instability but otherwise have little interest in politics. If one believes a purported strategy document leaked in February 2020, Russia's Presidential Administration has identified six population groups that require differentiated messaging: pensioners, "patriotically minded citizens," Putin loyalists, youth, the poor and "citizens with critical attitudes" toward the authorities.[27] Beyond these political groups, audiences can

---

[27] "В Кремле подготовили методички для привлечения населения
к голосованию за поправки в Конституцию" [The Kremlin prepares techniques to get people to vote for the Constitutional amendments], *MBK Media*, February 27, 2020, https://mbk-news.appspot.com/news/podgotovili-metodichku/.

be segmented by age, profession, hobbies and many other characteristics that can be precisely targeted over social networks.

Messaging Themes

Understanding that those messaging to Russian populations will pick their tone and target audiences depending on their goals, here are some content areas messaging might cover:

Putin

The figure of Putin evokes many different feelings among Russians. Judging from the leaked Kremlin strategy document, Russian officials themselves are highly sensitive to how he is viewed in different quarters. The document said that to promote the 2020 constitutional changes, "patriotically minded citizens" would be told the amendments would help Putin save Russia from the machinations of "Ukraine, Poland and Navalny." The message to young people would be that Putin aims to ensure social justice and better public benefits. Those who want to Putin gone would be told the new Constitution would do away with "authoritarianism and unchangeable leadership." (The strategy document was drawn up before the proposed constitution was modified to let Putin rule until 2036.)

Putin's personality and character are a potential third rail for messaging by outsiders, since even citizens who dislike a national leader tend to become defensive when foreigners criticize him. It is better to focus more on what Putin's policies have meant for Russia—based on documents and specifics—rather than to make personal or sarcastic attacks.

Political Freedom

Demonstrations in Russia for free elections have emboldened democratically minded citizens. Manipulation of official news media on issues like the coronavirus is a generally accepted fact. Communication to Russians on such issues should be in their own context, not that of Western democracies. Much material is available on the distortions of Russian media, including from former media employees. On political freedom issues, the most potent messengers for political freedom may be people from countries that once were Soviet-controlled but now have built functioning, if imperfect, democracies. For all the Russian resentment toward Ukraine, the free elections that vaulted a trendy young comedian into the presidency brought many approving posts on Russian social networks. Other post-Soviet countries have similar stories that can be told through Russian-speaking citizens. Accounts of pro-Russian politicians who have formed parties and entered parliament in various countries may be particularly effective with Russian audiences. Regrettable as their success may be for other reasons, their cases at least show that Russia does not always lose from democratic processes.

Corruption

Some believe it is hardly worth speaking to Russians about corruption, since it is so well known to them. However, two dimensions may not be. First, there are Putin's personal links to highly corrupt figures, including evidence that he has amassed a personal fortune from his position. By all accounts, Putin was furious over the Panama Papers' corruption allegations against his inner circle and believed the whole investigation was a plot by US intelligence. He apparently was far from nonchalant about citizens learning of the wealth around him.

Second, while Russians know that government and business corruption are widespread, its dimensions may be beyond anything they imagined. Ukrainians were stunned when President Viktor Yanukovych's Mezhyhirya estate was thrown open to the public after he fled the country in 2014. They wandered in astonishment through the 350-acre domain's mansions, manmade lakes, private zoo and automobile museum. Russian leaders and oligarchs, even on regional levels, may similarly enjoy luxury well beyond what citizens might consider appropriate.

More than 80 percent of Russians consider corruption a serious problem, but only 11 percent think progress against it is being made.[28] Much corruption that affects ordinary Russians is on a grinding, daily level—at work, in schools and at public institutions like clinics. Communication to Russian citizens could highlight successful anti-corruption efforts in other countries, including those aimed at petty, everyday exploitation that humiliates citizens.

Poverty, Prices and Services

The lives of Russia's poorest citizens, particularly pensioners and those in rural areas, are dramatically different from those of skilled workers and the well-connected. Russia is one of the world's leaders in wealth inequality. In mid-2019, 12.7 percent of the population, or

---

[28] "Генпрокуратура назвала лидеров по уровню коррупции—силовики, суды, исполнительная власть" [Prosecutor-general lists the leaders in corruption: law enforcement, courts and government executives], *Pasmi.ru*, October 22, 2019, https://pasmi.ru/archive/245653/.

18.6 million people, lived below the poverty line.[29] Russians also express great dissatisfaction with education and health services—sentiments likely only to rise as a result of the coronavirus. Pro-democracy engagement can emphasize the degree to which corruption and foreign adventures have contributed to this state of affairs. Other countries, including major Western powers, have their challenges in this area; the degree of public debate allowed over the issue and steps that have been taken would be of interest to Russian audiences.

Emigration

Russia has a rich history of killing or chasing out highly productive citizens, from successful farmers after the Bolshevik Revolution to its Jewish intelligentsia and modern-day entrepreneurs. Between 1.6 million and 2 million Russians are estimated to have left Russia, mostly for the West, since Putin came to power.[30] Many recent emigrants say they left for better economic opportunities. But since 2012, there has been a rise in those who quit their homeland over Russia's lack of rights and freedoms. Russia has suffered many losses among citizens who are entrepreneurial, young, well-educated and skilled in foreign languages. Why such emigration continues to happen is a strong theme for discussion. Many recent emigrants are more politicized than previous waves and sympathetic to the anti-

---

[29] "Росстат рассчитал численность населения с доходами ниже прожиточного минимума, установленного приказом Минтруда России для второго квартала 2019 года" [The Russian Statistical Service calculates the amount of the population with incomes below the living wage as established by order of the Russian Ministry of Labor for the second quarter of 2019], *Rosstat,* August 27, 2019, https://gks.ru/folder/313/document/60982.

[30] John Herbst and Sergei Erofeev, *The Putin Exodus: The New Russian Brain Drain* (Washington: Atlantic Council, February 2019), ix, https://www.publications.atlanticcouncil.org/putin-exodus/The-Putin-Exodus.pdf.

Putin opposition.[31] They could take part themselves in such communications.

Feminism

Russian women have long endured sexist media attitudes, exclusion from top jobs, and help-wanted ads that ask female applicants to send a full-length photo. Now a new feminist consciousness is rising. It targets not only sexism by public figures (as in the Pro Feminist group's "Sexist of the Year" awards[32]) but a legal system that continues to wink at domestic violence. Feminist bloggers like Zalina Marshenkulova have built large followings. Emphasizing feminist issues in message to Russia leverages unity with feminist causes in other countries and intersectionality with other campaigns for personal and political dignity.

Soviet Patriots

Many analysts of Russian attitudes consider those who revere Soviet times to be the hardest to reach. However, what these people remember about the Soviet Union (through severely rose-tinted glasses) is a nation of minimal corruption and united purpose. According to a Moscow sociologist, a shift has taken place "from [Soviet] nostalgia driven by the imperialist past toward a nostalgia driven by a demand for social justice and for equality."[33] As Peter Pomerantsev notes, while these people can be expected to continue to

---

[31] John Herbst and Sergei Erofeev, *The Putin Exodus.*

[32] https://sexist-award.ru/.

[33] Grigory Yudin of Moscow's Higher School of Economics, quoted in Matthew Luxmoore, "Flouting The Law In Nostalgia's Name: Russia's Growing Movement Of 'Soviet Citizens,' " *Radio Free Europe/Radio Liberty,* May 25, 2019, https://www.rferl.org/a/flouting-law-in-nostalgia-s-name-russia-s-growing-movement-of-soviet-citizens-/29962523.html.

idealize a Soviet model of society, they can also be highly critical of Putin's modern-day Russia.[34] It is worth experimenting to see what common cause might be struck with these citizens.

Local and Regional Issues

The past several years have seen a burst of NGA activity inside Russia on matters of local importance. Whether the issue is a church to be built in a Yekaterinburg park or a proposed dump near Arkhangelsk for Moscow's garbage, Russians feel a growing sense of agency. Increasingly, they are winning battles with nervous authorities. They do not only demonstrate; they mobilize to repair roads that the government will not fix and help fight forest fires the government cannot contain. During the coronavirus outbreak, activists formed groups to buy food for the elderly and intervene for citizens who never received results of their swab tests.[35] Authorities, claiming they wanted to prevent panic, ham-handedly threatened citizens who tried to buy masks for poorly equipped doctors.[36]

Such citizen action in the face of government failings can be a "gateway drug" for Russians to take bigger steps to control their lives. "Those who are involved in the garbage issue today will be in elections tomorrow," says Russian journalist Sergey Parkhomenko. "The key is to make the link for people not between the garbage plan and Putin,

---

[34] Peter Pomerantsev, personal communication with author, March 10, 2020.

[35] Lyubov Chizhova, Aleksandr Litoi, and Robert Coalson, "Contagious Solidarity: As Russia Faces Growing COVID-19 Crisis, Independent Activists Gear Up to Help," *Radio Free Europe/Radio Liberty,* March 25, 2019, https://www.rferl.org/a/contagious-solidarity-as-russia-faces-growing-covid-19-crisis-independent-activists-gear-up-to-help/30509363.html.

[36] Mark Krutov, " 'Вы сами что, бессмертные?' ФСБ не дает волонтерам помочь больнице" ["Are you immortal yourselves?" The FSB won't let volunteers help a hospital], *Radio Free Europe/Radio Liberty,* April 7, 2020, https://www.svoboda.org/a/30536721.html.

but between the garbage plan and the kind of system that lets these things happen—weak courts and so forth. The overall goal should not be to obsess about Putin. It should be more about building civil society."[37] During the coronavirus crisis, public confidence in the state's ability to protect them has been falling.[38] By some accounts, citizens have been increasingly resisting lockdowns, seeing them as a pretext for repression and profiteering.[39] Recent polling shows a sharp increase among Russians who look to "citizen organizations, volunteers and non-profits" to help them through the crisis.[40]

A perpetual local issue is the degree of autonomy cities and regions have from Moscow. Strong regional identities, and a feeling that distant parts of the country were being exploited by the Kremlin, were among the strains that brought down Mikhail Gorbachev and the Soviet Union. In July 2020, demonstrations against the arrest of the popular governor of Khabarovsk Krai, in the Russian Far East, took on a distinctly anti-Moscow tone. Democracy communicators need to be constantly alert to regional developments and be ready to "narrowcast" content to individual regions through social network microtargeting.

Russia's Place in the World

The Kremlin's foreign and military policies have isolated Russia from the major Western countries from which it has drawn inspiration and

---

[37] Sergey Parkhomenko, interview with author.

[38] "Исследование социальных эффектов пандемии COVID-19: Сводка #12" [Research on the social effects of the COVID-19 pandemic: 12th Edition], *Sotsiologicheskii Antikrizisny Tsentr,* http://sociocrisis.ru/files/sac_report_12.pdf.

[39] Kseniya Kirillova, "Russian Population Does Not Trust the Authorities but Still Believes the Propaganda," *Eurasia Daily Monitor,* April 28, 2020, https://jamestown.org/program/russian-population-does-not-trust-the-authorities-but-still-believes-the-propaganda/.

[40] "Исследование социальных эффектов пандемии COVID-19: Сводка #12."

strength since the time of Peter the Great. With the collapse of Communism, Russia had an opportunity to reunite with the West, but Putin has made continued separation a foundation of his regime. He has even declared that "Russia is not simply a country but really a separate civilization."[41]

Much of Russia's population seems to be falling out of love with hostility toward the West. From 2018 to 2020, the percentage of Russians who feel positively about the US and EU has risen by 70 percent to a near-majority. More than three-quarters of Russians believe their country should be a friend or partner of the West.[42] Russian citizens' enthusiasm for foreign adventures seems to be declining. A majority believe Russia should end its military involvement in Syria. Only 20 percent think Russia should annex eastern Ukraine.[43] Authorities suppress news of soldiers and mercenaries killed abroad.

Western messaging can emphasize that Putin's foreign adventurism has denied Russia's people the advantage of cooperation with democratic countries and continues to divert national resources to unproductive military ends. In April 2019, Putin promised, for at least the seventh time, that he would end military conscription—an obligation that terrifies many young Russians. Such groups as the Russian Committee of Soldiers' Mothers have fueled a whole movement dedicated to winning medical deferments and protecting

---

[41] "Путин назвал Россию отдельной цивилизацией" [Putin calls Russia a separate civilization], *Interfax,* May 17, 2020, https://www.interfax.ru/russia/709039.

[42] "Russia and the West," *Levada-Center,* February 28, 2020, https://www.levada.ru/en/2020/02/28/russia-and-the-west/.

[43] See "События в Сирии" [Events in Syria], *Levada-Center,* May 6, 2019, https://www.levada.ru/2019/05/06/sobytiya-v-sirii/?fromtg=1; Stepan Goncharov and Denis Volkov, "Russians Want Crimea; Prefer Luhansk and Donetsk Independent," *The Chicago Council on Global Affairs,* April 3, 2019, https://www.thechicagocouncil.org/publication/lcc/russians-want-crimea-prefer-luhansk-and-donetsk-independent.

conscripts from life-threatening hazing. [44] Military service, and the purposes to which soldiers are put, is fertile ground for communication. Many democracies have done away with conscription. The United States has strong anti-war and veterans' movements that will resonate with Russians with military experience. Both countries' tragic military adventures in Afghanistan should bring their soldiers and veterans even closer.

Western messaging might also point out that Russia's separation from the West leaves it on a geopolitical path to become, at best, a junior partner of China—at worst, an economic colony.

Internet Freedom

Although support by Russian citizens for an unfettered internet is hardly universal, it is likely high among young and politically aware Russians. Authorities increasingly monitor what its citizens do online, try to control conversation on Russian social networks through bots and other covert means, and block foreign sites Russians want to access. International broadcasters already distribute tips to avoid blockages.[45] Russians should welcome more advice on how to spot bots and browse and communicate without surveillance. This kind of messaging can be designed as non-political; it positions democratic nations as allies of those Russians who believe they should have free access to whatever internet content they want.

---

[44] http://ksmrus.ru/.

[45] See, for example, instructions from *Radio Free Asia* about circumventing censorship (https://www.rfa.org/about/help/web_access.html) and a Russian-language video from *Radio Free Europe/Radio Liberty's* Crimean service on using the Psiphon proxy to access its content (https://ru.krymr.com/a/video-bezopasniy-internet-krym-realii/27893486.html).

History

According to the Russian polling company VTsIOM, 47 percent of Russians aged from 18 to 24 have never heard of Stalin's terror.[46] Against that background, Yuri Dud, one of Russia's leading young video bloggers, found it important to produce a two-hour documentary about the history of the Gulag. Western communication about this period does not need to be presented as something Russians should be ashamed of. It can be a story of heroism. Some in Russia and its empire stood up to the excesses of communism, protected potential victims and chronicled the abuses of the period.

At the same time, communication about Soviet history cannot all be about Stalin. Despite his brutality, Stalin led a spectacular Soviet victory over Nazi Germany that Russians rightly continue to revere. One can also recount far more recent history, such as the Chechen war and the ecological devastation caused by atomic tests and ill-advised economic projects. In these cases, too, there are stories of heroism to tell.

The English Language

English is not only the key to world travel and business but is highly fashionable among educated Russians. English words are constantly being imported into Russian, from *menedzhment* to *no-khau*, and with them comes the implicit message that the outside world has ideas of value to Russia. Although for most Russians any content from outside needs to be in their language, we should not forget the power of English in addressing elites.

---

[46] "Репрессии XX века: память о близких" [Repressions of the 20th Century: remembering relatives], *VTsIOM*, October 5, 2018, https://wciom.ru/index.php?id=236&uid=9344.

The Messengers

The most direct means of foreign communication to Russian audiences is through established government channels, such as international broadcasters and embassy social media accounts. Their identities are transparent; there can be little doubt about who runs the *Voice of America* or the @UKinRussia Twitter feed. At the same time, these channels operate within boundaries. International broadcasters view themselves as bound by their journalistic agenda, and embassy communications reflect official policy. If the State Department decides not to involve itself in Russian internal affairs, the US Embassy's Twitter feed in Moscow is unlikely to act differently. If democracy activists want to do more messaging about Russian internal affairs than Western governments feel comfortable with, or to paint a brighter picture of Western democracy than is currently fashionable, they will need to look for other outlets. Some non-government initiatives outside Russia do their own messaging to Russian citizens, such as the young Ukrainians who recorded YouTube messages for their Russian counterparts and Georgia's Information Defense Legion. The legion runs a Facebook site aimed at Russian viewers.[47] Russia, however, has a substantial number of its own democracy-oriented NGAs, barely tolerated by the government but growing in number.

Russian NGAs

Russia is a tough place for NGAs. Police can surveil, harass and arrest people for activities they consider anti-government. Even short of arrests, they can search activists' homes and offices, harass them on the street and penetrate their computers. Fortunately for the NGAs, Russian authorities have tried to conduct their harassment under a

---

[47] https://www.facebook.com/infolegionrussian.

veneer of legality. Any citizen has the right to criticize the government, they like to say, but groups of citizens working together could be brewing illegal conspiracies.

Under these circumstances many activists have decided not to associate in any formal way, says Sergey Parkhomenko:

> Given these many risks, many types of civic communities find that it makes sense to exist without registration at all—to be "suspended in the air." In this model, there is no organization as such, only a network of people, a community built on horizontal rather than vertical ties. Such an organization is not a registered legal entity. It does not have an address, office, bank account, letterhead, computers, servers, executives, or accountants. [...] Such an organization has nothing that could be blocked, confiscated, or arrested. It is unclear how to demand official reports from such organizations, file lawsuits against them, or hold them liable for fictitious offenses.[48]

Mikhail Khodorkovsky dissolved his "Open Russia" organization after Russian authorities declared it a foreign agent, so that involvement with the group would not endanger Russian activists. Now its work is said to be carried out not by an organization, but by various "concerned people." Maria Logan, a spokesperson for Khodorkovsky, says, "How do the Russians attack something in a cloud"?[49] Other groups have switched their status from non-government organizations to businesses, since Russia's foreign agent laws are aimed mainly at civil society NGOs and media.

---

[48] Sergey Parkhomenko, "How Can Russian Civil Society Survive Putin's Fourth Term?" *Kennan Cable,* No. 32, April 2018, https://www.wilsoncenter.org/sites/default/files/media/documents/publication/ken nan_cable_32_-_parkhomenko.pdf.
[49] Maria Logan (spokesperson for Mikhail Khodorkovsky), interview with author, January 9, 2020.

Activists still face substantial risks, even if they are not members of a formal organization. Those who take the lead in encouraging "individual" activities can be seen as instigating group action. Also, as Parkhomenko notes, "a non-existent organization cannot apply for a grant, cannot accept funds from donors in a transparent manner, and cannot submit reports to satisfy the donors." Some activists try to handle no money at all. Individual people pay for printing services, equipment and so forth with their own funds without passing them through any central person or account.[50]

Western governments, activists and foundations are naturally sympathetic to these NGAs, but they need very much to avoid the syndrome of "I'm from Washington and I'm here to help." They must be careful not to provide, at least in any visible way, cash or in-kind support that authorities could use to declare activists foreign agents. Russia listed Alexei Navalny's Anti-Corruption Foundation as a foreign agent in 2019 on the strength of two contributions wired to its account from the United States and Spain totaling $2,250. Such designations are highly dangerous to Russian activists since the term "foreign agent" in Russian implies "foreign spy." Navalny has reputedly planted people in his crowds with instructions to accuse him of being a CIA agent, just so he can publicly deny it. Foreign agent designations for media in Russia force them to report in detail to the government on their activities and to label their publications as foreign agent products.

If there is a silver lining to prohibitions on NGAs receiving funds from abroad, it is that they guarantee the groups' local authenticity. Russian journalist Leonid Ragozin noted that the 2019 Moscow election protests were "led by an entirely organic opposition which—thanks to

---

[50] Sergey Parkhomenko, "How Can Russian Civil Society Survive Putin's Fourth Term?"

Putin's own draconian legislation on 'foreign agents'—is reliant neither on Western funding nor endorsement."[51]

NGAs, however, can use publicly available material and ideas from outside sources at their own initiative. Investigative stories from journalists abroad that reveal malfeasance by Russian authorities, tactics for civil activism and software for secure communications can all be helpful without requiring any direct contact between NGAs and Western organizations. Western human rights groups and governments can also give awards to Russian civil society activists (even if the recipients cannot take the risk of formally accepting them). Awards not only confer well-deserved recognition but may afford a measure of protection. It is more difficult for an authoritarian regime to prosecute or harass a person who has been the recipient of international honors. During the Cold War, Soviet dissidents who were frequently quoted on foreign radio broadcasts and praised by foreign governments were less likely to be arrested.

Independent Media Inside Russia

At a Brussels conference on disinformation at the start of 2020, speaker after speaker deplored what they called Vladimir Putin's total grip on Russian media. Roman Badanin, editor of the Moscow-based independent site *Proekt*, offered a sharply different view. He argued that dozens of media startups in Russia, some of them doing courageous investigative reporting, are fundamentally changing the media landscape.

Investigative reporting in Russia did not arise as a reaction to Putin. Under Gorbachev's glasnost policies, Russian reporters tore into the secrets of the Stalin period. They produced one revelation after

---

[51] Leonid Ragozin, "Moscow's Elections Show Putin Is Losing the War at Home," *Time*, September 10, 2019, https://time.com/5672235/putin-moscow-elections/.

another about labor camps, trumped-up prosecutions and secret burials of executed prisoners. Investigative journalism has been surprisingly resilient in Putin's Russia, targeting official corruption and many other sensitive topics. *Proekt* has been active in uncovering details of Russian mercenaries operating in Africa and the Middle East. It also reported on help by Russian advisors to leftist Bolivian leader Evo Morales in his ill-fated 2019 election campaign. *Proekt's* staff continues to report despite threats and cyber harassment. The Russia-based *Conflict Intelligence Team*, referred to earlier, also has focused on the activities of Russian mercenaries. *MediaZona*, which traces its lineage to the punk group Pussy Riot, concentrates on covering prison conditions. *The Bell* is dedicated to investigative reporting on topics important to businessmen.

While a few relatively large media outlets like the *Novaya Gazeta* newspaper, the *Dozhd* television network and *Ekho Moskvy* radio have the biggest international reputations for independence, newer online-only media like *Proekt* and *Romb* are forming a second wave of challengers to Kremlin media control. It is hard for Kremlin loyalists to assert (though some do) that these media are universally "anti-Russian" or Western puppets. These startups hold authorities to account from authentically Russian perspectives. Many are local media, concentrating on issues in their own cities and towns.

It is not always clear why authorities do not crack down on independent media more. Common lines of speculation include:

• tolerating them makes the government look like it believes in press freedom;

• they provide an escape valve for liberal energies without truly threatening the state;

• acting more strongly against them would create martyrs;

- powerful figures like using them to leak information that damages their enemies;

- senior officials need their reporting in a country prone to over-compartmentalizing information;

- the enormous number of print and online publications in Russia (nearly 150,000 officially registered and many unregistered) are simply too many for the government to monitor.[52]

These publications need no foreign assistance in gathering information inside their own country. They have broad networks of sources and a fairly good idea of what they can publish without drastic consequences. Some have "secure drop" mailboxes to receive documents from whistleblowers. Russian outlets routinely do far better than foreign correspondents at breaking stories from inside Russia. Much of what we know about Russian troll farms has come from stories in Russian media. Some independent Russian journalists could serve as instructors for reporters in other countries.

The best way for outsiders to assist these Russian publications would be for foreign media to include them in more joint ventures like the Panama Papers investigation. Foreign media—and governments—might also monitor these media more carefully to make the best use of the extensive reporting they do on Russia's activities abroad. This reporting, with the authenticity of coming from inside Russia, could have impact in the countries concerned if quickly translated and publicized—just as documents provided by a Russian NGA helped sink the Russian nuclear deal with South Africa. When major Western media cite work by Russian reporters, the publicity can help them

---

[52] "Перечень наименований зарегистрированных СМИ" [List of names of registered media], *Roskomnadzor*, accessed July 31, 2020, https://rkn.gov.ru/mass-communications/reestr/media/

financially and afford a small measure of personal protection.[53] "Star power" can also help. A human rights organization founded by George Clooney and his wife, Amal, sprang to the support of Russian journalist Svetlana Prokopyeva when she was tried for "justifying terrorism" in 2020.[54]

Russian reporters, like civil society NGAs, can also be honored with prizes. Mikhail Khodorkovsky has been sponsoring for four years his "Journalism as a Profession" awards for Russian-language journalism.[55] Major Western journalism contests should try to make Russian-language work eligible for their prizes.

Influencers

The relative freedom of the Russian internet has allowed a broad variety of social influencers to flourish. Yuri Dud's trenchant interviews and skeptical take on Russia's leadership have brought him seven million YouTube subscribers. Zalina Marshenkulova campaigns for laws against domestic violence. Ruslan Usachev mixes commentary on gaming and tech with politics. Alexander Gorbunov makes sarcastic comments about the government on his @Stalingulag Twitter account, and Boris Grebenshikov sings protest music.

Sometimes the state acts against the most aggressive bloggers, but with the same tentativeness it shows toward most political protesters. A

---

[53] Roman Badanin, "Russian indie media needs visibility—that's why the Pulitzer row matters," *OpenDemocracy*, May 14, 2020, https://www.opendemocracy.net/en/odr/russian-media-nyt-proekt-pulitzer-controversy/.

[54] "Clooney Foundation To Monitor Russian Journalist's Trial For 'Justifying Terrorism,'" *Radio Free Europe/Radio Liberty*, June 22, 2020, https://www.rferl.org/a/clooney-foundation-to-monitor-russian-journalist-s-trial-for-justifying-terrorism-/30684398.html.

[55] https://journalist.name/.

Moscow court in December 2019 handed down a three-year prison term against Yegor Zhukov, a college student charged with extremism for promoting anti-government protests on his video blog, but suspended the sentence. Occasionally, Russians are arrested for infractions as small as "liking" an anti-government post. This may be meant as a warning to others, but it has hardly stopped online criticism of state authorities. Overall, the Putin regime has used little of the crushing power it could exert against influencers, perhaps out of the same motives that could explain its tolerance of independent media. The Kremlin's main tactic against critical bloggers, as with critical media, appears to be either to drown them out with large volumes of pro-regime narratives or to create so much confusion around controversial issues that no one knows what is true. [56]

The West's best course of action toward online influencers is to avoid direct contact. Influencers are independent-minded people who will suspect, and may even expose, any attempt to recruit them for political ends. They also risk being named as foreign agents if Western actors try to give them financial support. Like independent journalists, influencers thrive on public recognition, so efforts to involve them in international competitions and technology workshops are likely to be welcome. Also, their video productions benefit from clips that can enhance their messages. During the 2019 election protests in Russia, bloggers made use of clips from *Radio Free Europe/Radio Liberty* and other online sources showing officials stuffing ballot boxes or intimidating opposition activists. This is an advantageous relationship for both parties: Russian bloggers obtain material they can use without any formal relationship with foreigners, and foreign media benefit

---

[56] On Russian efforts to create pro-regime viral content, see Julie Fedor and Rolf Fredheim, " 'We need more clips about Putin, and lots of them': Russia's state-commissioned online visual culture," *Nationalities Papers* (2016) 45:2, 161–181, https://www.cambridge.org/core/services/aop-cambridge-core/content/view/85A39DFF45D461EA01B1E6999338C934/S0090599200019231a.pdf/we_need_more_clips_about_putin_and_lots_of_them_russias_statecommissio ned_online_visual_culture.pdf.

from their content appearing on highly credible local platforms. Social media "backshops" can also send analytics and advice to influencers, even without receiving requests to do so.

Offshore Russian-Language Media

Western governments and NGAs enjoy much more latitude in aiding Russian-language media based outside Russia. This slowly growing ecosystem serves three quite different sets of consumers: those inside Russia, people in formerly Soviet countries who speak Russian as a first or second language, and the growing Russian diaspora in Western countries. The Kremlin sees Russia as the eternal headquarters of the Russian-speaking media world. Many Russian-speakers abroad, even if they are not Putin fans, watch Russian television for an emotional link to the homeland. However, Kremlin domination is not inevitable. Emigre Russian culture flourished in Paris, Berlin and elsewhere for various periods in the 20th century; "online" is a new location where it can comfortably live going forward. The question is whether media outside Kremlin control can attain the scale and quality to challenge the Russian state's prodigious and attractive production.

Fortunately, in today's world of atomized online content, the Russian media diaspora does not need to match Moscow's production on a movie-for-movie or channel-for-channel basis. There is obviously significant value to Moscow's raft of television channels that people can watch all day. At the same time, audiences are attracted increasingly to films, TV shows, articles and podcasts that circulate online as products in themselves, sometimes barely referencing the network or country they came from. Thus, it is not essential to match Kremlin-controlled production in total kilotons. Success can come from producing a limited amount of content that is truly memorable. The Latvia-based website *Meduza* offers an its attractive combination of political news, investigations, and light content like surveys and puzzles. It claims that 73 percent of its audience is inside Russia and that its Instagram account is the most popular of any Russian media organization.[57]

In hopes of generating more high-quality production in Russian, the European Endowment for Democracy (EED) created in 2016 a Creative Content Support Fund. The fund provides €2 million–3 million ($2.35 million–3.53 million, in July 2020) per year to create products including films, satire, documentaries, talent and cooking shows. The EED also funds online text and multimedia outlets.

The same year the Content Fund was created, EU and US donors funded the Prague-based Russian Language News Exchange. Its mission is to edit and distribute content produced by Russian-speaking newsrooms throughout the formerly Soviet world.

Projects like these have produced much high-quality work, but two issues hang over them. The first is sustainability. While *Meduza* says it covers 80 percent of its costs with advertising and events,[58] many other outlets still depend on government and foundation funding. Jerzy Pomianowski, EED's executive director, says it may take 12–15 years before some of the Russian media the endowment funds find successful business models.[59]

One strategy donors might follow is not to fund individual publications, or small syndicates that must cajole independent participants into providing useful material. Instead, donors should concentrate efforts on one or two large "content factories" that would produce material for multiple outlets. Like wire services, they would

---

[57] https://meduza.io/. Statistics from https://meduza.io/static/ads/mediakit-rus.pdf.

[58] Galina Timcheno (general director of Meduza), personal communication with author, May 12, 2020.

[59] Jerzy Pomianowski, interview with author.

have their own staffs, big enough to produce high-quality coverage. When published on many platforms, the material would have more impact and credibility.

The second challenge for media based outside Russia is their mission. Do they exist primarily to counter Russian IOs, or simply to provide good journalism that audiences will eventually gravitate to in preference to Kremlin-controlled outlets? The Amsterdam-based NGA Free Press Unlimited, which oversees the Russian Language News Exchange, says on its website that the exchange's goal is only to "increase the access to balanced and reliable Russian-language information." According to the website:

> The Minister of Foreign Affairs, Bert Koenders, emphasized that the purpose of the Dutch government [in supporting the news exchange] is not to oppose the state media, but to strengthen independent unbiased media. "Counterpropaganda is ineffective and goes against our democratic principles. We wish to support the work of independent media initiatives without dictating what they should write or broadcast."[60]

Similarly, Pomianowski says the EED does not tell its grantees, including the Creative Content Support Fund, what to do. "The EED doesn't micromanage. If they want to do satire, or whatever, EED doesn't interfere. There are no strings attached. The only issue is whether they're professional and ethical journalists."[61] This raises the question of whether Western tax and foundation money is intended simply to fund good journalism for its own sake—much as the EU funds arts projects—or whether there is at least some long game aimed

---

[60] "Russian-language news exchange supports independent media," *Free Press Unlimited*, accessed August 3, 2020,
https://www.freepressunlimited.org/en/projects/russian-language-news-exchange-supports-independent-media.
[61] Jerzy Pomianowski, interview with author.

at countering the messages of Kremlin-controlled media. Certainly, those carrying out these Russian-language projects are no fans of the Kremlin, but funders will have to be more specific if they want these media outlets to concentrate on producing some specific effect. The work is additionally complicated because of the sensitivities of the Russian diaspora, whose members may be critical of Kremlin policy but still feel affection and nostalgia for Russia itself.

Finally, the existence of robust Russian-language media is not necessarily the goal of every post-Soviet country. In the Baltic States and Ukraine there has been controversy over whether state funds should be devoted to reinforcing the language of a country that threatens them. Some government officials would prefer that their ethnically Russian citizens consume no content in Russian at all, but become comfortable in their countries' main national languages. Investment in Russian-language content ghettoizes Russian-speakers, these officials believe, rather than encouraging their assimilation into the countries' larger populations. However, since people are highly unlikely to just ignore content in the language they know the best, investment in Russian-language media continues to make sense.

Penetrating Russia's Information Space

The Runet in Peril

The internet in Russia has become the only means of widely distributing content critical of the authorities. For now, authorities have shown surprising indulgence toward the 75–80 percent of the population that uses the "Runet," as the internet in Russia is called. Officials block the webpages of "undesirable" foreign organizations and some critical domestic sites, but internet users can still access the vast majority of the world's business, political and information resources. That said, Russian authorities are slowly increasing their grip on the Runet and putting in place laws and tools to restrict content even more, especially from abroad.

In 2016, Russia blocked its citizens from accessing LinkedIn after the company refused to store information about its Russian users on servers inside Russia. A 2017 study found more than a dozen news sites had been blocked in Crimea, most of them Ukrainian but also the Crimea Service of *Radio Free Europe/Radio Liberty*. In many cases the sites had not been officially declared as blocked, making it harder to challenge the government over the actions.[62] In 2018, Russian began blocking citizens from the popular messaging service Telegram because its owner refused to give the FSB the keys to its encryption. Officials are trying to tighten control over news stories displayed by Yandex, the popular news aggregator and search engine.[63] During the Moscow election protests in July and August 2019, authorities slowed or blocked mobile internet service in downtown Moscow and told cafes to switch off their wireless hotspots.[64] Such tactics have been used during demonstrations outside Moscow as well.

In May 2019, Putin signed a law that would allow authorities to disconnect Russia from the worldwide internet in extreme situations. Although the measure's wording implies this would happen only in

[62] "Минимум 22 украинских Интернет-СМИ полностью или частично недоступны в Крыму - мониторинг" [At least 22 Ukrainian internet mass media fully or partially inaccessible in Crimea – monitoring], *Krymskaya Pravozashchitnaya Gruppa*, August 2, 2017, https://crimeahrg.org/ru/minimum-22-ukrainskih-internet-smi-polnostyu-ili-chastichno-nedostupnyi-v-kryimu-monitoring/.

[63] "The right stuff. How the Russian authorities forced the country's top news aggregator to purge unwanted stories," *Meduza*, August 16, 2019, https://meduza.io/en/feature/2019/08/16/the-right-stuff.

[64] Anna Pinchuk, "Интернет закончился. Почему на акциях протеста не было связи" [The internet is gone. Why there were no connections at the protests], *Radio Free Europe/Radio Liberty*, August 6, 2019, https://www.svoboda.org/a/30093866.html?ltflags=mailer?utm_source=newsletter&utm_medium=email&utm_campaign=smi&utm_content=article.

the case of major equipment failures or a cyberattack, the capability could conceivably be used to block foreign content at any time or to shield the Runet if Moscow decided to launch cyberattacks against foreign countries. A legislator who supported the bill, Nikolai Zemtsov, speculated that Russia and other formerly Soviet countries could cooperate to create a separate internet where news from critical Western media was restricted. "It could be that in our limited, sovereign internet we will only be stronger," he said.[65]

Substantial doubts persist as to whether the project to isolate the Runet is technically feasible. The internet was designed from the ground up to be resilient against attempts to divide it into pieces. For two years, Russian authorities have not been able to block Telegram throughout the country; in their blunderbuss attempts to shut off all IP address that could be linked to it, they cut off a host of foreign-based banking, file storage and other services essential to Russian citizens and businesses. (This suggests the West would have a powerful weapon against Russia if it executed an internet cutoff in reverse.)[66] Russian authorities have also found that local internet service providers, guided by their own technical, financial or ideological considerations, do not always follow government orders to block sites.[67]

---

[65] James Ellingworth, " 'A monopoly on information': Russia closes grip on internet," *The Associated Press,* April 11, 2019, https://apnews.com/262960a3495f4cdd97153be18444446c.

[66] For a proposal to cut off some or all internet services to authoritarian countries, see Richard A. Clarke and Rob Knake, "The Internet Freedom League," *Foreign Affairs,* September/October 2019, https://www.foreignaffairs.com/articles/2019-08-12/internet-freedom-league.

[67] Igor Valentinovich and Ksenia Ermoshina, "Exploring Online Media Filtering During the 2018 Russian Presidential Elections," *Open Technology Fund,* May 29, 2019, https://docs.google.com/gview?url=https://www.opentech.fund/documents/11/Measuring_Internet_Censorship_in_Disputed_Areas_Crimea_Russia_ICFP.pdf&embedded=true.

Beyond practical problems, cutting off the Russian internet—or even stepping up controls already in place—could threaten Russia's own technology sector. Western companies have already cut investments in Russia, and many Russian developers have emigrated. Technologies like deep-packet inspection, which Russian regulators plan to use to surveil online activity, could hamper tech and other businesses by slowing down traffic on the internet overall. In addition, Russian researcher Liliia Zemnukhova notes the social effects of trying to control the internet:

> [O]ver the last 20 years, Runet users have enjoyed free and unlimited access to the web, without perceptible barriers, filters or restrictions. [...] Today, any attempt to impose restrictions, as well as promoting the idea of a "good user" as a "good citizen," provokes confusion and criticism in Russia. But real monitoring and regulatory actions will become a training ground for creativity around "how to avoid blocking." Russia's project of a "sovereign internet" is doomed to failure, even when presented as an "information security" measure.[68]

Because of all the difficulties involved, Russia may never manage to isolate the Runet. (Some say cynically that the main drivers of the project are officials who want to buy billions in Chinese equipment at state expense, make it disappear and then black-market it abroad.) However, even if the ultimate project never comes to pass, Russian officials seem bent on restricting internet freedom by one means or another.

Using present technology, authorities could block the sites of outside news media, human rights groups and even entertainment content that has the slightest political cast. They can also block more sites

---

[68] Liliia Zemnukhova, "The Kremlin is pushing for a 'sovereign internet.' But at what cost?" *openDemocracy,* July 30, 2019, https://www.opendemocracy.net/en/odr/whats-wrong-with-internet-isolation-russia-en/.

inside Russia that are critical of the regime. All of this can be done by official decree or, to minimize protests, be carried out on a staggered basis with "technical difficulties" blamed for outages.

Russian citizens are likely to respond to such actions just as Zemnukhova describes—by developing and sharing ways to circumvent the impediments. Email is hard to block, and a simple way to transmit content. Some already use virtual private network (VPN) connections and proxies like Psiphon to access blocked sites and conceal their own locations. The makers of some smartphone apps used in Russia have built proxy technology into them. The *BBC*, *Deutsche Welle* and *Radio Free Asia* have created copies of their news sites that audiences can access securely using the Tor "dark web" browser. Other technologies, like the still-experimental Ouinet, can cache webpages on the computers of large numbers of users, creating alternative locations for citizens to obtain content when the original source is blocked.

A host of authoritarian countries have been working on ways to defeat VPNs and proxies. This would make web blockages impermeable in the absence of new penetration technologies. However, Western government agencies, human rights and civil society groups continue to work on new access tools in their arms race against censors, and often succeed.

Non-Internet Options

Suppose Russia did successfully cut off the Runet from the rest of the world or implemented other technologies, like throttling down internet speeds, to strangle the country's main information pipeline?

These are some alternatives for bringing content to Russians:

• *Local intranets*. Content can be redistributed within small areas through informal "intranets" separate from the internet itself. Mesh networks allow people to share files from multiple computers that are within Wi-Fi or Bluetooth range. The range can be expanded by additional routers. Such private internets already exist in parts of Russia where public internet speeds are too low to reliably handle video. To access fresh content if the internet is blocked, operators of private intranets could obtain it by means as simple as dialing by phone into internet nodes abroad. For private communications, cellphones can be securely linked directly to each other by Bluetooth connections, creating an intranet of their own in a limited area. Protesters used such techniques during the 2019 election demonstrations in Moscow.

• *Shortwave radio*. Shortwave radio was the main means of long-distance broadcasting for decades. The technology is still commonly used in Africa and Asia. Few Russians have shortwave radios anymore, and international broadcasters have dropped shortwave to Russia. However, radio hobbyists have created a whole line of "software-defined radio" (SDR) devices, some the size of a flash drive and costing as little as $20–$30. These can turn laptop computers and smartphones into radios that can access broadcasts over a broad range of frequencies, including shortwave. They only require an antenna. SDR software can even receive DRM, technology that allows transmitting multiple audio programs, as well as web content, on a single radio frequency. (Russia has been experimenting with DRM technology in its far northeast.) Medium-wave stations—commonly referred to in the US as AM radio—can also be heard for hundreds of miles, particularly at night. US international broadcasting still uses some medium-wave to Russia. Russian authorities could conceivably respond to a new round of shortwave or medium-wave broadcasting with jamming, though in the Cold War they found jamming a costly and only partially effective strategy.

• *Text messaging.* In August 2020, the United States sent text messages to the cellphones of Russians across the country offering a reward for information about Russian interference into US elections. The action showed that US authorities already consider such messaging a legitimate tool to use.[69]

• *Satellite broadcasting.* Satellite television can reach millions of Russians directly, with no dependence on the cooperation of authorities. People in Russia can buy a basic satellite receiver and dish for under $100 from local distributors, point the dish at the right satellite and watch hundreds of networks at no cost, including the US government-supported *Current Time* network in Russian. Some satellite receivers can also generate a Wi-Fi signal that could be shared over mesh networks. The problem is that very few people make the effort to receive satellite television this way. Those who get satellite TV at all, as opposed to cable, subscribe to packages offered by Russian satellite companies. The companies provide receivers set up for the channels they offer on the satellites they use. If significant numbers of people started receiving and recording foreign satellite programming themselves, satellite signals could be jammed by transmitters on the ground. Authorities could also start confiscating satellite dishes from homes, as they do in Iran. (Fortunately, new satellite antennas are less conspicuous and can even be flat.) It is also possible to send SMS messages from satellites to cell phones on existing cell frequencies, including to many phones at once through the kinds of alert systems used for severe weather warnings.[70] Satellite systems can offer two-way internet service. However, Russia is already blocking proposed

---

[69] Julian E. Barnes, "The Latest U.S. Tool to Fight Election Meddling: Text Messages," *The New York Times,* August 6, 2020, https://www.nytimes.com/2020/08/06/us/politics/election-meddling-texts-russia-iran.html.

[70] "Falklands testing ground for satellite system that could revolutionize mobile connectivity," *MercoPress,* March 26, 2020, https://en.mercopress.com/2020/03/26/falklands-testing-ground-for-satellite-system-that-could-revolutionize-mobile-connectivity.

satellite internet services like SpaceX's Starlink by refusing to guarantee clear frequencies for their operation in Russia.

- *Person-to-person.* Unlike in Soviet times, many Russians have wide networks of friends and family abroad. An internet shutdown might not ban email, an easy way to transmit text, photos and video. Russians travel heavily and can buy or be given content to take home. Bringing content into a country in such piecemeal fashion sounds inefficient. It is worth bearing in mind, however, that smuggled audio cassettes of speeches by Ayatollah Ruhollah Khomeini powered the 1979 Iranian revolution—and activists then had none of the redistribution technology available now. In Cuba, slow and restricted internet has empowered an industry of entrepreneurs who sell news and entertainment content from large hard drives, copying it to one customer at a time.[71]

- *In true emergencies,* radio and wi-fi signals can be broadcast from balloons or drones. This is extremely expensive, and the signals do not go far.

One can hope that none of these technologies, with all their limitations, will ever be needed to communicate with Russia's population. At the same time, the West needs to have a "Plan B" in case Moscow ever tries an internet cutoff, even for a limited time. Some of these methods, like satellite broadcasting, require resources that governments are best able to provide. Nothing stops NGAs or governments, however, from moving now to promote SDRs and mesh networks. This might best be done through gadget hobbyists and movie fans. NGAs and governments can also establish dialup phone lines, ready to serve content in the event of internet blocks. Russia will

---

[71] Mónica Rivero, "Cuba's Offline Quarantine," *Slate,* June 1, 2020, https://slate.com/technology/2020/06/cuba-internet-quarantine-coronavirus.html.

try to be a step ahead; it is already looking at ways to block mesh networks and the dark web.[72]

Meanwhile, the challenge remains to create content interesting enough that Russians will make an effort to get it.

---

[72] Anna Baydakova, "Russia Seeks to Block 'Darknet' Technologies, Including Telegram's Blockchain," *Coindesk*, March 11, 2020, https://www.coindesk.com/russia-seeks-to-block-darknet-technologies-including-telegrams-blockchain.

Chapter VI: The Covert Arts

Advocates and Opponents of Covert Action

As we have seen, widely different views exist about how serious a threat Russian IOs pose. Some believe that for all the West's frustration over Russian successes, they amount to nothing more than a few lucky breaks for a weak and declining country. The West's best overall strategy against the Kremlin, in their view, is "strategic patience" while we wait for the regime to collapse.[1] Many believe media literacy and fact-checking will suffice to protect the West—in tandem with efforts to cure the social and economic fragility that makes Western societies vulnerable to foreign IOs to begin with. These advocates sharply oppose Western countries trying to use IO techniques in the other direction.

Others believe the information threat is so existential as to justify the full force of whatever response the West can bring to bear. When the West has felt its interests profoundly threatened, it has dropped atomic bombs, staged coups, tampered with elections, bribed journalists, invaded countries and plotted assassinations. Compared to that, is deploying a few bots so bad?

---

[1] Peter Elstov, "The Best Way to Deal With Russia: Wait for It to Implode," *Politico*, August 3, 2019, https://www.politico.com/magazine/story/2019/08/03/russia-separatism-vladimir-putin-227498.

This chapter deals with the covert arts—the operational and ethical issues around responding by undercover means to adversary IOs that are often covert themselves. The term covert action, as we shall see, covers the widest range of activities, from a bit of quiet help to an investigative reporter to spreading flat-out disinformation.

Opposition to Western use of covert information tools rests on two arguments: ethics and practicality.

Opposition on Ethical Grounds

Those who oppose covert IOs are not necessarily information pacifists. They may still favor aggressive messaging about democratic principles. They may even support cyberattacks against adversary IO centers. What they resist is any kind of "fighting fire with fire"— Western information subterfuge that would involve falsifying where information comes from or "shaping the truth" to fit a specific goal. They feel that such action by the West risks undermining the whole global information system, which for many decades has allowed democratic countries to flourish. Some believe that when Russians and their allies lie, it does them little harm because their credibility is low to begin with; but if the West becomes outraged by Russian falsehoods and retaliates by inventing its own facts, it sets itself up for a phenomenon that Mervyn Frost calls "ethical trapping." According to Frost, of King's College London:

> [T]he trapping effect is achieved when the target state, ethically outraged, launches large-scale counterattacks that themselves violate fundamental ethical norms espoused by the target state itself and by the international community. The calculation here is simple: Do something unethical in order to provoke a much bigger unethical response. This then enables the small actor to point to the hypocrisy of the giant which purported to be the

defender of fundamental ethical standards. This results in a decrease in legitimacy of the great power(s).[2]

Frost had in mind ethical trapping of Western states by al-Qaeda, the Taliban, the Islamic State and Hamas, but it could just as well apply to Russia as the smaller actor. Russian IOs jump to publicize any suggestion that the West, which so prides itself on "truth," engages in propaganda itself.

Aversion to spreading false information is shared not only by many experienced Western diplomats but often by the West's own media and legislative bodies. Western intelligence agencies have endured repeated media, congressional and parliamentary disclosures of covert information activities, such as planting false stories in foreign publications. When US officials weigh a covert action proposal, it is common to ask: "Will it pass the *Washington Post* test?"

Opposition on Practical Grounds

Other opposition to covert IOs by democratic forces is based on practicality. Western governments are not built for treacherous activities, opponents say, so they do not execute them particularly well. This belief was expressed by the German Marshall Fund's Alliance for Securing Democracy, a staunch opponent of Russian IOs:

> [T]he U.S. government must resist emulating the tactics used by authoritarian regimes when responding to [authoritarian attacks on democracy]. We have learned from our history that when we seek to carry out covert subterfuge to undermine democratic

---

[2] Mervyn Frost, "Cognitive Warfare—Ethical Dimensions," public lecture to Defense Leaders' Breakfast, Barton ACT, Australia, August 30, 2019.

processes abroad, including elections, it frequently backfires, undermining our credibility and our values on the global stage.[3]

Opponents of US covert action readily acknowledge Russia's skills in IO tradecraft, honed by decades of dedication to the art. To do the same on our side, they say, would require a whole new culture of secrecy to keep operations from leaking and—if disinformation is part of the plan—a cynical disregard for truth. Opponents sometimes contend, with a touch of pride, that there is no aptitude for information warfare in the West's DNA—and therefore, any attempt to outplay the Russians at that sordid game is doomed to inauthenticity and failure. Opponents also fear the West would wind up propagandizing its own people. This could happen if propaganda we distributed elsewhere found its way back into the West's own media or if democratic governments became so enamored of psychological warfare tools that they intentionally turned them against their own citizens.

Advocates of Covert Action

Advocates of covert IOs against Russia can draw inspiration from at least as far back as Harry Truman, who declared that averting a third world war might depend on the strength and effectiveness of US psychological warfare. Advocates of covert action today believe that however much is invested in defensive programs like media literacy, the West has fought fire with fire in the past and it is not a hard call to do it again. Opponents of covert IOs like to say "that is not who we are," but it is certainly who we have been. Accounts of CIA and British covert activities in the Cold War suggest how capable and far-reaching

---

[3] Jamie Fly, Laura Rosenberger and David Salvo, *The ASD Policy Blueprint for Countering Authoritarian Interference in Democracies,* (Washington: Alliance for Securing Democracy, German Marshall Fund, June 26, 2018), 19, http://www.gmfus.org/file/25928/download.

Western operations were—and conceivably could be again. The CIA obtained from Israel and leaked to the public Nikita Khrushchev's 1956 "secret speech," which electrified the world with its revelations of Stalin's terror. It set up a fake news agency—Continental Press Service—to spread anti-Soviet material abroad. The agency published a Russian-language edition of *Doctor Zhivago* for smuggling into the Soviet Union, where it had been banned. It secretly funded the Congress for Cultural Freedom, a platform for European intellectuals who were already anti-Communist. As participant Arthur Schlesinger Jr. later recalled:

> During the last days of Stalinism [...] the non-Communist trade-union movements and the non-Communist intellectuals, were under the most severe, unscrupulous, and unrelenting pressure. For the United States government to have stood self righteously aside at this point would have seemed to me far more shameful than to do what, in fact, it did—which was through intermediaries to provide some of these groups subsidies to help them do better what they were doing anyway.[4]

The CIA also secretly ferried money and a radio transmitter to Solidarity activists in Poland. UK agents worked covertly to counteract Soviet influence during elections in Italy and France. They produced large numbers of anti-Communist publications through a front publisher, and tried to influence *Reuters'* news reporting from the Middle East.[5] France used disinformation to hold on to its African colonies, warning that "Communism" could otherwise triumph.[6]

---

[4] "Liberal Anti-Communism Revisited: A Symposium," *Commentary*, Vol. 44, No. 3, September 1, 1967, 70.
[5] Guy Faulconbridge, "Britain secretly funded Reuters in 1960s and 1970s: documents," *Reuters*, January 13, 2020, https://www.reuters.com/article/us-britain-media/britain-secretly-funded-reuters-in-1960s-and-1970s-documents-idUSKBN1ZC20H.
[6] See, for example, Klass Van Walraven, "Decolonization by Referendum: The Anomaly of Niger and the Fall of Sawaba, 1958–1959," *The Journal of African*

After the Cold War, the United States and other NATO allies deployed psychological operations forces during the war in Yugoslavia. The US was reported to have planted false news stories to undermine Muammar Qaddafi in Libya.[7] In recent years, several allies have run covert operations against al-Qaeda and the Islamic State. The US Central Command was reported, in 2011, to have contracted for a capability that would allow one operator to control up to ten fake online personas in the information war with Islamist extremists.[8]

All this demonstrates that the West's DNA is not without a capability for undercover action. Even political liberals in the United States, who generally are quite wary of such activities, have been known to engage in them domestically when they feel the chips are down. In advance of the 2020 presidential election, Democrats were reported to be preparing to use artificial intelligence and network analysis to identify pro-Trump narratives on social platforms and boost counter-messaging through paid social influencers.[9]

Many democratic nations today feel tepid about any information offensive, let alone a covert one, against Russian IOs. Yet, an openness

---

History 50, No. 2 (2009): 269–292, available from
https://www.jstor.org/stable/25622024.
[7] Leslie H. Gelb, "Administration is accused of deceiving press on Libya," *The New York Times,* October 3, 1986,
https://www.nytimes.com/1986/10/03/world/administration-is-accused-of-deceiving-press-on-libya.html.
[8] Nick Fielding and Ian Cobain, "Revealed: US spy operation that manipulates social media," *The Guardian,* March 17, 2011,
https://www.theguardian.com/technology/2011/mar/17/us-spy-operation-social-networks.
[9] Isaac Stanley-Becker, "Technology once used to combat ISIS propaganda is enlisted by Democratic group to counter Trump's coronavirus messaging," *The Washington Post,* May 1, 2020,
https://www.washingtonpost.com/politics/technology-once-used-to-combat-isis-propaganda-is-enlisted-by-democratic-group-to-counter-trumps-coronavirus-messaging/2020/05/01/6bed5f70-8a5b-11ea-ac8a-fe9b8088e101_story.html.

to new covert efforts to affect public attitudes has built up among some Western government officials, military officers and NGAs. In 2020, Congress specifically authorized the Defense Department "to conduct military operations, including clandestine operations, in the information environment [...] including in response to malicious influence activities carried out against the United States or a United States person by a foreign power." The act includes approval for operations outside of zones of armed conflict.[10]

A Sliding Scale of Ethics

Much of the controversy over covert pro-democracy IOs comes from matters of definition. As soon as the word "covert" is mentioned, the minds of some leap to tactics like disinformation and forgery. Since they reject the most underhanded forms of covert action, they jump to declare that transparency should be the watchword of all information efforts.

However, the continuum of covert action goes for a long way before it reaches the most extreme end. Consider these hypothetical situations:

---

[10] National Defense Authorization Act for Fiscal Year 2020, https://www.govinfo.gov/content/pkg/BILLS-116s1790enr/pdf/BILLS-116s1790enr.pdf. Over the next five years, US Special Operations Command will enhance its Joint Military Information Support Operation (MISO) WebOps Center to provide "improved messaging and assessment capabilities, shared situational awareness of adversary influence activities, and coordinated internet-based MISO globally." See "Statement of Gen. Richard D. Clarke before the Subcommittee on Intelligence, Emerging Threats and Capabilities," House Armed Services Committee, April 9, 2019, https://armedservices.house.gov/_cache/files/7/9/7970f176-0def-4a2d-beb3-a7d5d69e513b/9C80F888EEE40D8E82ABFF5336C012C3.hhrg-116-as26-wstate-clarker-20190409.pdf.

• A US diplomat, on condition of anonymity, gives a newspaper documents proving a local politician has received money from the Russian embassy. The documents are genuine and the newspaper splashes the story.

• A local NGA creates a popular website that satirizes the country's authoritarian leader. To improve the site, the producers win a small grant from a foreign embassy to buy video cameras and editing software. The NGA decides there is no need to mention the foreign funding on the site.

• A free press organization wants to help an independent news outlet inside Russia. To protect the outlet from being labeled a foreign agent, it sends money through a hard-to-trace bitcoin transfer.

All these situations are technically covert, but most people would find them benign. In the first, officials give newspapers anonymous information all the time. In the second, why undermine a successful satirical site by forcing a foreign funding reference over a couple of video cameras? In the third, it would be reckless to transfer money to the Russian news outlet in a way that would endanger its staff. The International Senior Lawyers Project, a press freedom-oriented NGA, had no moral qualms about smuggling money into Crimea to help a journalist in legal trouble pay for a defense lawyer and buy groceries.[11]

One could argue that these operations would easily pass the "*Washington Post* test" (especially given the antipathy of major US media these days toward Russia). They demonstrate that information efforts do not divide neatly into overt and moral on one hand, or covert and morally dubious on the other. Sometimes the best way to

---

[11] Richard Winfield, "ISLP Media Law Volunteers Defend Freedom Worldwide," *Experience Magazine,* January/February 2020, 24, available from https://www.americanbar.org/groups/senior_lawyers/publications/experience/2020/january-february/islp-media-law-volunteers-defend-freedom-worldwide/.

accomplish a virtuous outcome with the least risk to the people involved is through non-transparent means.

Some assert that any use of covert tools "makes us just like the Russians." This is quite the overstatement. To begin with, Russia did not invent covert action. Engaging in unattributed communication puts us just as much in the tradition of Octavius and Mark Antony, the anonymous authors of *The Federalist Papers*, and many others in history who found disguised messaging useful in information conflicts. Beyond that, for Western powers to be "just like" hostile information operators would mean fueling racial hatred and denying historical facts. It would mean spreading word that (to reverse a 2020 narrative about Bill Gates and George Soros) the coronavirus was a plot by Russian oligarchs to slash the world's population.[12] Being "just like" Russian IOs is not a risk that Western governments are likely to run in the foreseeable future.

The best way to assess the acceptability of a planned covert action is not to measure it against some fixed standard of righteousness, but to ask a brutally practical question: How will it look when it all comes out? Most covert operations will be revealed sooner or later. Viewed in hindsight, will they be considered to have been legal, properly controlled and ethically justifiable? Veteran diplomat Joseph Nye sets three ethical standards for a government action: whether the goal was worthy, whether there was proper analysis of the chances for success, and what unintended consequences the action brought on.[13]

---

[12] For similar narratives from Russia and its allies, see "The Virus to Liberate us from Freedom," *EUvsDisinfo, https://mailchi.mp/euvsdisinfo/dr188-881685?e=fb718b27db.*

[13] Joseph Nye, "Do Morals Matter?" Walter Roberts Annual Lecture, George Washington University, video, January 30, 2020, https://www.youtube.com/watch?v=uX-8jneY3tU.

Beyond Nye's ethical criteria, the US intelligence community has identified certain operational conditions that characterize successful covert operations. They include using covert activities to the minimum extent necessary—as just one part of a well-thought-out overall policy. Officers should be given as much flexibility as possible to adapt plans to changing circumstances. US operators also believe it is extraordinarily difficult to quickly bring about a sudden sea change in public attitudes; the best covert information action provides only a marginal push at a key time. To that end, information efforts should first try to benefit from pre-existing views and trends. Then they should work to gently move people to a middle ground—and, finally, at the right tactical moment, to the beliefs needed for the desired outcome.

Examples of Covert IOs

While the overall debate continues about the advisability of covert action in support of democracy, covert operators—governments and NGAs—have not been idle. They have launched some activities directed at foreign states and discussed many more. The three kinds of "benign" covert action described at the start of this chapter, such as leaking true information about corruption to a newspaper, are examples. Moving further along the "sliding scale" to illustrate its broad range, here are examples of covert or on-the-edge activities that have come to the minds of those working against Kremlin disinformation:

• Using social media accounts with false identities to campaign for democratic causes or against disinformation. The goal of these accounts—run by humans or automated processes—would be to spread true information and pro-democracy points of view at scale, including to niche platforms outside the usual "bubbles." The latest tools of social targeting would be used to reach populations most receptive to the messages. Content could be original, or consist of retweets of posts by other people and organizations with pro-democracy outlooks. Messages could also be sent via SMS, which would have a very direct personal impact on recipients.

• Paying social network "hired guns" to make friendly sites appear more credible by running up their numbers of followers and "likes."

• Covertly funding social network influencers to challenge the narratives of Russian IOs and their allies.

• Putting popular sports and entertainment hashtags on political tweets to draw attention to them.

• Obtaining (through hacking or other means) documents that expose corrupt officials and spreading them by anonymous means. The information could be shared in small, "story-sized" packages that news media can quickly use, or they could be "dumped" in enormous quantities to tempt large teams of investigative journalists to analyze them in detail.

• Using "active reconnaissance"—communicating under false identities with known hostile accounts to develop a sense of what they are thinking and the campaigns they may launch next.

• Using fake accounts or identities to play hoaxes on anti-democracy forces, ranging from local disinformation agents and corrupt politicians to Russian soldiers.

• Creating websites that imitate the look of pro-Russian sites and have similar URLs but carry material with an opposite point of view.

• Creating clickbait websites or news sites filled with non-political stories, without identifying who is behind them. As they grow, gradually seeding them with political content.

• Creating news sites, even if the content is true, without fully disclosing the organizations behind them.

• Running a social media campaign and, simultaneously, what appears to be a counter-campaign opposing it. Monitor those spreading the counter-campaign's messages to identify bots and trolls. When interest in the exchanges grows, slowly change the counter-campaign's posts to "give in" to the main campaign's arguments.

• At the extreme end, creating intentionally false information.

Whether to use strategies like those above is something each organization must decide in line with its own ethical taste. One overall distinction among them might be drawn between using covert means to gather information or harass hostile operators, on the one hand, and deceiving the public on the other.

Gathering information would include tactics like active reconnaissance under false identities to smoke out adversary intentions as well as hacking to uncover genuine documents showing corrupt acts. True, false identities could be a violation of social platforms' terms of service. Hacking violates the law in most jurisdictions. Still, one could imagine that depending on the targets, such acts might not be met by universal ethical outrage. Facebook's terms of service did not come down from Mount Sinai, and activists who do hacking for public benefit have many defenders.

Deceiving the audience is a different story. Using bots with false identities to make a post appear more popular than it is, paying hired guns to drive up numbers of "likes," or simulating an opposition movement that does not exist means conning the very populations democracy advocates are supposedly out to protect. Justifying such acts requires a belief that they need to be deceived because they do not know what is ultimately good for them. This smacks of the elitism that angers populations and drives them to anti-democratic views to begin with.

Cyber

When most people think of cyber operations, they think of damaging an adversary's economic or military infrastructure. They do not think of the information conflict—other than the hacking of documents to discredit a target. In the last decade, however, cyber tools have been used increasingly in information warfare. They are being marshaled to attack the social network feeds or computer systems of news media, either to plant false information or to take them off the air.

In 2013, hackers claiming to support Syrian President Bashar al-Assad gained access to the Twitter feed of *The Associated Press*, posting a false report that there had been an explosion at the White House and President Barack Obama had been injured.[14] Stock markets plunged, with the S&P 500 losing more than $130 billion before *AP* could get word out that the tweet was a hoax. In 2015, agents claiming to be from the Islamic State but apparently with Russian connections knocked out worldwide broadcasts by the French television network *TV5 Monde* and seized its website.[15] A 2019 cyberattack against Georgia's information infrastructure put two major broadcasters,

---

[14] "2 Syrian nationals indicted in pro-Assad hacking scheme," *The Associated Press*, May 17, 2018, https://www.ap.org/ap-in-the-news/2018/2-syrian-nationals-indicted-in-pro-assad-hacking-scheme.

[15] "Russian hackers likely behind 'IS group cyber attack' on French TV network," *France 24*, June 10, 2015, https://www.france24.com/en/20150610-france-cyberattack-tv5-television-network-russia-hackers.

Maestro and *Imedi TV*, off the air.[16] In 2020, the Lithuanian *Kauno Diena* newspaper said a fake story was posted on its website saying an American soldier in Lithuania was infected with the coronavirus.[17] (Previous intrusions into Lithuanian media computers, widely blamed on Russia, included the posting in 2019 of a story saying the Lithuanian defense minister had accepted bribes.[18])

Some retaliatory activity by Western actors against adversary information centers has been reported. The United States staged a broad cyberattack, codenamed Glowing Symphony, against the Islamic State's propaganda network in 2016, deleting accounts and destroying material on servers.[19] The US reportedly attacked the Internet Research Agency on the day of the 2018 US midterm elections, cutting off staffers there from the internet.[20] The US may have engaged in other operations against Russian disinformation sources.

Such actions raise questions of escalation. While the Islamic State may not have much potential for cyber counterattacks, Russia does. Fear of Russian capabilities is a significant deterrent to action against Russia's IO infrastructure by Western countries. Another question is

---

[16] "Georgia hit by massive cyber-attack," *BBC*, October 28, 2019, https://www.bbc.com/news/technology-50207192.

[17] John Vandiver, "Hacking leads to fake story claiming US soldier in Lithuania has coronavirus," *Stars and Stripes*, February 3, 2020, https://www.stripes.com/news/europe/hacking-leads-to-fake-story-claiming-us-soldier-in-lithuania-has-coronavirus-1.617404.

[18] Valdas Saldžiūnas, "How Lithuanian defense minister became a target: cyber and fake news attack was just the beginning," *Delfi.en*, April 13, 2019, https://en.delfi.lt/politics/how-lithuanian-defense-minister-became-a-target-cyber-and-fake-news-attack-was-just-the-beginning.d?id=80897865.

[19] Dina Temple-Raston, "How the US Hacked ISIS," *NPR*, September 26, 2019, https://www.npr.org/2019/09/26/763545811/how-the-u-s-hacked-isis.

[20] Julian E. Barnes, "U.S. Begins First Cyberoperation Against Russia Aimed at Protecting Elections."

what Western attacks can accomplish. Two US scholars who have studied cyber escalation concluded, in 2019, that unless accompanied by significant economic or diplomatic actions, cyber action against Russian information operators can impose "friction" on their actions (making their work harder) but is unlikely to change Moscow's behavior in the long term. They went on to caution:

> It's not clear that U.S. military hacking of Russian internet connections will put a damper on Putin's global information warfare campaign. It's also not yet clear whether there will be—or even has already been—any sort of retaliation. There may be a point at which the conflict escalates, threatening the electricity grid, civic groups, private homes or voting systems. It's valuable for the U.S. to introduce friction against enemies who seek to harm the American way of life. But it's equally important to consider the potential for escalation to more widely harmful forms of conflict. This type of cyber offensive may succeed at pushing back Russian disinformation. Or it may just be the government's attempt to do something—anything—to convince the public it's engaging the threat. Quick wins, like shutting down a troll factory for a few days, could produce much bigger longer-term consequences in a connected world.[21]

For Western governments, much depends on whether Russia considers their cyber actions against its IO capabilities a true threat, or simply a shot across the bow—a form of "signaling" that Russian actions have been seen and analyzed, and that tools are available to retaliate if Kremlin IOs reach a certain level. At the same time, Russia must engage in its own calculus of escalation, especially if it is considering cyberattacks that could result in significant economic damage. The danger would be that the use of cyber in a tit-for-tat

---

[21] Benjamin Jensen and Brandon Valeriano, "Waging war against the troll farms," *Navy Times,* March 13, 2019, https://www.navytimes.com/news/your-navy/2019/03/13/waging-war-against-the-troll-farms/.

contest over information operations would spill into non-information areas with unpredictable results for both sides.

NGAs have more freedom to maneuver in the cyber realm than do governments. Unless NGA actors are extremely lucky, they are not likely to put *RT* off the air. However, some NGAs have been involved in hacking for information. In 2016, the Ukrainian group InformNapalm published an archive of emails from the account of Vladislav Surkov, then a top advisor to Putin. The emails were stolen by the CyberHunta, one of at least four Ukrainian hacker groups that have preyed on Russian targets.[22] In 2019, transparency advocates published a stunning 175 gigabytes of documents that various players had obtained from the files of Russian politicians, journalists, church officials and others.[23] It should be noted that, at least officially, many governments oppose any hacking by non-governmental organizations, even in retaliation for hacking against them. The French government–inspired "Paris Call," a 2018 document signed by 78 countries to establish ethical guardrails in cyberspace, called for signatories to "prevent non-state actors, including the private sector, from hacking-back, for their own purposes or those of other non-State actors."[24] The United States and Russia were not among the signers.

---

[22] Christopher Miller, "Inside the Ukrainian 'Hacktivist' Network Cyberbattling the Kremlin," *Radio Free Europe/Radio Liberty*, November 2, 2016, https://www.rferl.org/a/ukraine-hacktivist-network-cyberwar-on-kremlin/28091216.html.

[23] Scott Shane, "Huge Trove of Leaked Russian Documents Is Published by Transparency Advocates," *The New York Times*, January 25, 2019, https://www.nytimes.com/2019/01/25/world/europe/russian-documents-leaked-ddosecrets.html.

[24] "The 9 principles," *Paris Call*, accessed August 7, 2020, https://pariscall.international/en/principles.

Disinformation

Finally comes the domain of disinformation—intentionally making up and distributing information that is false. Ideally, the proper response to adversary disinformation would always be correct information. As a RAND Corp. study put it, "For democracies, the best antidote to disinformation campaigns is compelling factual evidence supplied in a timely manner."[25] With the evaporation of many of the West's Cold War talking points against Russia (its economic failure, its closed borders), respect for truth (at least as we see it) is one of the greatest remaining differentiators between democratic countries and the Kremlin. A strong argument exists that if we violate that value, however much we may be provoked, the whole democratic project loses much of its moral high ground. In this view, disinformation is the information equivalent of chemical warfare: something to defend against, but never moral to use offensively.

The use of disinformation is never likely to remain secret for long. The reason Russia can use it so effectively is that it does not really care if a false narrative is traced back to Moscow. Information is simply a tool to be used to an end. In contrast, many diplomats, intelligence officials and legislators interviewed for this story were adamant that disinformation should be off the table for Western use. During the Falklands war, when the UK broadcast radio programs to undermine the morale of Argentine soldiers, the programs' producers were instructed that "no lies are to be told."[26]

---

[25] Linda Robinson et al., *Modern Political Warfare: Current Practices and Possible Responses* (Santa Monica, Calif. : RAND Corporation, 2018), 232, https://www.rand.org/content/dam/rand/pubs/research_reports/RR1700/RR1772/R AND_RR1772.pdf.

[26] Chris Greenway, "Radio Atlantico del Sur," November 27, 2017, https://radioatlanticodelsur.blogspot.com/2017/11/no-lies-are-to-be-told.html.

In 1986, Bernard Kalb resigned as State Department spokesperson over the reported US plan to plant false news stories that would make Muammar Qaddafi think his aides were disloyal and the United States was about to attack him. In 2002, a news report claimed that the Pentagon's Office of Strategic Influence was preparing to plant false stories in foreign newspapers. The Pentagon ordered an investigation and said the reports were not true, but the uproar over the claim forced then–Defense Secretary Donald Rumsfeld to close the office.

That said, the West has a long history of engaging in disinformation. Allied "black broadcasts" that used false information to confuse and demoralize Germans in World War II were highly effective. (Winston Churchill said, "In wartime, truth is so precious that she should always be attended by a bodyguard of lies.")

In the Cold War, the CIA launched operations in Hungary and North Vietnam to create the impression that anti-Communist resistance groups existed there when they in fact did not. Under the Reagan administration, the Office of Public Diplomacy planted newspaper articles and spread false information to boost support for the Nicaraguan Contras. The UK forged documents and invented non-existent opposition groups to undermine Soviet front organizations and build up resistance to Kremlin influence in Africa.[27]

One can argue that even disinformation has a sliding scale of ethics, depending on the target. Today, many would be comfortable with almost any information campaign that dissuaded young men and women from going to Syria to be killed fighting for the Islamic State. Some argue disinformation is permissible in narrow tactical situations to confuse enemy forces.

---

[27] Lee Richards, "IRD Special Operations: An Initial Survey of the Covert Propaganda Activities of the Information Research Department," *Psywar.org,* January 26, 2020, https://www.psywar.org/content/irdSpecialOperations.

To many officials in major Western countries, Russian IOs are simply not existential enough to justify pulling the red handle of disinformation. NGAs in the eye of the storm may feel differently. For actors who genuinely fear Russian armed attack or that the next election will tip their nation into decades of corrupt, authoritarian rule, almost any action may seem worth trying. An activist interviewed for this study insisted that his own group would never spread disinformation. But he said his counterparts in countries that face stronger Russian IO threats have the right to feel otherwise. "We have a sense of respect for their fight," he said. "We shouldn't judge them because we don't walk in their shoes."

Another NGA member, from a Central European country, said a legacy of the Soviet era is that people have "a flexible view of ethics." He recalled that people in Soviet times used to say, "If you're not stealing from the state, you're stealing from your own family." People brought up with such a results-oriented mindset may not obsess over the fine points of messaging integrity.

Alert to the prospect of NGAs engaging in disinformation, a group of experts who collaborated in 2017 on anti-disinformation strategies said, "It may be important to have today's NGOs sign up to an ethical charter [prohibiting disinformation and propaganda] in return for funding."[28]

One danger is that false information planted by NGAs will make its way back to Western politicians and reporters, who would take it to be genuine and use it in policymaking and reporting. US intelligence agencies are under specific instructions to avoid this kind of

---

[28] Nicholas J. Cull, Vasily Gatov, et al., *Soviet Subversion, Disinformation and Propaganda: How the West Fought Against It* (London: LSE Consulting, October 2017), 57, http://www.lse.ac.uk/iga/assets/documents/arena/2018/Jigsaw-Soviet-Subversion-Disinformation-and-Propaganda-Final-Report.pdf.

"blowback" from covert action. Others may not share this concern—
or even see it as an opportunity.

'How much do we want to know about this?'

When judging disinformation or any covert action, Western countries
and funders must make two decisions.

The first is whether a course of action is so morally offensive that they
would never engage in it. The second is whether they can live with it
being done by someone else whom they are associated with.

We tend to think of covert strategies as something government
planners consider around a conference table and can simply decide to
discard if too unethical or risky. Potentially more common are
situations where governments or funders discover that an action has
already been launched by activists they work with. The choice then
becomes whether to intervene to stop it.

Consider this situation: A funder has a long relationship with a pro-
democracy group engaged in traditional overt activities like social
network campaigning and investigative journalism. The funder then
learns that some group members are paying hackers to steal
documents, and are creating false social media accounts to spread
untrue accounts of anti-democracy figures' private lives. The funder
would never have approved either course but is now confronted with
a *fait accompli*.

The activists involved will likely say they are doing this on their own,
not as part of the official work the funder is supporting. They might
also say the danger from Russian IOs in their country is existential and
that they do not need to be lectured to by foreigners about the morality
of their response. Should the funder revoke all support for the group

and its good works? Or should it just insist that the group's "official" activities be clean, ignoring what some members do on—as they will assert—their own time?

One consideration in this situation is whether the local situation really is existential enough to merit such conduct. The other is the degree to which the funder can keep at a safe distance from what is going on. In other words, "How much do we want to know about this?" Closely aligned to that is another question: "Can we know so little about this that if it all blows up, we can say we basically had no idea?" Implementers and other intermediaries offer a possible buffer that could let governments and funders support the main thrust of an NGA's activities without being fully aware of everything that people do in their spare time. However, if the actions the NGA engages in are objectionable enough, it is highly likely the original funder will eventually be identified and called to account. Funders will have to assess the specific covert tactics involved and their own stomach for risk—ethical, operational and reputational.

It seems reasonable, however, that even if no decision to use covert action is ever made, an array of capabilities should be at hand. Preparing for covert information warfare is not like creating biological weapons—mixing up something that has never been created before. Covert IOs, including spreading disinformation, use largely the same technology routinely used for advertising and the distribution of true information. However, skill sets and targeting data cannot be acquired overnight. Learning to target audiences on a rapidly growing number of social media platforms is a complex and ever-changing process. News and information brands must be created well in advance if they are to have any meaning in a crisis. SMS communication requires constantly updated lists of numbers. If we believe that Russian IOs are currently or potentially an existential threat to democratic nations, all means of opposing them should be available.

Chapter VII: Recommendations

This chapter summarizes recommendations from throughout this study on the best responses to IOs by Russia and its allies. I advocate a significantly stepped-up campaign for democratic values and against disinformation, better-organized and more assertive than most of what is currently being done. Russian citizens should be among the target audiences. The recommendations attach central significance to the role of non-government actors. I call for strengthening NGAs significantly through the resources of both government and non-government funders.

As we have seen, Western countries have periodically responded to Russian information activities by legal, diplomatic and economic means. It is rare to find officials of these states who feel these responses have been effective. At the same time, few have the ambition to take new, potentially risky steps in these areas. This leaves information strategies, which have been much less discussed, as a remaining domain for increased action.

The recommendations are limited in number because it is easy to disperse energy among many courses of action. I have tried to identify a small group of strategies that will have the most impact. Many of them can be carried out either by governments or NGAs, depending on which institutions are more committed or energetic in a country.

The proposals do not require any sudden hardening of attitudes toward Russia by top Western political leaders. This is unlikely in the short term. Even if there is a change in power in the White House in 2021 and Western countries begin to move more assertively against Russian IOs, tactics along the lines of those enumerated here are likely still to be the most effective.

IDENTIFY PROBLEMS AND GOALS

• **Determine to what degree Russian IOs are the problem.** It is dangerous to overstate the power of Russian IOs. They may not be the key source of anti-democratic or pro-Russian beliefs. In many countries, conflicts in society—and sources of disinformation—may be organic and local, fueled by genuine political divisions or local conspiracy theorists. Russian IOs should be spotlighted only if they clearly exist and have impact. Otherwise, looking for "Russians under the bed" only helps to advance the mystique of Russian power and ultimately will not be credible.

• **Identify goals.** This may require making a distinction between the fundamental requirements of democracy, such as political liberties, the rule of law and an independent judiciary, and a "values agenda" that includes social causes like abortion rights or welcoming immigrants. Decide if values goals threaten basic democracy goals and prioritize what is most important. The best message might be that democracy is not intrinsically linked to any social agenda, but gives all citizens a voice in deciding what social policies should be adopted. That said, there is no reason for democracy activists to accept hateful policies, however widely they are publicly supported.

STRENGTHEN THOSE OPPOSING RUSSIAN IOS

• **Recognize government strengths and weaknesses.** Democratic governments can be rich sources of funding and training to counter

Russian IOs. They can also mobilize public opinion and impose economic and diplomatic costs on Moscow. However, many either fail to grasp the danger of Russian IOs or lack the courage and coordination to respond effectively. Governments are often incapable of fast, flexible messaging.

• **Empower NGAs.** In many countries, non-government actors such as civil society groups, journalists and fact-checking organizations will be the most effective and authentic opponents of Russian IOs. Governments can play a decisive role in aiding them with funding and advice, while NGAs are likely to prove the most creative and flexible messengers. They are also less prone than governments to worry about "propaganda"; in their view, they are simply stating the truth.

• **Prioritize projects that can be conducted at scale.** To increase their impact, NGAs should concentrate on larger projects, carried out by full-time staffs with a clear chain of command. NGAs must realize that despite the virtues of being all-volunteer organizations, true effectiveness requires raising or accepting money in order to operate at scale. Small NGAs should try to join bigger efforts. Projects should be aimed at diverse audiences, including working-class citizens and those in rural areas.

• **Create regional "backshops" to sharply improve NGAs' social media capabilities.** "Backshops" would monitor hostile narratives and actors and spread word of new campaigns quickly to NGAs and journalists. Their expertise would give them credibility when they contact social networks to expose inauthentic activity. They would provide fast analytics to help NGAs tune their messaging for the greatest effect. Backshops could also take a more offensive role— identifying population segments worth targeting, driving up the visibility of posts by pro-democracy groups and helping NGAs create videos and memes.

• **Increase collaboration among NGAs of different countries.** In addition to occasional in-person conferences, develop day-to-day cross-border consulting mechanisms, similar to the regular collaboration of international fact-checkers and investigative reporters. Many disinformation narratives circulate from country to country. Collaboration saves time in rebutting them and helps identify key disinformation nodes.

• **Encourage intersectionality.** When it helps pro-democracy goals, align NGA efforts with causes like economic equality, women's and workers' rights, public safety, climate activism, anti-extremism and press freedom. Seek opportunities to collaborate with religious groups on moral issues.

• **Protect activists.** NGA organizations and funders should improve security procedures to protect activists, their families, documents and communications. Outside funders should make clear what they can and cannot do to protect activists working in dangerous situations.

STRENGTHEN FUNDING MECHANISMS

• **Prioritize large-scale projects for grants.** Give fewer grants, but for bigger projects. Encourage NGA groups to work together in large projects, even if they pursue different lines of work within that funding. Adjust funding structures to facilitate multi-year grants.

• **Reduce burdens on grant recipients.** Reduce paperwork and speed the decision-making process. Focus reporting metrics on indicators that truly reflect whether the grant's goals were achieved. Reduce micromanagement of grants and imposition of funder agendas that do not match local needs.

• **Provide support for underlying costs.** Provide resources for NGAs' infrastructure, including office personnel and expenses. The operation of pro-democracy projects at scale depends on infrastructure that can support large-scale undertakings. Allow NGAs to accept advertising on their sites.

• **Increase donor coordination.** Donors should jointly identify large-scale projects to which they will all contribute, rather than sponsoring many small undertakings that may duplicate each other or attain minimal results. Funders should be prepared to subordinate niche goals that particular donors cherish in favor of big-picture democratic goals.

COMBAT HOSTILE DISINFORMATION

• **Block or not?** Blocking Russian information outlets is counterproductive because it can raise audience interest in "forbidden fruit." Blocking also buys into the Kremlin's notion that governments should rule over the information its citizens receive. However, democratic countries that create content for Russian citizens have a basis to demand that access to audiences be the same in both directions.

• **Attack or soothe?** Based on local situations, determine whether the best strategy against disinformation is to attack hostile operators with the same aggressiveness and snark they use, or to encourage more reasonable, respectful conversation in the hope it will lead to less polarization and more democratic outcomes. The determination should be based not on personal preference, but on testing.

• **Respond better to disinformation that gains traction.** Much disinformation should be ignored, but some claims are harmful enough that they need to be denied immediately. If governments cannot respond quickly and vigorously, NGAs must fill the gap, using their own subject-matter experts and graphic and meme capabilities. Call out by name the source of the disinformation. Explain the hypocrisy behind the claim or the motivations likely at work. In breaking news situations, it may be necessary to point out that the truth is simply unknowable at that moment, and to briefly note the welter of contradictory theories just to make clear that baseless narratives exist on all sides.

• **Kill the messenger.** Whenever possible, focus not on responding to specific disinformation claims but on the credibility of the outlets that originate them. Use a few examples of obviously false or bizarre content to make clear that nothing from those outlets should be trusted. Use "crossing their channels" to expose compartmentalized, hypocritical disinformation techniques.

• **Defund and degrade disinformation outlets.** Campaign to deny advertising to disinformation outlets and to boycott companies whose ads appear on their sites. Pressure advertising networks not to serve ads to disinformation outlets that have been identified by reliable NGAs. (An appeal process should exist for sites that feel they were wrongly listed.) Web hosting and other technical support services should be urged to drop disinformation outlets as customers. NGAs should expose social media mercenaries who promote hostile narratives or help disinformation sites falsify their number of followers.

• **Set achievable tasks for social networks.** No matter how many people demand it, social networks will never be able to remove all disinformation—especially considering that even factual information can be used to misleading ends. Achievable tasks for the networks would be to make their staffs easily reachable at any hour by governments and NGAs to take down clearly harmful material; to step up their own monitoring of content; to further fund fact-checking efforts; to make sure that fact checks travel to anyone who saw or engaged with false information; and to ban precision targeting of messages on political and other controversial subjects.

STRENGTHEN PRO-DEMOCRACY MESSAGING

• **Do not be ashamed of democracy.** No society can completely fulfill its citizens' expectations. However, this does not mean that people elsewhere do not still admire democracies or want to bring liberty to their countries. Defend democracy, despite its failings, as the best route to the future that most people want. Emphasize the contributions of organizations like the European Union and NATO to the prosperity and security of their members and partners.

• **Define a message and stay on it.** Establish a set of overarching "bumper sticker" messages for each audience and come back to them repeatedly. The most useful overall themes will likely be free speech, prosperity, the struggle against corruption, charity and compassion and (to the degree the target audience is interested in Russia) the failings of Kremlin policy. The word "democracy" itself may or may not be effective, depending on whether it has been well-enshrined as a public value, or if anti-democratic forces have besmirched the term into uselessness.

• **Segment the audience.** Devise a message subset and tone for each audience, and target that group through social networks, chain emails or whatever vehicle that group uses most. Do not neglect political elites; even in countries where Russian IOs are not active, knowledge of Kremlin practices can build immunity to future operations.

• **Cultivate effective, economical messaging vehicles.** Develop podcasts, memes, graphic novels, computer animations, video games, low-power radio and other inexpensive vehicles to carry pro-democracy messaging. The goal should be to create and promote a small number of highly popular, viral productions in place of dispersing energy among projects with less visibility. Work to increase the visibility of existing content created by others—TV shows, video blogs, satire, etc.—that carries desirable messages. Attract attention on social networks by buying search terms, creating special-interest sites and developing chatbots.

• **Target support for independent journalism and fact-checking to larger-scale players.** Focus support on a small number of independent media and fact-checking groups in order to maximize their staffing and market share. Unless media projects in individual cities and regions have their own successful revenue models, encourage them to operate under the umbrellas of larger organizations. To build audience, urge publishers and fact-checkers to include entertainment, business and sports content along with political themes. Promote involvement in cross-border reporting and fact-checking projects. Create an NGA-run offshore center to fact-check statements by Russian officials. Provide international recognition for successful and courageous work. Urge international news agencies and foundations to provide news, photos and video at concessional rates to media in at-risk countries.

• **Leverage the strength of international broadcasters.** In addition to creating their own programming, international broadcasters should function as production houses for programs prepared by NGAs. They should lend support in writing, reporting and production of broadcast and web materials. The broadcasters should then aggregate the best of this content into their own output, clearly identifying the organization responsible for each. For their own programming, international broadcasters should seek to define more clearly if they should be rigidly objective, part of their countries' diplomatic "soft power" or something in-between—and align their output with that definition.

IMPROVE CONTENT FOR RUSSIAN-SPEAKING AUDIENCES

• **Decide on goals.** This will determine both tone and content. For citizens inside Russia, the wisest goals at present are to encourage slow, positive change in Russian society and keep a line of communication open for future contingencies, rather than try to bring about sudden change. For the Russian diaspora, balance content critical of Kremlin policy with respect for audience affection and nostalgia for their Russian heritage.

• **Segment the Russian audience.** Recognize political differences among Russian-speaking populations, and appreciate that some people are not particularly interested in politics at all. Pitch communication to the interests of each group, but do not send contradictory messages that could be grist for Russian efforts to "cross our channels."

• **Encourage independent voices inside Russia—carefully.** Russian civil society, independent media, bloggers and influencers are critical to democratic development in Russia. However, outsiders must be careful not to jeopardize their safety with actions that could lead them to be branded "foreign agents." The safest and most effective assistance is likely to be training; the posting of video clips and other content that they can use without a contractual relationship; involvement in cross-border reporting projects; republishing of their content by outside networks and sites; and international recognition and awards.

• **Strengthen the content of Russian-language outlets based outside Russia.** Outlets should define and transparently state their mission: journalism with a political intent, fully objective journalism or just "good reading"? The organization should then focus its work on those goals for the greatest effectiveness. Develop joint projects among outlets, to be published by all of them for the greatest impact. Instead of many fragmented outlets, work toward a smaller number of organizations, each with larger reporting, editing and multimedia capabilities. Prioritize unified organizations with strong editing structures over looser groups that try to "coordinate" the efforts of independent organizations.

• **Prepare for Kremlin efforts to block communication to its citizens.** Anticipate increasing interference with pro-democracy communication to Russian citizens, as well as added blocking of content from within Russia that the government considers disloyal. Develop workarounds and begin raising consciousness among Russian citizens about the threat and alternative ways to access content.

UNDERSTAND THE RISKS AND BENEFITS OF COVERT ACTION

• **Minimize covert activities.** Covert methods are difficult to manage and keep secure. If they must be used, they should be part of a well-conceived overall policy that includes transparent elements as well. Recognize that the degree to which a situation justifies covert action may vary in the eyes of local activists and more distant funders.

• **Set operational and ethical boundaries.** Create clear definitions of actions that are almost always acceptable (such as discreet funding mechanisms to protect endangered NGAs); actions that require deliberation case by case; and acts that may consider unacceptable at the current stage of the information war, like spreading disinformation. Consider whether a covert strategy under consideration is targeted only at adversary actors, or if it also has the effect of deceiving the very population one is trying to protect from authoritarianism.

• **Assume exposure.** Assume that covert actions will be exposed sooner or later, and that they will need to be publicly justified in terms of their goals and the need for them to have been covert.

• **Prepare for everything.** If we believe that IOs by Russia and its allies are currently or potentially an existential threat to democratic nations, no means of opposing them should be off the table. These could include cyberattacks against information hubs and spreading disinformation. These tactics are best used in quite limited situations to "signal" a capability that could be deployed more extensively, depending on the adversary's future behavior.

Bibliography

"2 Syrian nationals indicted in pro-Assad hacking scheme," *The Associated Press,* May 17, 2018, https://www.ap.org/ap-in-the-news/2018/2-syrian-nationals-indicted-in-pro-assad-hacking-scheme.

"95% subscriber growth in less than 3 years: How a news startup is driving reader revenue with its own CRM," *What's New In Publishing,* September 25, 2019, https://whatsnewinpublishing.com/95-subscriber-growth-in-less-than-3-years-how-a-news-startup-is-driving-reader-revenue-with-its-own-crm.

2018 Ranking of countermeasures by the EU28 to the Kremlin's subversion operations, Kremlin Watch Report (Prague: European Values Center for Security Policy, 2018), https://www.kremlinwatch.eu/userfiles/2018-ranking-of-countermeasures-by-the-eu28-to-the-kremlin-s-subversion-operations.pdf.

Africa Check, Chequeado, and Full Fact, "Fact checking doesn't work (the way you think it does)," *Full Fact,* June 20, 2019, https://fullfact.org/blog/2019/jun/how-fact-checking-works/.

A multi-dimensional approach to disinformation: Report of the independent High Level Group on fake news and online disinformation (Brussels: European Union, 2018), http://ec.europa.eu/newsroom/dae/document.cfm?doc_id=50271.

"Ansip uncovered: Commission Vice-President on disinformation, Huawei, copyright," *EurActiv,* January 23, 2019, https://www.euractiv.com/section/cybersecurity/interview/ansip -uncovered-commission-vice-president-on-disinformation- huawei-copyright/.

"An Update on How We Are Doing At Enforcing Our Community Standards," Facebook, May 23, 2019, https://about.fb.com/news/2019/05/enforcing-our-community- standards-3/.

"April 2020 Coordinated Inauthentic Behavior Report," Facebook, May 5, 2020, https://about.fb.com/news/2020/05/april-cib- report/.

Badanin, Roman, "Russian indie media needs visibility—that's why the Pulitzer row matters," *OpenDemocracy,* May 14, 2020, https://www.opendemocracy.net/en/odr/russian-media-nyt- proekt-pulitzer-controversy/.

Barbashin, Anton, "Improving the Western strategy to combat Kremlin propaganda and disinformation," *Atlantic Council,* June 11, 2018, 6, https://www.atlanticcouncil.org/wp- content/uploads/2018/06/Improving_the_Western_Strategy.pdf.

Barker, Alex, "Third of top brands likely to suspend social media spending, survey finds," *Financial Times,* June 30, 2020, https://www.ft.com/content/aa723316-67e6-41a3-9f37- e9c6b8855edb?utm_campaign=meetedgar&utm_medium=social &utm_source=meetedgar.com.

Barnes, Julian E., "The Latest U.S. Tool to Fight Election Meddling: Text Messages," *The New York Times,* August 6,

2020, https://www.nytimes.com/2020/08/06/us/politics/election-meddling-texts-russia-iran.html.

Barnes, Julian E., "U.S. Begins First Cyberoperation Against Russia Aimed at Protecting Elections," *The New York Times,* October 28, 2018, https://www.nytimes.com/2018/10/23/us/politics/russian-hacking-usa-cyber-command.html

Baydakova, Anna, "Russia Seeks to Block 'Darknet' Technologies, Including Telegram's Blockchain," *Coindesk*, March 11, 2020, https://www.coindesk.com/russia-seeks-to-block-darknet-technologies-including-telegrams-blockchain.

"Boosting Immunity to Disinformation: Ukrainian students better detect false information after teachers integrate media literacy into standard subjects," *IREX*, https://www.irex.org/sites/default/files/node/resource/evaluation-learn-to-discern-in-schools-ukraine.pdf.

Bradshaw, Samantha and Phillip N. Howard, *The Global Disinformation Order: 2019 Global Inventory of Organised Social Media Manipulation"* (Oxford: Oxford Internet Institute, September 26, 2019), https://comprop.oii.ox.ac.uk/wp-content/uploads/sites/93/2019/09/CyberTroop-Report19.pdf.

Bradshaw, Samantha, Lisa-Maria Neudert, and Philip N. Howard, *Government responses to malicious use of social media* (Riga: NATO Stratcom Centre of Excellence, 2018), https://www.stratcomcoe.org/download/file/fid/79655.

"Briefing on Disinformation and Propaganda Related to COVID-19 (remarks by Lea Gabrielle), US State Department, March 27, 2020, https://www.state.gov/briefing-with-special-envoy-lea-gabrielle-global-engagement-center-on-disinformation-and-propaganda-related-to-covid-19/.

Broderick, Ryan, "Trump Supporters Online Are Pretending To Be French To Manipulate France's Election," *Buzzfeed*, January 24, 2017, https://www.buzzfeednews.com/article/ryanhatesthis/inside-the-private-chat-rooms-trump-supporters-are-using-to#.tfQGYyveA.

"Brussels Forum 2020: A Conversation with Josep Borrell," video, German Marshall Fund, June 22, 2020, https://www.youtube.com/watch?v=LrEdjsmB3j8&list=PLRlpW88SeBSPD79WFzP9jpawQGDyapjYM&index=16&t=905s.

Buyniski, Helen, "Just (MSM-approved) facts, ma'am! Response to FB's political ad decision shows 'media literacy' was just cover for thought-police," *RT*, January 9, 2020, https://www.rt.com/usa/477861-facebook-factcheck-political-ad-targeting/.

Cabinet Office, "Semantic Visions wins $250,000 Tech Challenge to Combat Disinformation, news release, March 11, 2019, https://www.wired-gov.net/wg/news.nsf/articles/Semantic+Visions+wins+$250000+Tech+Challenge+to+Combat+Disinformation+11032019112000?open.

"Četiri aviona sa medicinskom pomoći i lekarima iz Rusije sleteli u Batajnicu" [Four planes with medical aid and doctors from Russia land in Batajnica], *N1*, April 3, 2020, http://rs.n1info.com/Vesti/a585344/Avioni-sa-medicinskom-pomoci-i-lekarima-iz-Rusije-sleteli-u-Batajnicu.html.

Chaguaceda, Armando, "El Oso va a Occidente" [The Bear Heads West], *Foreign Affairs Latinoamérica*, Vol. 18, No. 3, July–September 2018, https://www.academia.edu/38165496/El_oso_va_a_Occidente._La_agenda_rusa_en_Latinoam%C3%A9rica.

Chizhova, Lyubov, Aleksandr Litoi, and Robert Coalson, "Contagious Solidarity: As Russia Faces Growing COVID-19 Crisis, Independent Activists Gear Up to Help," *Radio Free Europe/Radio Liberty,* March 25, 2019, https://www.rferl.org/a/contagious-solidarity-as-russia-faces-growing-covid-19-crisis-independent-activists-gear-up-to-help/30509363.html.

"Civil Society Tracks Trolls and Fakes, Prompts Facebook Action in Moldova," *Internews,* February 21, 2019, https://internews.org/story/civil-society-tracks-trolls-and-fakes-prompts-facebook-action-moldova.

Clarke, Richard A. and Rob Knake, "The Internet Freedom League," *Foreign Affairs,* September/October 2019, https://www.foreignaffairs.com/articles/2019-08-12/internet-freedom-league.

"Clooney Foundation To Monitor Russian Journalist's Trial For 'Justifying Terrorism,'" *Radio Free Europe/Radio Liberty*, June 22, 2020, https://www.rferl.org/a/clooney-foundation-to-monitor-russian-journalist-s-trial-for-justifying-terrorism-/30684398.html.

Collins, Ben, "Jenna Abrams, Russia's Clown Troll Princess, Duped the Mainstream Media and the World," *Daily Beast,* November 3, 2017, https://www.thedailybeast.com/jenna-abrams-russias-clown-troll-princess-duped-the-mainstream-media-and-the-world.

Conger, Kate and Nathaniel Popper, "Behind the Scenes, 8chan Scrambles to Get Back Online," *The New York Times,* August 5, 2019, https://www.nytimes.com/2019/08/05/technology/8chan-website-online.html.

Cook, Lorne and Samuel Petrequin, "Legal opinion: Poland, Hungary, Czechs broke EU migrant law," *The Associated Press,* October 31, 2019, https://apnews.com/353b99a01ae949958d730b59737ee0a2.

Coppock, Alexander, Andrew Guess, et al., "When Treatments are Tweets: A Network Mobilization Experiment over Twitter," *Political Behavior,* 38 (2016), available from https://link.springer.com/article/10.1007/s11109-015-9308-6#page-1.

Corasaniti, Nick, "How Immigrant Twin Brothers Are Beating Trump's Team on Facebook," *The New York Times,* May 18, 2020, https://www.nytimes.com/2020/05/18/us/politics/occupy-democrats-facebook.html.

"Coronavirus: an unprecedented challenge to democracy?" *Euronews,* April 9, 2020, https://www.euronews.com/2020/04/09/coronavirus-an-unprecedented-challenge-to-democracy.

"COVID-19 in CEE," *GLOBSEC,* April 17, 2020, https://mailchi.mp/GLOBSEC/covid-19-in-cee-weekly-roundup_corona-disinfo-and-impact-on-democracy-k4kbhjppfm?e=9421bc0cee.

"COVID-19 Infodemic: Push and Pull Factors," video, GLOBSEC, May 28, 2020, https://www.facebook.com/GLOBSECforum/videos/2741100437 80526.

Cull, Nicholas J., Vasily Gatov, et al., *Soviet Subversion, Disinformation and Propaganda: How the West Fought Against It* (London: LSE Consulting, October 2017), http://www.lse.ac.uk/iga/assets/documents/arena/2018/Jigsaw-Soviet-Subversion-Disinformation-and-Propaganda-Final-Report.pdf.

Cull, Nicholas J., "The Tightrope to Tomorrow: Reputational Security, Collective Vision and the Future of Public Diplomacy," *The Hague Journal of Diplomacy 14 (2019)*, https://nsiteam.com/social/wp-content/uploads/2019/06/Cull-Conclusion_HJD_014_01-02.pdf.

Cyber-enabled Information Operations, Hearing of the Subcommittee on Cybersecurity, Senate Armed Services Committee, April 27, 2017, https://www.armed-services.senate.gov/imo/media/doc/Waltzman_04-27-17.pdf.

"Debunk.eu: Countering disinformation with AI," video, *Google*, February 14, 2020, https://youtu.be/u1MThnflDTA.

"Democratic Rights Popular Globally but Commitment to Them Not Always Strong," *Pew Research Center*, February 27, 2020, topline questionnaire, https://www.pewresearch.org/global/wp-content/uploads/sites/2/2020/02/PG_2020.02.27_global-democracy_TOPLINE.pdf.

"Денег нет, но вы держитесь" [There's no money, but you hold on there], *Meduza*, May 24, 2016, https://meduza.io/shapito/2016/05/24/deneg-net-no-vy-derzhites.

Department of State, "President Putin's Fiction: 10 False Claims about Ukraine," fact sheet, March 5, 2014, archived at https://www.liveleak.com/view?t=2b0_1394109329.

Department of State, Press Release No. 94, February 4, 1952, quoted in Jonathan P. Herzog, *The Spiritual-Industrial Complex* (Oxford: Oxford University Press, 2011), 128.

"Disinformation Can Kill," *EUvsDisinfo,* March 26, 2020, https://euvsdisinfo.eu/disinformation-can-kill/.

Dlhopolec, Peter, "Checkbot educates and warns. It never tells the truth," *The Slovak Spectator,* November 22, 2019, https://spectator.sme.sk/c/22266109/checkbot-educates-and-warns-it-never-tells-the-truth-bringing-world-to-the-classroom.html.

"Доклад А.А. Климова на комиссии СФ по итогам работы мониторинговой группы за период с 30 мая по 12 сентября 2019 года" [Report of A.A. Klimov to the commissions of the Federation Council on the results of the work of the Monitoring Group from May 30 to September 12, 2019], Federation Council of the Russian Federation, October 8, 2019, http://council.gov.ru/media/files/cWoDECZrNAv9hKQ2ZOPk OpA6vPHLgAUG.pdf.

Effron, Daniel A. and Medha Raj, "Misinformation and Morality: Encountering Fake-News Headlines Makes Them Seem Less Unethical to Publish and Share," *Psychological Science,* November 21, 2019, available from https://journals.sagepub.com/doi/abs/10.1177/0956797619887896.

Elstov, Peter, "The Best Way to Deal With Russia: Wait for It to Implode," *Politico,* August 3, 2019, https://www.politico.com/magazine/story/2019/08/03/russia-separatism-vladimir-putin-227498.

"Эмиграционные настроения" [Mood toward emigration], *Levada-Center,* November 26, 2019, https://www.levada.ru/2019/11/26/emigratsionnye-nastroeniya-4.

Eslas, Urve, "Estonian Forces Neutralize Disinfo Attack," *Center for European Policy Analysis,* April 10, 2018, http://infowar.cepa.org/Briefs/Est/Estonia-Neutralizes-Sputniks-Disinformation-Attack.

"EU Assistance to Serbia," The Delegation of the European Union to the Republic of Serbia, http://europa.rs/eu-assistance-to-serbia/?lang=en.

European Commission, "Action Plan Against Disinformation," December 5, 2018, https://eeas.europa.eu/sites/eeas/files/action_plan_against_disinformation.pdf

European Commission, "The Multiannual Financial Framework: The External Action Financing Instruments," news release, December 11, 2013, https://ec.europa.eu/commission/presscorner/detail/en/MEMO_13_1134.

European Council, "Countering hybrid threats: Council calls for enhanced common action," news release, December 10, 2019, https://www.consilium.europa.eu/en/press/press-releases/2019/12/10/countering-hybrid-threats-council-calls-for-enhanced-common-action/.

European Union, "Questions and Answers—The EU steps up action against disinformation," news release, December 4, 2018, https://ec.europa.eu/commission/presscorner/detail/en/MEMO_18_6648.

European Union, "Speech of Vice President Věra Jourová on countering disinformation amid COVID-19 'From pandemic to infodemic,'" news release, June 4, 2020, https://ec.europa.eu/commission/presscorner/detail/en/SPEECH_20_1000.

"Facebook Reports Fourth Quarter and Full Year 2019 Results," Facebook, January 29, 2020, https://www.prnewswire.com/news-releases/facebook-reports-fourth-quarter-and-full-year-2019-results-300995616.html.

"Falklands testing ground for satellite system that could revolutionize mobile connectivity," *MercoPress*, March 26, 2020, https://en.mercopress.com/2020/03/26/falklands-testing-ground-for-satellite-system-that-could-revolutionize-mobile-connectivity.

Faulconbridge, Guy, "Britain secretly funded Reuters in 1960s and 1970s: documents," *Reuters*, January 13, 2020, https://www.reuters.com/article/us-britain-media/britain-secretly-funded-reuters-in-1960s-and-1970s-documents-idUSKBN1ZC20H.

Fedor, Julie and Rolf Fredheim, " 'We need more clips about Putin, and lots of them': Russia's state-commissioned online visual culture," *Nationalities Papers* (2016) 45:2, 161–181, https://www.cambridge.org/core/services/aop-cambridge-core/content/view/85A39DFF45D461EA01B1E6999338C934/S0090599200019231a.pdf/we_need_more_clips_about_putin_and_lots_of_them_russias_statecommissioned_online_visual_culture.pdf.

Fielding, Nick and Ian Cobain, "Revealed: US spy operation that manipulates social media," *The Guardian,* March 17, 2011, https://www.theguardian.com/technology/2011/mar/17/us-spy-operation-social-networks.

"Fighting hoaxes with Slovak YouTubers—case study," video, *GLOBSEC,* November 14, 2017, https://www.youtube.com/watch?v=RJdwJzM89jo.

Fly, Jamie, Laura Rosenberger, and David Salvo, *The ASD Policy Blueprint for Countering Authoritarian Interference in Democracies* (Washington: Alliance for Securing Democracy, German Marshall Fund, June 26, 2018), 19, http://www.gmfus.org/file/25928/download.

Fonseca, Brian, "Russian Deceptive Propaganda Growing Fast in Latin America," *Diálogo,* July 24, 2018, https://dialogo-americas.com/articles/russian-deceptive-propaganda-growing-fast-in-latin-america/.

Foreign & Commonwealth Office, "UK steps up fight against fake news," news release, July 7, 2019, https://www.gov.uk/government/news/uk-steps-up-fight-against-fake-news.

Freed, Daniel and Alina Polyakova, *Democratic Defense Against Disinformation* (Washington: Atlantic Council, March 5, 2018), https://www.atlanticcouncil.org/in-depth-research-reports/report/democratic-defense-against-disinformation/.

Freedberg Jr., Sydney J., "'Desperate Need For Speed' As Army Takes On Chinese, Russian, ISIS Info Ops," *Breaking Defense,* August 21, 2019, https://breakingdefense.com/2019/08/desperate-need-for-speed-as-army-takes-on-chinese-russians-isis-trolls/.

Freier, Nathan, "The Darker Shade of Gray: A New War Unlike Any Other," *Center for Strategic & International Studies,* July 27, 2018, https://www.csis.org/analysis/darker-shade-gray-new-war-unlike-any-other.

"From 'Memory Wars' to a Common Future: Overcoming Polarisation in Ukraine," Arena Project, London School of Economics and Political Science, July 2020, https://www.lse.ac.uk/iga/assets/documents/Arena-LSE-From-Memory-Wars-to-a-Common-Future-Overcoming-Polarisation-in-Ukraine.pdf.

Frost, Mervyn, "Cognitive Warfare - Ethical Dimensions," public lecture to Defense Leaders' Breakfast, Barton ACT, Australia, August 30, 2019.

Frost, Mervyn and Nicholas Michelson, "Strategic communications in international relations: practical traps and ethical puzzles," *Defence Strategic Communication* 2 (Spring 2017), https://stratcomcoe.org/download/file/fid/75915.

"FY 2019 Performance and Accountability Report," US Agency for Global Media, November 2019, https://www.usagm.gov/wp-content/uploads/2019/11/USAGM-FY2019-PAR.pdf.

"FY 2021 Congressional Budget Justification," US Agency for Global
Media, February 10, 2020, https://www.usagm.gov/wp-
content/uploads/2020/02/FINAL-USAGM-FY-2021-
Congressional-Budget-Justification_2_9_2020.pdf.

Gabuyev, Alexander, "Нет никакой объективности" [There is no
objectivity], *Kommersant,* April 7, 2012,
https://www.kommersant.ru/doc/1911336.

Gatov, Vasily, "How to Talk with Russia," *The American Interest,*
February 26, 2018, https://www.the-american-
interest.com/2018/02/26/how-to-talk-with-russia/.

"GEC Special Report: Pillars of Russia's Disinformation and
Propaganda Ecosystem," Global Engagement Center, August
2020, https://www.state.gov/wp-
content/uploads/2020/08/Pillars-of-Russia%E2%80%99s-
Disinformation-and-Propaganda-Ecosystem_08-04-20.pdf.

Gelb, Leslie H., "Administration is accused of deceiving press on
Libya," *The New York Times,* October 3, 1986,
https://www.nytimes.com/1986/10/03/world/administration-is-
accused-of-deceiving-press-on-libya.html.

"Генпрокуратура назвала лидеров по уровню коррупции—
силовики, суды, исполнительная власть" [Prosecutor-general
lists the leaders in corruption: law enforcement, courts and
government executives], *Pasmi.ru,* October 22, 2019,
https://pasmi.ru/archive/245653/.

"Georgia hit by massive cyber-attack," *BBC,* October 28, 2019,
https://www.bbc.com/news/technology-50207192.

Gerasimov, Valery, "Ценность науки в предвидении" [The value of science in prediction], *Voenno-Promyshlenny Kurier,* No. 8 (476), February 27–March 5, 2013, https://vpk-news.ru/sites/default/files/pdf/VPK_08_476.pdf.

Giles, Keir, "Countering Russian Information Operations in the Age of Social Media," *Council on Foreign Relations,* November 21, 2017, https://www.cfr.org/report/countering-russian-information-operations-age-social-media.

Gleicher, Nathaniel, "Removing More Coordinated Inauthentic Behavior From Russia," Facebook blog, October 30, 2019, https://about.fb.com/news/2019/10/removing-more-coordinated-inauthentic-behavior-from-russia/.

Goble, Paul, "Pandemic Has Changed Russians, But Can It Change Russia?" *Eurasia Daily Monitor,* April 21, 2020, https://jamestown.org/program/pandemic-has-changed-russians-but-can-it-change-russia.

"Going viral: lessons from the COVID-19 crisis for fighting disinformation," video, European Policy Centre, June 12, 2020, http://www.epc.eu/en/events/Going-viral-lessons-from-the-COVID-19-crisis-for~33df4c.

Goncharov, Stepan and Denis Volkov, "Russians Want Crimea; Prefer Luhansk and Donetsk Independent," *The Chicago Council on Global Affairs,* April 3, 2019, https://www.thechicagocouncil.org/publication/lcc/russians-want-crimea-prefer-luhansk-and-donetsk-independent.

Gontmakher, Yevgeny, "Никто не подставит российской власти плечо в момент ее обрушения" [No one will offer the Russian authorities a hand at the moment of their collapse], *Moskovsky*

Komsomolets, March 6, 2020,
https://www.mk.ru/politics/2019/03/04/nikto-ne-podstavit-
rossiyskoy-vlasti-plecho-v-moment-ee-obrusheniya.html.

Greenfield, Rebecca, "The Economics of Netflix's $100 Million New
Show," *The Atlantic,* February 1, 2013,
https://www.theatlantic.com/technology/archive/2013/02/econo
mics-netflixs-100-million-new-show/318706/.

Greenway, Chris, "Radio Atlantico del Sur," November 27, 2017,
https://radioatlanticodelsur.blogspot.com/2017/11/no-lies-are-
to-be-told.html.

Greenpeace International, "Massive forest fires in Siberia is a climate
emergency," news release, August 5, 2019,
https://www.greenpeace.org/international/press-
release/23660/massive-forest-fires-iSn-siberia-is-a-climate-
emergency/.

Grossman, Shelby, Daniel Bush, and Renée DiResta, "Evidence of
Russia-Linked Influence Operations in Africa," Stanford
Internet Observatory, October 29, 2019, https://fsi-live.s3.us-
west-1.amazonaws.com/s3fs-public/29oct2019_sio_-
_russia_linked_influence_operations_in_africa.final_.pdf.

Harding Luke, and Jason Burke, "Leaked documents reveal Russian
effort to exert influence in Africa," *The Guardian,* June 11, 2019,
https://www.theguardian.com/world/2019/jun/11/leaked-
documents-reveal-russian-effort-to-exert-influence-in-africa.

Heisbourg, François, "From Wuhan to the World: How the
Pandemic Will Reshape Geopolitics," *IISS Blog,* May 11, 2020,
https://www.iiss.org/blogs/survival-blog/2020/05/from-wuhan-
to-the-world.

Herbst, John and Sergei Erofeev, *The Putin Exodus: The New Russian Brain Drain* (Washington: Atlantic Council, February 2019), https://www.publications.atlanticcouncil.org/putin-exodus/The-Putin-Exodus.pdf.

Hicks, Kathleen H., Melissa Dalton, et. al., *By Other Means, Part II: U.S. Priorities in the Gray Zone* (Washington: Center for Strategic & International Studies, August 2019), https://csis-prod.s3.amazonaws.com/s3fs-public/publication/Hicks_GrayZone_II_full_WEB_0.pdf.

Himma-Kadakas, Marju, " 'Sparing time from fact-checking': Journalists' skills and competences in recognizing and publishing false information," video, International Fact-Checking Network, June 17, 2020, https://www.youtube.com/watch?v=XrS7IHYNYj4&list=PLEcKYh_fjP9hsDdFjnRkxFdDKARmivAPg&index=2.

HM Government, "Government Communication Plan 2019/20," 2019, https://gcs.civilservice.gov.uk/communication-plan-2019/strengthening-our-democracy/.

Hovhannisyan, Tatev, "Revealed: US-funded website spreading COVID misinformation in Armenia," *openDemocracy,* May 28, 2020, https://www.opendemocracy.net/en/5050/us-money-armenia-misinformation-covid-vaccines/.

"How Effective Are Fact-Checkers?" *Alto Analytics,* July 12, 2019, https://www.alto-analytics.com/en_US/fact-checkers/.

"How the Kremlin Bankrolled An Online Comedy Channel," *Radio Free Europe/Radio Liberty,* November 17, 2019, https://www.rferl.org/a/how-the-kremlin-bankrolled-an-online-comedy-channel/30273568.html.

H.R. 5515 National Defense Authorization Act for Fiscal Year 2019, Sec. 1284, Modifications to Global Engagement Center, https://www.congress.gov/115/bills/hr5515/BILLS-115hr5515enr.pdf.

"Inauthentic *Sputnik*-Linked Pages Target the Armenian Diaspora," DFR Lab post, *Medium*, September 5, 2019, https://medium.com/dfrlab/inauthentic-sputnik-linked-pages-target-the-armenian-diaspora-3e4ed8923525.

"Interview with The Financial Times," President of Russia website, June 27, 2019, http://en.kremlin.ru/events/president/news/60836.

Ireton, Cherilyn, and Julie Posetti, *Journalism, 'Fake News' & Disinformation: Handbook for Journalism Education and Training* (Paris: UNESCO, 2018), http://unesdoc.unesco.org/images/0026/002655/265552E.pdf

"Исследование социальных эффектов пандемии COVID-19: Сводка #12" [Research on the social effects of the COVID-19 pandemic: 12th Edition], *Sotsiologicheskii Antikrizisny Tsentr*, http://sociocrisis.ru/files/sac_report_12.pdf.

Jakes, Lara, "As Protests in South America Surged, So Did Russian Trolls on Twitter, U.S. Finds," *The New York Times*, January 20, 2020, https://www.nytimes.com/2020/01/19/us/politics/south-america-russian-twitter.html.

Jensen, Benjamin and Brandon Valeriano, "Waging war against the troll farms," *Navy Times*, March 13, 2019, https://www.navytimes.com/news/your-navy/2019/03/13/waging-war-against-the-troll-farms/.

Johnson, Tim, "Security certificate yanked from Russia-backed website, hurting ability to divide voters," *McClatchy DC*, January 2, 2019, https://www.mcclatchydc.com/news/policy/technology/cyber-security/article223832790.html.

Кампания НЕТ! "Онлайн-митинг «За жизнь»" [Online rally 'For Life'], YouTube video, 2:53:07, April 28, 2020, https://www.youtube.com/watch?v=gYDkz-tjn7E.

Kent, Thomas, "Congress needs to clarify mission and oversight of Voice of America," *The Hill*, April 28, 2020, https://thehill.com/opinion/technology/494957-congress-needs-to-clarify-mission-and-oversight-of-voice-of-america.

Kent, Thomas, "The Case for Democratic Optimism," *The American Interest*, March 2, 2018, https://www.the-american-interest.com/2018/03/02/case-democratic-optimism/.

Kirillova, Kseniya, "Russian Population Does Not Trust the Authorities but Still Believes the Propaganda," *Eurasia Daily Monitor*, April 28, 2020, https://jamestown.org/program/russian-population-does-not-trust-the-authorities-but-still-believes-the-propaganda/.

Kosečeková, Rebeka, " 'Hudbou proti hoaxom' bojujú v novej kampani aj Sajfa či Gogo" [Saijfa and Gogo join the new 'music against hoaxes' campaign], *Mediálne*, December 6, 2018, https://medialne.trend.sk/marketing/hudbou-proti-hoaxom-bojuju-novej-kampani-aj-sajfa-gogo.

Krekó, Péter, Csaba Molnár, and András Rácz, *"Mystification and Demystification of Putin's Russia* (Budapest: Political Capital, March 2019), https://politicalcapital.hu/pc-

admin/source/documents/pc_mystification_and_demystificatio
n_of_russia_eng_web_20190312.pdf.

Krutov, Mark, " 'Вы сами что, бессмертные?' ФСБ не дает
волонтерам помочь больнице" ["Are you immortal
yourselves?" The FSB won't let volunteers help a hospital], *Radio
Free Europe/Radio Liberty*, April 7, 2020,
https://www.svoboda.org/a/30536721.html.

" 'Krymnash' Meme Part of Russian Society's Return to Late Soviet
Times," *Euromaidan Press,* June 10, 2015,
http://euromaidanpress.com/2015/06/10/krymnash-meme-part-
of-russian-societys-return-to-late-soviet-times/.

Lansdale, James, "Russia-linked hack 'bid to discredit' UK anti-
disinformation campaign - Foreign Office," *BBC*, December 10,
2018, https://www.bbc.com/news/uk-46509956.

Lenzi, Massimilliano, "Libertà superflua per 2 italiani su 3" [For 2
Italians out of 3, freedom is superfluous], *Il Tempo,* April 18,
2020,
https://www.iltempo.it/cronache/2020/04/18/news/coronavirus-
app-tracciamento-liberta-spostamenti-italiani-sondaggio-
covid19-1316880/.

"Liberal Anti-Communism Revisited: A Symposium," *Commentary,*
Vol. 44, No. 3, September 1, 1967, 70.

Limits on Freedom of Expression (Washington: Library of Congress,
June 2019), https://www.loc.gov/law/help/freedom-
expression/limits-expression.pdf.

Lindborg, Nancy, "Revolutions of our time: Freedom without US
leadership," *The Hill*, November 2019,

https://thehill.com/opinion/civil-rights/471481-revolutions-of-our-time-freedom-without-us-leadership.

Lucas, Edward, "How the West should punish Putin," *CapX*, October 31, 2016, https://capx.co/playing-russia-at-its-own-game/.

Lucas, Edward and Peter Pomerantsev, *Winning the Information War Redux* (Washington: Center for European Policy Analysis, April 2017), https://docs.wixstatic.com/ugd/644196_264a764d8fc04714a8833 55f4ac682b9.pdf.

Luxmoore, Matthew, "Flouting The Law In Nostalgia's Name: Russia's Growing Movement Of 'Soviet Citizens,' " *Radio Free Europe/Radio Liberty,* May 25, 2019, https://www.rferl.org/a/flouting-law-in-nostalgia-s-name-russia-s-growing-movement-of-soviet-citizens-/29962523.html.

Lyashchuk, Vitalya, "Обращение студентов Украины к студентам России" [Ukrainian students' appeal to the students of Russia], February 10, 2015, https://www.youtube.com/watch?v=7uCK73eU--Q.

Mackintosh, Eliza, "Finland is winning the war on fake news. What it's learned may be crucial to Western democracy," *CNN*, May 2019, https://edition.cnn.com/interactive/2019/05/europe/finland-fake-news-intl/.

Macron, Emmanuel, "Pour une Renaissance européenne [For a European renaissance]," Elysée, March 4, 2019, https://www.elysee.fr/emmanuel-macron/2019/03/04/pour-une-renaissance-europeenne.

Mantas, Harrison, "Fact-checkers fighting the COVID-19 infodemic drew a surge in readers," *Poynter,* June 9, 2020, https://www.poynter.org/fact-checking/2020/fact-checkers-fighting-the-covid-19-infodemic-drew-a-surge-in-readers/.

Mantas, Harrison, "Fact-checkers use new tools of engagement to fight fast-moving hoaxes," *Poynter,* June 10, 2020, https://www.poynter.org/fact-checking/2020/fact-checkers-use-new-tools-of-engagement-to-fight-fast-moving-hoaxes/.

"Maria Stephan on What We Get Wrong About Protest Movements," *On Peace,* podcast, United States Institute of Peace, December 19, 2019, https://www.usip.org/publications/2019/12/maria-stephan-what-we-get-wrong-about-protest-movements.

Marquardt, Alex, "State Department suspends funding of anti-Iran group which targeted journalists and activists," *CNN,* June 5, 2019, https://www.cnn.com/2019/06/05/politics/us-suspends-funding-anti-iran-group/index.html.

Mattis, James, address to IRI Freedom Dinner, May 15, 2018, https://www.youtube.com/watch?v=YsnyeGt7kng.

Mazmanian, Adam, "DOD shutters two 'influence' websites covering Africa," *FCW,* February 13, 2015, https://fcw.com/articles/2015/02/13/african-web-sites.aspx.

"Media Freedom Groups Express Unease Over Ukrainian Disinformation Bill," *Radio Free Europe/Radio Liberty,* January 23, 2020, https://www.rferl.org/a/media-freedom-groups-express-unease-over-ukrainian-disinformation-bill/30393814.html.

"Merkel droht Russland wegen Hackerangriff mit Konsequenzen"
[Merkel threatens Russia with consequences for hacking],
Frankfurter Allgemeine Zeitung, May 13, 2020,
https://www.faz.net/aktuell/politik/ausland/merkel-droht-
russland-wegen-hackerangriff-mit-konsequenzen-
16767763.html.

Miller, Christopher "Inside the Ukrainian 'Hacktivist' Network
Cyberbattling the Kremlin," *Radio Free Europe/Radio Liberty,*
November 2, 2016, https://www.rferl.org/a/ukraine-hacktivist-
network-cyberwar-on-kremlin/28091216.html.

Mishra, Prankaj, "Democracy Is on the March, Not in Retreat,"
Bloomberg News, November 2, 2019,
https://www.bnnbloomberg.ca/democracy-is-on-the-march-not-
in-retreat-1.1341836.

"Moldova's Orthodox Church Lashes Out At 'Anti-Christ Plot' To
Develop Virus Vaccine," *Radio Free Europe/Radio Liberty,* May
20, 2020, https://www.rferl.org/a/moldova-s-orthodox-church-
lashes-out-at-anti-christ-plot-to-develop-virus-
vaccine/30624250.html.

"Москва обратится к США и ФРГ из-за вмешательства во
внутренние дела России" [Moscow will address the USA and
Germany about interference in the internal affairs of Russia],
RIA-Novosti, August 4, 2019,
https://ria.ru/20190804/1557158646.html.

Nakashima, Ellen, "U.S. Cybercom contemplates information
warfare to counter Russian interference in 2020 election," *The
Washington Post,* December 25, 2019,
https://www.washingtonpost.com/national-security/us-
cybercom-contemplates-information-warfare-to-counter-

russian-interference-in-the-2020-election/2019/12/25/21bb246e-
   20e8-11ea-bed5-880264cc91a9_story.html.

Nakashima, Ellen, "U.S. Cyber Command operation disrupted
   Internet access of Russian troll factory on day of 2018
   midterms," *The Washington Post,* February 27, 2019,
   https://www.washingtonpost.com/world/national-security/us-
   cyber-command-operation-disrupted-internet-access-of-
   russian-troll-factory-on-day-of-2018-
   midterms/2019/02/26/1827fc9e-36d6-11e9-af5b-
   b51b7ff322e9_story.html.

National Defense Authorization Act for Fiscal Year 2020,
   https://www.govinfo.gov/content/pkg/BILLS-
   116s1790enr/pdf/BILLS-116s1790enr.pdf.

"Непопулярная версия: американский БПЛА сбил украинский
   'Боинг-737' в небе над Ираном" [An unpopular version: An
   American drone shot down the Ukrainian Boeing 737 in the sky
   over Iran], *Federalnoe Agentstvo Novostei,* January 8, 2020,
   https://riafan.ru/1240427-nepopulyarnaya-versiya-amerikanskii-
   bpla-sbil-ukrainskii-boing-737-v-nebe-nad-iranom.

"New collaboration steps up fight against disinformation," *BBC,*
   September 9, 2019,
   https://www.bbc.co.uk/mediacentre/latestnews/2019/disinforma
   tion?ns_linkname=corporate&ns_mchannel=social&ns_campai
   gn=bbc_press_office&ns_source=twitter.

"No need to install: Microsoft has controversial fake news filter
   NewsGuard built into mobile browser," *RT,* January 23, 2019,
   https://www.rt.com/news/449530-newsguard-edge-browser-
   media-integrated/.

"Notice of Funding Opportunity: PAS-CHISINAU-FY18-08," US Embassy Chisnau, April 15, 2018, https://s3-us-west-2.amazonaws.com/instrumentl/grantsgov/303573.pdf.

Nye, Joseph, "Do Morals Matter?" Walter Roberts Annual Lecture, George Washington University, video, January 30, 2020, https://www.youtube.com/watch?v=uX-8jneY3tU.

Nye, Joseph, "Soft Power," *The Atlantic,* November 2007, https://www.theatlantic.com/magazine/archive/2007/11/soft-power/306313/.

Oates, Sarah, "When Media Worlds Collide: Using Media Model Theory to Understand How Russia Spreads Disinformation in the United States," paper for the Annual Meeting of the American Political Science Association, August 24, 2018, available from https://dx.doi.org/10.2139/ssrn.3238247.

"On Peace," podcast, United States Institute of Peace, April 29, 2020, https://play.google.com/music/listen?u=0#/ps/Iijmiabq66jjzbtkv6v3rzn3ycq.

Operation Secondary Infektion (Washington: DFR Lab, 2019), https://docs.wixstatic.com/ugd/9d177c_3e548ca15bb64a85ab936d76c95897c7.pdf.

Örsek, Baybars, "Fact-checking and the IFCN made big strides in 2019. Here's what's coming in 2020," *Poynter,* December 18, 2019, https://www.poynter.org/fact-checking/2019/the-state-of-fact-checking-and-the-ifcn-in-2019-and-whats-around-the-corner-for-2020/.

"Отношение к Владимиру Путину" [Feelings about Vladimir Putin], *Levada-Center,* April 14, 2020, https://www.levada.ru/2020/04/14/otnoshenie-k-vladimiru-putinu-4/.

Papineau, Philippe, "Collaborer contre la désinformation aux élections" [Collaborating against election disinformation], *Le Devoir*, March 1, 2019, https://www.ledevoir.com/culture/medias/548950/collaboration-contre-la-desinformation-aux-elections.

Parkhomenko, Sergey, "How Can Russian Civil Society Survive Putin's Fourth Term?" *Kennan Cable,* No. 32, April 2018, https://www.wilsoncenter.org/sites/default/files/media/documents/publication/kennan_cable_32_-_parkhomenko.pdf.

Pavlenko, Dmitri, "Правящая партия ЮАР готовится отнять землю у белых фермеров" [RSA ruling party prepares to seize land from white farmers], *Tsargrad TV,* December 22, 2017, https://tsargrad.tv/articles/unizhenie-belyh-chjornyj-peredel-prevratit-juar-v-novoe-zimbabve_102121.

"People Power in a Pandemic," video, United States Institute of Peace, May 19, 2020, https://www.youtube.com/watch?v=YOwmydRwxDo.

"Песков заявил, что в Кремле трезво оценивают уровень благосостояния россиян" [Peskov declares that the Kremlin is seriously evaluating Russians' well-being], *Tass,* May 30, 2019, https://tass.com/politics/1060833.

Pomerantsev, Peter, "The Death of the Neutral Public Sphere," *The American Interest,* September 18, 2019, https://www.the-american-interest.com/2019/09/18/the-death-of-the-neutral-public-sphere/.

Pomerantsev, Peter, "Peter Pomerantsev on information wars, Trump, Putin, and regulations," *Coda,* October 16, 2019, https://codastory.com/disinformation/disinfo-newsletter/pomerantsev-information-wars-trump-putin-regulations/.

Prosser, Michael B., "Memetics—A Growth Industry in US Military Operations," (MA diss., Marine Corps University, 2006), https://apps.dtic.mil/dtic/tr/fulltext/u2/a507172.pdf.

"Путин назвал Россию отдельной цивилизацией" [Putin calls Russia a separate civilization], *Interfax,* May 17, 2020, https://www.interfax.ru/russia/709039.

"Q1 2019 Earnings Report," Twitter, April 28, 2020, https://s22.q4cdn.com/826641620/files/doc_financials/2019/q1/Q1-2019-Slide-Presentation.pdf.

Ragozin, Leonid, "Moscow's Elections Show Putin Is Losing the War at Home," *Time,* September 10, 2019, https://time.com/5672235/putin-moscow-elections/.

Reno, R.R., *Return of the Strong Gods* (Washington: Regnery Gateway, 2019).

Report of the Select Committee on Intelligence on Russian Active Measures, Campaigns and Interference in the 2016 US Election, Volume 2: Russia's Use of Social Media with Additional Views (Washington: United States Senate), July 25, 2019, https://www.intelligence.senate.gov/sites/default/files/documents/Report_Volume2.pdf.

"Репрессии XX века: память о близких" [Repressions of the 20th Century: remembering relatives], *VTsIOM*, October 5, 2018, https://wciom.ru/index.php?id=236&uid=9344.

Reuters Institute Digital News Report (Oxford: Reuters Institute for the Study of Journalism, 2020), https://reutersinstitute.politics.ox.ac.uk/sites/default/files/2020-06/DNR_2020_FINAL.pdf.

"RFP Countering Russian Propaganda in Ukraine," Democracy Council, November 25, 2019, https://demcouncil.org/?p=2877.

Richards, Lee, "IRD Special Operations: An Initial Survey of the Covert Propaganda Activities of the Information Research Department," *Psywar.org*, January 26, 2020, https://www.psywar.org/content/irdSpecialOperations.

Richter, Monika L., *The Kremlin's Platform for 'Useful Idiots' in the West: An Overview of RT's Editorial Strategy and Evidence of Impact* (Prague: European Values, September 18, 2017), https://www.europeanvalues.net/wp-content/uploads/2017/09/Overview-of-RTs-Editorial-Strategy-and-Evidence-of-Impact-1.pdf.

Rivero, Mónica, "Cuba's Offline Quarantine," *Slate*, June 1, 2020, https://slate.com/technology/2020/06/cuba-internet-quarantine-coronavirus.html.

Robinson, Linda et al., *Modern Political Warfare: Current Practices and Possible Responses* (Santa Monica, Calif. : RAND Corporation, 2018), https://www.rand.org/content/dam/rand/pubs/research_reports/RR1700/RR1772/RAND_RR1772.pdf.

Rogachev, Sergei and Vilovatykh, Anna, "Информационное обеспечение внешнеполитической деятельности в условиях цифровой реальности" [Informational security for foreign political activity in the conditions of digital reality], *Problemy Natsionalnoi Strategii,* No. 6 (57) 2019, https://riss.ru/analitycs/65672/.

Room, Tony, "Zuckerberg: Standing For Voice and Free Expression" (full text of Zuckerberg speech), *The Washington Post,* October 17, 2019, https://www.washingtonpost.com/technology/2019/10/17/zuckerberg-standing-voice-free-expression/.

"Российский медиаландшафт-2020" [Russian media landscape 2020], *Levada-Center,* April 28, 2020, https://www.levada.ru/2020/04/28/rossijskij-medialandshaft-2020/.

"Росстат рассчитал численность населения с доходами ниже прожиточного минимума, установленного приказом Минтруда России для второго квартала 2019 года" [The Russian Statistical Service calculates the amount of the population with incomes below the living wage as established by order of the Russian Ministry of Labor for the second quarter of 2019], *Rosstat,* August 27, 2019, https://gks.ru/folder/313/document/60982.

Royce, Marie, "A Strategy to Fight Digital Disinformation: Digital Communicators Network," State Department blog, February 19, 2020, Google cache copy: http://webcache.googleusercontent.com/search?q=cache:1o24N V95XMwJ:https://blogs.state.gov/stories/2018/09/20/en/strategy -fight-digital-disinformation-digital-communicators-network&client=firefox-b-1-d&hl=en&gl=us&strip=1&vwsrc=0.

Rozhdestvensky, Iyla, Michael Rubin, and Roman Badanin, "Шеф и повар. Часть третья" [Master and chef. Part 3], *Proekt,* April 11, 2019, https://www.proekt.media/investigation/prigozhin-polittekhnologi/.

"Ru media uses humor to justify aggressive politics," video, Ukraine Crisis Media Center, March 11, 2019, https://www.youtube.com/watch?v=h1tbxlyV9GE&feature=youtu.be.

"Russia and the West," *Levada-Center,* February 28, 2020, https://www.levada.ru/en/2020/02/28/russia-and-the-west/.

Russian Disinformation Attacks on Elections: Lessons from Europe, hearing of the Subcommittee on Europe, Eurasia, Energy and the Environment, House Foreign Affairs Committee, July 16, 2019, https://www.youtube.com/watch?v=U3heju1HIQE&feature=youtu.be&t=2545.

"Russian hackers likely behind 'IS group cyber attack' on French TV network," *France 24,* June 10, 2015, https://www.france24.com/en/20150610-france-cyberattack-tv5-television-network-russia-hackers.

"Russian Information Operations in East Europe," video, Harriman Institute, Columbia University, April 2, 2020, https://www.facebook.com/TheHarrimanInstitute/videos/593326268194157/.

Saldžiūnas, Valdas, "How Lithuanian defense minister became a target: cyber and fake news attack was just the beginning," *Delfi.en,* April 13, 2019, https://en.delfi.lt/politics/how-lithuanian-defense-minister-became-a-target-cyber-and-fake-news-attack-was-just-the-beginning.d?id=80897865.

Schoen, Fletcher and Christopher J. Lamb, "Deception, Disinformation, and Strategic Communications: How One Interagency Group Made a Major Difference," *Strategic Perspectives* 11, Institute for National Strategic Studies, June 2012, https://ndupress.ndu.edu/Portals/68/Documents/stratperspectiv e/inss/Strategic-Perspectives-11.pdf.

Schultz, Teri, "Why the 'fake rape' story against German NATO forces fell flat in Lithuania," *Deutsche Welle,* February 23, 2017, https://www.dw.com/en/why-the-fake-rape-story-against-german-nato-forces-fell-flat-in-lithuania/a-37694870.

Shane, Scott, "Huge Trove of Leaked Russian Documents Is Published by Transparency Advocates," *The New York Times,* January 25, 2019, https://www.nytimes.com/2019/01/25/world/europe/russian-documents-leaked-ddosecrets.html.

Siegel, Jacob, "Is America Prepared for Meme Warfare?" *Vice,* January 31, 2017, https://www.vice.com/en_us/article/xyvwdk/meme-warfare.

Sinaiee, Maryann, "Iranian News Agency Targeted by US Sanction Resorts to Hacking To Get Domain Back," *Radio Free Europe/Radio Liberty,* January 25, 2020, https://en.radiofarda.com/a/iranian-news-agency-targeted-by-us-sanction-resorts-to-hacking-to-get-domain-back-/30396680.html.

Sippitt, Amy, *What is the impact of fact checkers' work on public figures, institutions and the media?* (Africa Check, Chequeado and Full Fact, February 2020), https://fullfact.org/media/uploads/impact-fact-checkers-public-figures-media.pdf.

Sirotnikova, Miroslava German, "Disinformation Nation: The Slovaks fighting in defence of facts," *Balkan Insight,* June 7, 2019, https://balkaninsight.com/2019/06/07/disinformation-nation-the-slovaks-fighting-in-defence-of-facts/.

"События в Сирии" [Events in Syria], *Levada-Center,* May 6, 2019, https://www.levada.ru/2019/05/06/sobytiya-v-sirii/?fromtg=1.

"*Sputnik* Moldova Painted Media Forum as a Coup Factory," *Polygraph.info,* November 1, 2019, https://www.polygraph.info/a/fact-check-sputnik-moldova/30248595.html.

Stanley-Becker, Isaac, "Technology once used to combat ISIS propaganda is enlisted by Democratic group to counter Trump's coronavirus messaging," *The Washington Post,* May 1, 2020, https://www.washingtonpost.com/politics/technology-once-used-to-combat-isis-propaganda-is-enlisted-by-democratic-group-to-counter-trumps-coronavirus-messaging/2020/05/01/6bed5f70-8a5b-11ea-ac8a-fe9b8088e101_story.html.

"Stemming the Tide of Global Disinformation," conference transcript, Council on Foreign Relations, October 11, 2019, https://www.cfr.org/event/stemming-tide-global-disinformation.

Steshin, Dmitry, "14 добрых и дельных советов американскому Майдану" [14 friendly and useful suggestions for the American Maidan], *Komsomolskaya Pravda,* May 30, 2020, https://www.kp.ru/daily/27136.5/4227260/.

Stencel, Mark, and Joel Luther, "Update: 237 fact-checkers in nearly 80 countries … and counting," *Duke Reporters' Lab,* April 3, 2020, *https://reporterslab.org/category/fact-checking/#article-2656.*

Stengel, Richard, *Information Wars: How We Lost the Global Battle Against Disinformation and What We Can Do About It* (New York: Atlantic Monthly Press, 2019).

"Страхи" [Fears], *Levada-Center,* October 29, 2019, https://www.levada.ru/2019/10/29/strahi-4/.

"Strengthening America & Countering Global Threats," Republican Study Committee, US House of Representatives, June 10, 2020, https://rsc-johnson.house.gov/sites/republicanstudycommittee.house.gov/files/%5BFINAL%5D%20NSTF%20Report.pdf.

Sukhanin, Sergey, "The Kremlin's Controversial 'Soft Power' in Africa (Part Two)," *Eurasia Daily Monitor,* December 10, 2019, https://jamestown.org/program/the-kremlins-controversial-soft-power-in-africa-part-two/.

"Supporting People Striving for Democracy," EED Annual Report, 2018, https://www.democracyendowment.eu/en/component/attachments/attachments.html?id=289.

Surkov, Vladislav, "Владислав Сурков: Долгое государство Путина" [Vladislav Surkov: Putin's long state], *Nezavisimaya Gazeta,* February 11, 2019, http://www.ng.ru/ideas/2019-02-11/5_7503_surkov.html.

Tardáguila, Cristina, "The rest of the world's fact-checkers collaborate on big elections—why won't they in the U.S.?" *Poynter*, June 26, 2019, https://www.poynter.org/fact-checking/2019/the-rest-of-the-worlds-fact-checkers-collaborate-on-big-elections-why-wont-they-in-the-u-s/.

Taylor, Philip M., *Munitions of the mind: A history of propaganda* (Manchester: Manchester University Press, 2003), 313.

Temple-Raston, Dina, "How the US Hacked ISIS," *NPR,* September 26, 2019, https://www.npr.org/2019/09/26/763545811/how-the-u-s-hacked-isis.

Teperik, Dmitri, "Does the West Dare to Open the Eastern Front of Information War?" ICDS Blog, June 8, 2020, https://icds.ee/does-the-west-dare-to-open-the-eastern-front-of-information-war/?fbclid=IwAR1-RP8We46yrziJuSSqt2NLvPRJsU_ZQU5h9ARgOyhRWYO38Tnq4LKMbLk.

"The New Rules of War: Victory in the Age of Durable Disorder, with Sean McFate," video, Carnegie Council, March 13, 2019, https://www.carnegiecouncil.org/studio/multimedia/20190313-new-rules-war-victory-age-durable-disorder-sean-mcfate.

The Quarter-Billion Dollar Question: How is Disinformation Gaming Ad Tech? (Global Disinformation Index, September 2019), 4, https://disinformationindex.org/wp-content/uploads/2019/09/GDI_Ad-tech_Report_Screen_AW16.pdf.

"The Virus to Liberate us from Freedom," *EUvsDisinfo*, https://mailchi.mp/euvsdisinfo/dr188-881685?e=fb718b27db.

The White House, *National Cyber Strategy of the United States of America,* September 2018, https://www.whitehouse.gov/wp-content/uploads/2018/09/National-Cyber-Strategy.pdf.

"Three Ways to Counter Disinformation," *GEC Counter-Disinformation Dispatches #2*, Global Engagement Center, February 11, 2020, https://commons.america.gov/article?id=69&site=content.america.gov.

Troianovski, Anton, "Fighting False News in Ukraine, Facebook Fact Checkers Tread a Blurry Line," *The New York Times,* July 26, 2020, https://www.nytimes.com/2020/07/26/world/europe/ukraine-facebook-fake-news.html.

"Trust and the coronavirus," Edelman, March 6, 2020, https://www.edelman.com/sites/g/files/aatuss191/files/2020-03/2020%20Edelman%20Trust%20Barometer%20coronavirus%20Special%20Report_0.pdf.

Unger, Arthur, " 'Let Poland Be Poland' - is the program really that bad? Closer look at an international special finds some unpredicted meaning," *The Christian Science Monitor*, February 5, 1982, https://www.csmonitor.com/1982/0205/020500.html.

United States Efforts to Counter Russian Disinformation and Malign Influence, hearing of the Subcommittee on State, Foreign Operations, and Related Programs, House Foreign Affairs Committee, video, July 10, 2019, https://appropriations.house.gov/events/hearings/united-states-efforts-to-counter-russian-disinformation-and-malign-influence.

US Department of State, "State Department and US Agency for International Development (USAID) FY 2021 Budget Request:

Fact Sheet," February 10, 2020, https://www.state.gov/state-department-and-u-s-agency-for-international-development-usaid-fy-2021-budget-request/.

"US Envoy: A Unified Effort Is Going To Make A Difference in Fighting COVID" (interview with US Ambassador Lynne Tracy), *Radio Free Europe/Radio Liberty,* June 4, 2020, https://www.youtube.com/watch?v=hGkFfzFw2LI&feature=youtu.be&t=1123.

"US Relations With the USSR," National Security Decision Directive No. 75, January 17, 1983, https://www.reaganlibrary.gov/sites/default/files/archives/reference/scanned-nsdds/nsdd75.pdf.

Valášek, Tomáš, "How Not to Lose Friends and Alienate People," *Carnegie Europe,* March 1, 2018, https://carnegieeurope.eu/strategiceurope/75677.

Valentinovich, Igor and Ksenia Ermoshina, "Exploring Online Media Filtering During the 2018 Russian Presidential Elections," *Open Technology Fund*, May 29, 2019, https://docs.google.com/gview?url=https://www.opentech.fund/documents/11/Measuring_Internet_Censorship_in_Disputed_Areas_Crimea_Russia_ICFP.pdf&embedded=true.

Vandiver, John, "Hacking leads to fake story claiming US soldier in Lithuania has coronavirus," *Stars and Stripes,* February 3, 2020, https://www.stripes.com/news/europe/hacking-leads-to-fake-story-claiming-us-soldier-in-lithuania-has-coronavirus-1.617404.

Van Walraven, Klass, "Decolonization by Referendum: The Anomaly of Niger and the Fall of Sawaba, 1958–1959," *The*

Journal of African History 50, No. 2 (2009): 269–292, available from https://www.jstor.org/stable/25622024.

Vice, Margaret, *Publics Worldwide Unfavorable Toward Putin, Russia,* (Washington: Pew Research Center, 2017), https://www.pewresearch.org/global/wp-content/uploads/sites/2/2017/08/Pew-Research-Center_2017.08.16_Views-of-Russia-Report.pdf.

Vilmer, Jean-Baptiste Jeangène, Alexandre Escorcia, et al., *Les Manipulations de l'Information* [*The Manipulation of Information*] (Paris: CAPS-IRSEM, August 2018), https://www.diplomatie.gouv.fr/IMG/pdf/les_manipulations_de_l_information_2__cle04b2b6.pdf.

Vilmer, Jean-Baptiste Jeangène, *The "Macron Leaks" Operation: A Post-Mortem,* (Washington: Atlantic Council/IRSEM, June 2019), https://www.atlanticcouncil.org/wp-content/uploads/2019/06/The_Macron_Leaks_Operation-A_Post-Mortem.pdf.

"В Кремле подготовили методички для привлечения населения к голосованию за поправки в Конституцию" [The Kremlin prepares techniques to get people to vote for the Constitutional amendments], *MBK Media,* February 27, 2020, https://mbk-news.appspot.com/news/podgotovili-metodichku/.

Voice of America, "*Voice of America* experiences record audience numbers due to its robust global coverage of COVID-19," news release, April 7, 2020, https://www.usagm.gov/2020/04/07/voice-of-america-experiences-record-audience-numbers-due-to-its-robust-global-coverage-of-covid-19/.

Voices of Central and Eastern Europe (Bratislava: Globsec, June 23, 2020), https://www.globsec.org/wp-content/uploads/2020/06/Voices-of-Central-and-Eastern-Europe_read-version.pdf.

"Voluntary contributions by fund and by contributor, 2018," World Health Organization, May 9, 2019, https://www.who.int/about/finances-accountability/reports/A72_INF5-en.pdf?ua=1.

Von Hafften, Marie, "Ahead of Brazil's election, Twitter bot Fátima spreads fact-checked information," *Ijnet* (International Journalists' Network), October 5, 2018, https://ijnet.org/en/story/ahead-brazils-election-twitter-bot-f%C3%A1tima-spreads-fact-checked-information.

Walker, Christopher, "What is 'Sharp Power?'" *Journal of Democracy,* July 2018, https://www.ned.org/wp-content/uploads/2018/07/what-is-sharp-power-christopher-walker-journal-of-democracy-july-2018.pdf.

Wallin, Matthew, *A New American Message: Fixing the Shortfalls in America's Message to the World* (Washington: American Security Project, December 2019), https://www.americansecurityproject.org/wp-content/uploads/2019/12/Ref-0233-A-New-American-Message.pdf.

Warrick, Joby, "How a U.S. team uses Facebook, guerrilla marketing to peel off potential ISIS recruits," *The Washington Post,* February 6, 2017, https://www.washingtonpost.com/world/national-security/bait-and-flip-us-team-uses-facebook-guerrilla-marketing-to-peel-off-potential-isis-recruits/2017/02/03/431e19ba-e4e4-11e6-a547-5fb9411d332c_story.html.

Watts, Clint, "Advanced Persistent Manipulators, Part Two: Intelligence-led Social Media Defense," *Alliance for Securing Democracy*, April 24, 2019, https://securingdemocracy.gmfus.org/advanced-persistent-manipulators-part-two-intelligence-led-social-media-defense/.

Watts, Clint, *Messing with the Enemy* (New York: HarperCollins, 2018).

Webb, Alban, "Iron Curtain: How did the BBC's response to the descending Iron Curtain shape its Cold War broadcasting style?" *History of the BBC,* undated web presentation, https://www.bbc.com/historyofthebbc/100-voices/coldwar/iron-curtain.

Weiss, Andrew S. and Eugene Rumer, "Nuclear Enrichment: Russia's Ill-Fated Influence Campaign in South Africa," *Carnegie Endowment for International Peace,* December 16, 2019, https://carnegieendowment.org/2019/12/16/nuclear-enrichment-russia-s-ill-fated-influence-campaign-in-south-africa-pub-80597.

Wesolowsky, Tony, and Robert Coalson, "Teflon Putin? Over 20 Years In Power, Scandals Don't Seem To Stick To The Russian President," *Radio Free Europe/Radio Liberty,* August 8, 2019, https://www.rferl.org/a/putin-20-years-power-corruption-scandals/30100279.html.

Whitmore, Brian, "The Latin American Front: Russian Propaganda in Venezuela and Western Responses," (Washington: Center for European Policy Analysis, February 2019),

https://docs.wixstatic.com/ugd/644196_a56b7c0167314e15bed79
392ef24495b.pdf/.

Wike, Richard, et al., "Trump Ratings Remain Low Around Globe,
While Views of U.S. Stay Mostly Favorable" (Washington: Pew
Research Center, January 8, 2020),
https://www.pewresearch.org/global/2020/01/08/trump-ratings-
remain-low-around-globe-while-views-of-u-s-stay-mostly-
favorable/.

Williams, Martin, "EU vs Fake News: The truth about Brussels' fight
against disinformation," *4News*, December 18, 2018,
https://www.channel4.com/news/eu-vs-fake-news-the-truth-
about-brussels-fight-against-disinformation.

Winfield, Richard, "ISLP Media Law Volunteers Defend Freedom
Worldwide," *Experience Magazine*, January/February 2020, 24,
available from
https://www.americanbar.org/groups/senior_lawyers/publicatio
ns/experience/2020/january-february/islp-media-law-
volunteers-defend-freedom-worldwide/.

Wittemore, Hank, *CNN: The Inside Story* (Boston: Little, Brown,
1990).

Woodberry, Robert D., "The Missionary Roots of Liberal
Democracy," *American Political Science Review*, Vol. 106, No. 2
(May 2012), https://doi:10.1017/S0003055412000093.

Zechmeister, Elizabeth J. and Noam Lupu (Eds.), *Pulse of Democracy*
(Nashville: LAPOP, 2019),
https://www.vanderbilt.edu/lapop/ab2018/2018-
19_AmericasBarometer_Regional_Report_10.13.19.pdf.

Zemnukhova, Liliia, "The Kremlin is pushing for a 'sovereign internet.' But at what cost?" *openDemocracy,* July 30, 2019, https://www.opendemocracy.net/en/odr/whats-wrong-with-internet-isolation-russia-en/.

Zhegulev, Ilya, "I want to serve my country," *Meduza,* February 28, 2019, https://meduza.io/en/feature/2019/03/01/i-want-to-serve-my-country-that-s-always-been-my-main-motivation.

Acknowledgements

I am deeply grateful to the more than 160 diplomats, military and intelligence officials, civil society activists and academic specialists on four continents who contributed to the research for this book. Each of them generously shared their recommendations for countering Russian information operations. Several were kind enough to review and comment on my initial conclusions. Many of these experts could not speak on the record because of government or military regulations, but their thinking deeply informed my research. Any factual errors are, of course, my responsibility.

The book has profited greatly from guidance from Glen Howard, president of The Jamestown Foundation, my patient editor at Jamestown, Matthew Czekaj, and from my colleagues at the Harriman Institute of Columbia University. The research was conducted under a generous grant from the Smith Richardson Foundation, and publication was made possible, in part, by a grant from the Harriman Institute.

About the Author

Thomas Kent is a specialist on disinformation, journalism and Russian affairs. Until September 2018, he was president and CEO of *Radio Free Europe/Radio Liberty*. He now teaches at Columbia University's Harriman Institute, is a Senior Fellow of The Jamestown Foundation, and consults on disinformation, journalism and ethics for government, media, NGO and corporate clients.

He has spoken at professional forums in 22 countries and writes frequently for general and specialized publications.

Previously, Kent was standards editor of *The Associated Press*, responsible for the credibility, balance and fairness of *AP's* content. His *AP* assignments included bureau chief in Moscow, chief of *AP* operations in Tehran during the Iranian revolution, EU correspondent in Brussels and international editor of the *AP*.

He has served twice as a juror for the Pulitzer Prizes in international reporting and has held board or advisory positions with the Online News Association, the Ethical Journalism Network, the Society of Professional Journalists and the Organization of News Ombudsmen and Standards Editors.

He was raised in Shaker Heights, Ohio, holds a degree in Russian and East European Studies from Yale University, and speaks Russian, French and Spanish.

https://linkedin.com/in/tjrkent